D0887003

COMBATING TERRORISM
Evolving Asian Perspectives

COMBATING TERRORISM

Evolving Asian Perspectives

Editor

Shruti Pandalai

INSTITUTE FOR DEFENCE STUDIES & ANALYSES
NEW DELHI

PENTAGON PRESS LLP

Combating Terrorism: Evolving Asian Perspectives
Editor: Shruti Pandalai

First Published in 2019

Copyright © Institute for Defence Studies and Analyses, New Delhi

ISBN 978-93-86618-81-8

Published by
PENTAGON PRESS LLP
206, Peacock Lane, Shahpur Jat
New Delhi-110049
Phones: 011-64706243, 26491568
Telefax: 011-26490600
email: rajan@pentagonpress.in
website: www.pentagonpress.in

In association with
Institute for Defence Studies and Analyses
No. 1, Development Enclave,
New Delhi-110010
Phone: +91-11-26717983
Website: www.idsa.in

Printed at Aegean Offset Printers, Greater Noida, U.P.

Contents

Foreword

The world's geo-economic pivot may have shifted to Asia, but terrorism continues to be one of the core impediments in the realisation of the Asian Century. Threats that were earlier contained within national boundaries have now become transnational challenges. While the issues confronting Asia and the global order have multiplied, a cohesive response to them has remained elusive. In an era of protracted uncertainty and instability in global affairs, intensifying social and cultural cleavages driven by the backlash against globalisation, closing of borders as well as heightened nationalism within countries, have all served to complicate matters further. The arc of terrorism now encompasses Europe as much as it does the whole of Asia. As India has reiterated time and again in various fora, terrorism remains the most pervasive and serious challenge to international security.

Developing a serious global response to the scourge of terrorism is imperative, but is seemingly difficult to achieve. Even though, in principle, there is a global consensus on combating terrorism, we remain bogged down by conflicting definitions of what constitutes terrorism. Geopolitical constraints have prevented concerted action. On the other hand, with time, terrorist outfits have evolved and exploited sophisticated means of technology, tools of communication and complicated webs of finance to fund their nefarious activities. Terrorist groups recruit globally and strike across national boundaries, yet nations have adopted a fragmented approach in meeting this challenge. India seeks a more coherent approach on the part of the entire international community through its advocacy of an early conclusion of a Comprehensive Convention on International Terrorism (CCIT).

This book *Combating Terrorism: Evolving Asian Perspectives* is an anthology of essays that explores the inconsistencies in the global war on terror, and brings together diverse perspectives from academia, practitioners and civil society from Asia. Based on the deliberations of the 19th Asian Security Conference, IDSA's flagship security event, this book captures the wide-ranging debates on regional efforts in countering terrorism, including first person accounts of from the heart of conflict zones in Syria, Libya, Iraq and Afghanistan. The book begins with an exploration of India's efforts to revive the push for the adoption of the CCIT, first submitted by India as a proposal in the UN General Assembly over two decades ago. While India's efforts have received support from the global community that lives increasingly in the shadow of terrorism, consensus on the language has remained elusive. It is for this reason that India, through the Convention, has sought to identify an acceptable definition of terrorism that would be acceptable to all 193 members of the UNGA. The aim is to ban all terror groups and shut down terror camps regardless of their objectives, to prosecute all terrorists under special laws, and to make cross-border terrorism an extraditable offence worldwide. To build an Asian consensus on the issue, India has also consistently suggested that violent extremism needs to be delinked from religion, ethnicity or identity. Recognising the transnational nature of terrorism today, India has been pushing for a global regime on terrorism that reinforces notions of assigning responsibility and accountability.

The role of Asia in this discourse is central. With seven out of the top ten countries with the highest impact from terrorism being from Asia, and four of the five deadliest terror outfits in the world also found in Asia, the initiative of a global response, understandably, has to come from nations within Asia. A strong regional example from Asia will exert more pressure globally to adopt a cohesive framework and join hands to fight all terrorist activities. Ironically, it is in Asia, where countries which acknowledge the scourge of terrorism on the word stage, have in reality shied away from pushing for a more global response to the threat owing to geopolitical pressures, affiliations and rivalries.

For India in particular, Asia is critical. India's ties with other Asian countries go back several centuries. India is dependent on other Asian countries for more than 60 per cent of its oil and gas imports. India's trade with its immediate and extended neighbours amounts to more than US$ 200 billion. The growth and prosperity of the region, over the years, has become interdependent and India cannot afford to distance itself from events in other Asian countries. Not only do acts of terror challenge the very ethos of democracy and secularism, it also impedes economic growth and development, as evident in many countries. The economic and opportunity costs arising from terrorism globally have increased approximately eleven-fold during the last 15 years and now stand at a staggering US$ 52 billion. (Global Terrorism Index 2018)

It is within this larger framework, that the authors in this book endeavour to navigate the conceptual challenges encountered in countering terrorism, identifying the ideologies and drivers fuelling the transnational resurgence of extremist violence and examining how technology is changing the nature of conflict from South West Asia, to South Asia and South East Asia. Most importantly, they debate the absence of counter-narratives to deal effectively with the spectre of terrorism and offer ideas to build a corpus of best practices in counter terrorism efforts. A shared understanding of the perils of terrorism will go a long way in lifting the roadblocks. The book echoes the belief that a global regime built on a strong foundation of effective regional practices is bound to find wider acceptability.

It is hoped that the book adds value and fresh perspective to this defining challenge to global and Asian Security and that readers find it insightful.

March 2019

Sujan R. Chinoy
Director General
IDSA

Acknowledgements

The Asian Security Conference is the Institute for Defence Studies and Analyses' (IDSA) flagship security conference and it was an honour and a privilege for me to coordinate this prestigious event. I would like to express my sincere thanks to the former Director General of IDSA, Shri Jayant Prasad for entrusting me with this responsibility and his guidance as we deliberated upon the curation of this conference. I am also grateful to Shri Sujan R.Chinoy, DG, IDSA for helping me bring out this anthology of essays, which hopefully will help take the conversation on this global challenge further.

It would have been impossible for me to take on a conference of this scale, without the unwavering support and encouragement shown by Maj Gen (Retd.) Alok Deb, Deputy Director General of IDSA. I would like to thank him for his confidence in me and for ensuring that I had the institutional support which is essential for the successful conduct of the conference. My efforts were ably supported by the Assistant Director Col. A.K. Chugh (Retd.) and his team, especially the IDSA Conference Cell and I would take this opportunity to thank Aparna Krishna, Ameeta Narang and Sumit for their efficient conduct of all administrative procedures.

The core of any such conference are the paper presenters. We had an excellent mix of academia, practitioners, technologists and civil society voices from the heart of conflict zones in Asia, who took time to travel to New Delhi and exchange ideas. I would like to thank each one of them for their diverse perspectives and their contributions which saw thought-provoking ideas and excellent audience participation.

The ASC conference team especially Shibani Mehta, Nikhil Raj Aggarwal and Natallia Khaniejo made invaluable contributions to the conduct of the ASC and the bringing out of this volume. Last but not the least, I would take this opportunity to thank my family, Ravi, Shymala and Smriti Pandalai, Rajiv and Mina Sain, but most importantly Mohit and Tara for always supporting me.

I hope this volume adds value and finds resonance in many more conversations on the subject.

New Delhi   **Shruti Pandalai**

List of Abbreviations

AI	Artificial Intelligence
APCs	Armoured Personnel Carriers
APEC	Asia-Pacific Economic Cooperation Forum
AQAP	Al-Qaeda in the Arabian Peninsula
AQIM	Al-Qaeda in the Islamic Maghreb
ARF	ASEAN Regional Forum
ASEAN	The Association of Southeast Asian Nations
ASG	Abu Sayyaf Group
ASWJ	Ahle Sunnat Wal Jamaat
AU	African Union
BCCI	Board of Control for Cricket in India
BEI	Bangladesh Enterprise Institute
BIMSTEC	Bay of Bengal Initiative for MultiSector Technical and Economic Cooperation
BJP	Bharatiya Janata Party
BRICS	Grouping referring to Brazil, Russia, India, China and South Africa
CBRN	Chemical, Biological, Radiological and Nuclear
CCIT	Comprehensive Convention on International Terrorism
CDMA	Code Division Multiple Access
CIA	Central Intelligence Agency
CIS	Commonwealth of Independent States
CoE	Council of Europe
COIN	Counter-Insurgency
CRSV	Conflict-related Sexual Violence
CSTO	Collective Security Treaty Organisation
CT	Counter-terrorism
CTAG	Counterterrorism Action Group
CTC	Counterterrorism Committee
CTED	Counter Terrorism Committee Executive Directorate

CTITF	Counterterrorism Implementation Task Force
CVE	Countering Violent Extremism
DDR	Demobilisation, Disarmament and Reintegration
EU	European Union
FATA	Federally Administered Tribal Areas
FATF	Financial Action Task Force
FBI	Federal Bureau of Investigation
FIF	Falah-i-Insaniyat Foundation
FIU	Financial Intelligence Units (FIU)
G8	Group of Eight
GCC	Gulf Cooperation Council
GCHQ	General Communications Headquarters
GCT	Global Counterterrorism Strategy
GoSL	Government of Sri Lanka
GPS	Global Positioning System
HM	Hizbul Mujahideen
HUJI-B	Harkat-ul-Jihad al-Islami Bangladesh
ICSVE	International Center for the Study of Violent Extremism
IDF	Israel Defense Forces
IEDs	Improvised Explosive Devices
IM	Indian Mujahideen
IP	Internet Protocol
IPDR	Internet Protocol Detail Record
IRA	Irish Republican Army
ISA	Internal Security Act
ISB	Islamic State of Bangladesh
ISI	Inter-Services Intelligence
ISIL	Islamic State of Iraq and the Levant
ISIS	Islamic State of Iraq and Syria
J&K	Jammu and Kashmir
JeM	Jaish-e-Mohammad
JI	Jamaat-e-Islami
JKLF	Jammu and Kashmir Liberation Front
JMB	Jamaat-ul-Mujahideen Bangladesh
JSOC	Joint Special Operations Command
JuD	Jaamat-ud-Dawa
JVP	Janatha Vimukthi Peramuna

SOF	Special Operations Forces
SoP	Standard Operating Procedure
SSP	Sipah-e-Sahaba Pakistan
TOPSIS	Threat-Oriented Passenger Screening Integrated System
TTP	Tehrik-e-Taliban Pakistan
TV	Television
UAE	United Arab Emirate
UAVs	Unmanned Aerial Vehicles
UK	United Kingdom
UN	United Nations
UNGA	United Nations General Assembly
UNODC	United Nations Office on Drugs and Crime
UNSCR	United Nations Security Council Resolution
US	United States
USSR	Union of Soviet Socialist Republics
VHF	Very High Frequency
VoIP	Voice over Internet Protocol
WMDs	Weapons of Mass Destruction

List of Tables and Figures

Introduction

India's Quest for a Global Convention on Combating Terrorism: An Overview of Regional Responses and Recurring Challenges

Shruti Pandalai

The first time a treaty to counter-terrorism found global consensus was in 1937, when the League of Nations came up with the Convention for the Prevention and Punishment of Terrorism.[1] The League was triggered into action by France after the assassination of King Alexander I of Yugoslavia and French foreign minister Louis Barthou in Marseilles.[2] India then represented by Sir Denys de Saumarez Bray, was among the 24 countries at the League of Nations that signed the convention in 1937 and was one of the first countries to ratify it in 1941.[3] The convention, according to accounts by Indian experts, was not enforced due to the inability of many signatory states to act on the issue of "extradition or prosecution".[4] With the dissolution of the League, the convention, along with the archives of the League of Nations, was transferred to the UN in 1946.

Since 1963, the international community has elaborated 19 international legal instruments to prevent terrorist acts, reacting to evolving threats, however a consensus on a global regime has still remained elusive.[5] Within the United Nations General Assembly (UNGA), according to observers, there have been three distinct phases in the evolution of counter-terrorism efforts.[6] The first, from 1972 to 1991, is defined and characterised by the terms used in resolutions: proposals of "measures to prevent terrorism". Within this timeframe (1972 to 1989) consideration of terrorism as a general problem was assigned primarily to the Sixth Committee of the General Assembly under an agenda item entitled "Measures to prevent international terrorism".[7] At that time, there was a clear disagreement within the member states as to whether terrorism should be prevented through cooperation in suppressing its manifestations or removal of its root causes.[8] It was only in September 1972, after 11 members of the Israeli contingent were killed in a terror attack during the Munich Olympics that the UNGA galvanised and adopted the first UNGA resolution on countering terrorism.[9] That resolution established the Ad Hoc Committee on International Terrorism in 1972, consisting of 35 countries, including India, to carve out a multilateral legal framework to counter-terrorism. With India as its chair in 1979, The ad hoc committee, submitted its report to the UNGA, which included a proposal for the negotiation of an additional international convention, or conventions, based inter alia "on the principle of extradition or prosecution to combat acts of international terrorism not yet covered by other similar international conventions".[10] The UNGA asked the UN secretary general, on the basis of views of member states, to follow up on this proposal. No consensus emerged.

A second phase from period 1993 to 2001 saw an emphasis on human rights and terrorism and measures to eliminate international terrorism, reflecting broader agreement that the existence of root causes did not justify terrorist acts.[11] The third phase, defined by the events of 11 September 2001 (9/11 attacks) did much to change the orientation of the General Assembly's counter-terrorism policy. Since then the concept and terminology have evolved towards discussion of measures to eliminate terrorism. The day after the 11 September attacks, both the UNSC and UNGA adopted unanimous resolutions condemning the acts of terrorism and urging all states to bring the perpetrators, organisers, and sponsors of the attacks to justice. UNSC Resolution (UNSCR) 1368 was important because it linked the right to self defence as enshrined in Article 51 of the UN Charter with the response to international terrorism.[12] The UNSC also passed UNSCR 1373, requiring member states to criminalise terrorism and its financing, and providing guidelines for enhanced cooperation on law enforcement and intelligence sharing. Although UNSCR 1373 provides the foundational requirements to international counter-terrorism efforts, some countries have criticised it saying it oversteps the legislative authority of the UNSC by imposing its will on member states.[13] There have been several legal and normative efforts to combat terrorism, however threat perceptions of member states have stayed uneven and the frameworks for implementation non-binding. This will be elaborated upon in further sections.

Overall, the global counter-terrorism regime continues to suffer from three inherent weaknesses.[14] First, lack of universal consensus over what constitutes terrorism, hinders efforts to formulate a concerted global response. Second, multilateral action is ineffective due to inadequate compliance and enforcement of existing instruments. Third, although counter-radicalisation and de-radicalisation initiatives have gained some attention, progress is uneven and lacking. This chapter is meant to serve first, as an overview on the glaring inconsistencies in the global war on terror that have precipitated Indian efforts to revive its push for a global regime to combat terror, second, to assess responses to India's efforts and discuss what the landscape of recurring and future challenges look like, and third, offer a closer examination of evolving responses from within nations in Asia to this mutating threat. The discussion on conceptualisation of challenges and responses, will be brought forth as short introductions to the wide-ranging perspectives and issues covered by the impressive list of contributors in this volume.

Inconsistencies in the Global War on Terror

The landscape for counter-terrorism activity since 2001 has been vast but clearly lacking coherence. Within the United Nations (UN) alone are more than thirty agencies dedicated to CT efforts.[15] It now oversees sixteen conventions that target different aspects of terrorism, including terrorist financing, hijacking, acquiring weapons of mass destruction, and hostage taking, to name a few. To monitor the implementation of resolutions post 9/11 the UNSC established the Counter-terrorism Committee (CTC), and the CTC Executive Directorate (CTED).[16] The CTC is mandated with assessing states' efforts to implement resolutions, evaluating gaps in state capacity, and facilitating donor coordination for technical and financial counter-terrorism assistance. The CTED works to coordinate and strengthen implementation of UNSC resolutions, as also to conduct country specific assessments. Both bodies, however, have uneven support across the UN membership.

To push for a more a coordinated effort and increase legitimacy to UN's mandate, the UNGA unanimously adopted in 2006 the Global Counter-terrorism Strategy (GCT).[17] Although the GCT provides an important normative and operational foundation for counter-terrorism work at the UN, a report by the Centre on Global Counter-terrorism Cooperation released ahead of the 2010 review conference notes that it has earned little attention or traction even among most UN member states.[18] The main onus of implementing the GCT is with member states, but its institutional operation is supported by the Counter-terrorism Implementation Task Force (CTITF) which includes more than thirty UN entities plus INTERPOL.[19] However, since it is composed of representatives from different agencies within the UN system, each agency's to mandate and priorities often take precedence, undermining the goals and effectiveness of the task force. [20] Again, despite being created to help coordinate, a concerted effort remains elusive.

UN-sponsored sanctions have seen limited success in addressing state sponsorship of terrorism.[21] This is particularly true in the case of non state actors operating within state boundaries. Following the UN Security Council Resolution

1267, the Al-Qaeda and Taliban Sanctions Committee and Monitoring Team were created to implement and enforce this and subsequent resolutions. It is a consolidated list of people and entities it has determined as being associated with Al Qaeda or the Taliban, and laws which must be passed within each member nation to implement the sanctions. Observers [22] argue that the list's "name and shame" tactic has had negligible impact given the lack of regular updates and the expansion of the list, making it an inflexible mechanism. This combined with the lack of provisions for legal due process makes it less effective as an appeals mechanism. Except for the UNSC's role in resolutions imposing sanctions, nobody is responsible for ensuring that member states meet their commitments under UN terrorism conventions or resolutions and there is no mandate for penalisation.

Outside the UN, other multilateral and regional bodies and initiatives have also ramped up their efforts to address terrorism given the resurgence of extremist attacks and movements since 9/11. The Financial Action Task Force (FATF) and the Group of Eight (G8) Counter-terrorism Action Group (CTAG), for instance, have independent mandates and have found varying degrees of success.[23] The FATF created in 1989 to combat money laundering and tasked with countering terrorist financing following 11 September, has resulted in making countries more conscious about practices to deter or limit terrorist financing within their borders. The CTAG's efforts, experts say, have suffered from a lack of direction and declining motivation among member states.[24]

A number of regional organisations, have delivered formal statements outlining their shared commitment to counter-terrorism and invested in frameworks, however the scale of capacity, funding and political will to aggressively pursue counter-terrorism strategies has remained diffused.

For example an assessment by experts in the report from the Center on Global Counter-terrorism Cooperation made some very critical observations.[25] It concluded that while the African Union (AU) has adopted a broad-based normative framework to combat terrorism via its 1999 counter-terrorism convention, 2002 protocol, and 2004 counter-terrorism plan of action, unfortunately that framework has yet to be implemented by many of its 53 member states. In Central Asia, mechanisms of the the Commonwealth of Independent States (CIS), the Collective Security Treaty Organisation (CSTO), and the Shanghai Cooperation Organisation (SCO) , the report argues have largely focused on improving joint military operations aimed at preventing drug trafficking, arms smuggling, and terrorism. Despite the overlapping membership in the three regional bodies, there is a lack of coordination among them and considerable substantive duplication of effort, including in their counter-terrorism activities. It summarised that Europe has the most developed regional architecture, with the Council of Europe (CoE), the European Union (EU), and the Organisation for Security and Cooperation in Europe, but each plays important yet sometimes overlapping roles in pursuing a regionally coordinated response. The report further added that in the Middle East and North Africa (MENA) the Organisation of the Islamic Conference (OIC) and the League of Arab States (LAS) have seen progress in promoting counter-terrorism cooperation among states but have seen limited follow-up activities within members. In South east Asia, the Asia-Pacific Economic Cooperation Forum (APEC), the Association of Southeast Asian Nations (ASEAN), the ASEAN Regional Forum (ARF), have made considerable strides in regional counter-terrorism cooperation, however due to the region's relatively weak multilateral bodies and poor track record of cooperation among states and those bodies, many of their efforts are carried out with insufficient coordination with other relevant actors either within the region or at the global level. It is a similar story with South Asia, where relative lack of subregional counter-terrorism cooperation should hardly come as a surprise. Different perceptions of the threat of terrorism, intra-regional rivalries and often tense relations between and among countries have generally limited the ability of subregional bodies, principally the South Asian Association for Regional Cooperation (SAARC) and the Bay of Bengal Initiative for Multi Sector Technical and Economic Cooperation (BIMSTEC) to develop and carry forward action-oriented counter-terrorism initiatives.[26]

India having consistently committed to efforts to combat global terrorism and has advocated over the last several decades in various international fora, a policy of zero tolerance on terrorism. In this context, in 1996, India proposed to the UNGA the adoption of the 'Comprehensive Convention on International Terrorism' (CCIT).

India's Push for the Comprehensive Convention on International Terrorism

Over twenty years after its first proposition, India has revived its efforts to secure a global consensus on the Comprehensive Convention on International Terrorism (CCIT). Officials from the government described the push for the treaty as 'the first serious attempt to approach terrorism from a regime perspective'[27] as it seeks to identify an acceptable definition of terrorism that all 193 members of the UNGA would be able to adopt legally. The CCIT purports to undertake the weeding out of terrorism through the denial of funds, safe havens, arms and technologies. Its main tenets aim to unite the international community, to ban all terror groups and shut down terror camps, to outline special laws under which all terrorists could be prosecuted and to make cross-border terrorism an extraditable offence worldwide.[28] Within this framework, the State Party, in the territory of which the alleged offender is present, has to submit the case without undue delay to its competent authorities for prosecution.[29] Offences set forth in this convention shall be deemed to be extraditable offences in any extradition treaty existing between any of the State Parties.[30] CCIT would also include the act of 'Naming and Shaming' countries that serve as financiers and havens for terrorist activities.[31]

Authoritative accounts on India's efforts traced back to November 1996, recall that when India first took the initiative to circulate a "first draft" of a CCIT, within the ad hoc committee, it was decided to keep this draft in suspension until the sectoral negotiations on the Convention on Suppression of Terrorist Bombings and the Convention on the Suppression of Financing of Terrorism were completed.[32] Work on the CCIT was further delayed when the ad hoc committee decided to complete work on a Convention on Suppression of Acts of Nuclear Terrorism, which eventually adopted in 2005.[33] A working group was eventually formed in 2005, when the 6th Committee of the UNGA decided to review the draft. In April 2013, the working group considered a proposal to address the outstanding issues by incorporating them in a UNGA resolution while adopting the CCIT as a purely legal instrument to deal with the crime of terrorism. This proposal was not agreed upon by all the countries.[34] Years later, the main issues of discord among the participants in the ad hoc committee on the drafting of a CCIT have not changed very much.

However India's renewed push on the CCIT, has been bolstered by the belief that the CCIT draft under current deliberation is able to effectively counter the opposition from the three main blocs that have raised objections: the U.S., the Organisation of Islamic Countries and the Latin American countries.[35] All three have objections over the "definition of terrorism" and have sought exclusions to safeguard their strategic interests. For example, the OIC wants exclusion of national liberation movements, especially in the context of Israel-Palestinian conflict and as observers suggest to prevent action against Pakistan.[36] The US wanted the draft to exclude acts committed by military forces of states during peacetime and Latin American countries had concerns about human rights law.[37]

India's engagement to support the a global regime on terrorism have also included active participation in several counter-terrorism discussions,[38] such as drafting a Global Counter-Terrorism Strategy in the General Assembly in 2006, serving as a founding members of the Global Counter-Terrorism Forum (GCTF), and supporting counter-terrorism mechanisms established by UN Security Council Resolutions, such as Resolutions 1267, 1988, and 1989 related to sanctions against

Al-Qaeda/Taliban, Resolution 1373 establishing the Counter-Terrorism Committee, and Resolution 1540 addressing the non-proliferation of Weapons of Mass Destruction to terrorist organisations.[39] During India's tenure on the Security Council in 2011–2013, it served as the chair of the Counter-Terrorism Committee.[40] India is also party to the 13 sectoral conventions on terrorism adopted by the UN.[41]

India's attempts have received traction as the world seems to be in the shadow of constant terror, with an increase in the footprint of global terrorist groups, especially in the West and South East Asia. Having been subjected to and resisted such acts against humanity, India is engaged in persuading responsible governments across the world to take a more united stand on the matter.[42] During his speech to the UNGA in 2014, India's Prime Minister Narendra Modi, reiterated the need for developing a Comprehensive Convention on International Terrorism. He re-emphasised the Indian position that the distinction between good terrorism and bad terrorism cannot be accepted and such actions merely underlie the lack of intent in eradicating this global threat.[43] At the UNGA held in September 2015, the foreign minister Sushma Swaraj, also exhorted the UN to consider taking a stronger stance on the issue:[44]

'International terrorism can only be defeated by organized international action. The world must demonstrate that it has zero tolerance for terrorists who kill and maim innocent civilians with action based on the principle of prosecute or extradite. Countries that provide financing to terrorists and safe havens for their training, arming and operations must be made to pay a heavy price by the international community [...] importantly, an international legal regime, under the Comprehensive Convention on International Terrorism can no longer be held up. 19 years ago, in 1996, India had made this proposal at the United Nations but we have been unable to adopt it and entangled ourselves in the issue of definition. We have to understand that there can be no distinction between good and bad terrorists. Neither can terrorism be linked to any religion. A terrorist is a terrorist; one who commits crimes against humanity cannot have any religion. Therefore, my appeal to all of you is that we should come together in this 70th anniversary year of the United Nations and pledge to unanimously adopt the CCIT.'

The foreign minister also appealed to the UNGA to take up the issue in September 2017 during the General Debate of the 72nd Session:[45]

Terrorism is at the very top of problems for which the United Nations is searching for solutions. We have been the oldest victims of this terrible and even traumatic terrorism. When we began articulating about this menace, many of the world's big powers dismissed this as a law and order issue. Now they know better. The question is: what do we do about it? [...] Although India proposed a Comprehensive Convention on International Terrorism (CCIT) as early as in 1996, yet two decades later the United Nations has not been able to agree upon a definition of terrorism. If we cannot agree to define our enemy, how can we fight together? If we continue to differentiate between good terrorists and bad terrorists, how can we fight together? If even the United Nations Security Council cannot agree on the listing of terrorists, how can we fight together?

Since a decision on the CCIT was not adopted at the UNGA in 2017, India has pivoted to a new strategic approach, holding bilateral meetings with opposing states to persuade them towards a compromise or agreement. India's Foreign Minister for instance held bilateral meetings with her counterparts at the Gulf Cooperation Council and from the 22-member Arab League.[46] Counter-terrorism initiatives have also been a major part of the bilateral relationship with the US and China,[47] particularly vis-à-vis Pakistan, a country, India accuses of sponsoring cross-border terrorism. India has also established a number of Joint Working Groups on Counter-Terrorism (JWG-CT) as part of its bilateral relationships with several countries.[48] In these exchanges, as well as during high-level exchanges at the Ministerial and Head of State/Government levels, India has lobbied for support for the adoption of the CCIT.[49] Indian officials have claimed that there is a growing resonance among UN members on the need for such a legal framework and that the initiative has seen 'a lot of progress' as a result of India's advocacy.[50] In answer to a question in the Indian Parliament on the progress of the CCIT, the Minister of State for External Affairs in July 2017 clarified:

> There is growing international support for this initiative. In the World Summit held in September 2005, leaders stressed the need to make every effort to reach an agreement on and conclude a comprehensive convention on international terrorism in that session itself. Several countries including the five permanent members of the UN Security Council have voiced support for such a convention. Leaders of prominent multilateral groupings, during their recently concluded Summits, such as NAM (September 2016), BRICS (October 2016) and SCO (June 2017) have also called for the early finalization of a CCIT.[51]

Indian observers[52] have long argued that while no country in the UN has opposed the need for a CCIT, the shortcoming lies in the fact, that UN resolutions are the result of political compromises between the members, especially the permanent members, of the UNSC. They elaborate from experience that the preferred approach of the major UNSC resolutions to counter-terrorism (1267 and 1989, 1373 and 1540) has been to condemn terror acts, recall obligations of member states to fight against terrorism, including the concept of "zero tolerance" of terrorism, offer support for capacity building in member states to counter-terrorism, and introduce sanctions in specific cases.[53] India has taken a position that, the embryo of building a unified response exists[54] in frameworks like the Financial Action Task Force (FATF) that sets standards with respect to combating money laundering and terrorist financing, the Egmont Group, which is an informal network of Financial Intelligence Units (FIU) and through instruments such as the 'United Nations Security Council committee pursuant to resolutions 1267 (1999) 1989 (2011) and 2253 (2015) concerning ISIL (da'esh) al-qaida and associated individuals groups, undertakings and entities'. However, to have impact, there has to be concerted effort, as these provisions in their current state, do not yet provide an effective global response for reasons of national expediency.

Since Asia has suffered the largest impact of terrorism globally, to build an Asian consensus on the issue, India has also repeatedly suggested that violent extremism needs to be delinked from religion, ethnicity or identity. Recognising the transnational nature of terrorism today, India has been pushing for a global regime on terrorism that enforces concepts of - assigning responsibility and ensuring accountability.[55]

Recurring Challenges and Future Considerations

It is within context that the contributors of this anthology of essays, debate and discuss recurring challenges, future considerations and immediate deliverables in the evolving debate on countering terrorism. The chapters are organised around distinctive themes that help locate the current dilemmas on the subject and aim to:

1. Evaluate the norm building efforts in countering global terrorism, understanding the geo-political realities and defining the Asian and global response to terrorism.

2. Identify ideologies and drivers fuelling this transnational resurgence of extremist violence, with an eye on the role of terror finance in exacerbating conflict in the region.

3. Examine how technology is changing the nature of conflict and the rising challenges there-in to Asian security.

4. Assess the threat of terrorism in Asia, from South West Asia, to the extended outposts in South Asia and South East Asia.

5. Debate the absence of effective counter-narratives, and building upon a reservoir of best practices of counter-terrorism efforts by countries in the region.

Authors have taken positions in their reflections based on their perspectives and national identities and since this a conversation on mitigating divergences, the book allows for it.[56]

The book begins with a special insight on the situation in Afghanistan and the implications for the Global War on Terror by H.E. Mhd. Hanif Atmar, National Security Advisor of Afghanistan (2014–2018). He succinctly explains as to what went wrong in global efforts in countering terrorism since 9/11 and makes a scathing critique of inadequate regional responses. He reiterated the responsibility of Pakistan to eliminate the safe havens for its own and regions stability. The former NSA of Afghanistan argues that a breakdown on consensus on countering terrorism is not just to the detriment of Afghanistan but that of the entire region. Interestingly, in the first chapter of the book, Maj. Gen. Durrani, the former National Security Advisor to Pakistan, has in his submission sought to flesh out a way to developing a common denominator to fight terrorism in Asia. Lamenting on why Pakistan and India have failed to cooperate against terrorism, his chapter concludes by taking stock of the current state of affairs between these countries and attempting to present a few guidelines in the form of common denominators which if agreed to by all nations will support the common objective of destroying terrorism in the region.

Abdel Bari Atwan, draws from his experience as a veteran journalist from the Arab world to demystify the 'geopolitics of global jihad'. He takes the case of the Islamic State and discusses the various factors that led to the rise, proliferation and various points of narrative resonance that give the group its ideological influence. He concludes by delineating the responses that have emerged in an effort to contain and control the rampant spread of this threat and the steps that need to be taken in the future to prevent it from resurfacing. Looking at this issue from the Indian perspective, one of India's foremost investigative journalists, Praveen Swami, attempts to trace such terrorism in the Indian Subcontinent and outline similarities that occur in most modern Islamist movements as well. He begins by citing the incident of the Darmapatnam suicide bombers as a means to describe how religious violence has occurred across geographies and histories and the means used for the proliferation of political agendas. Two and a half centuries on, as Indians contemplate the rise of the Islamic State, the story of the suicide-attackers of Darmapatnam serves as a means to illuminate the structural and hierarchical conflations between religion and politics that have existed in the Indian subcontinents' history as well. From the author's perspective it is hoped that such re-examinations of the past would provide means through which current threats can be contextualised and contained as well.

Going back to the absence of norms and binding frameworks to counter the scourge of terrorism, Ehsan Monawar, a counter-terrorism specialist from Afghanistan, delves into his experiences to argue the need for sustainable efforts and peace building to re-establish socio-political and legal order in the region. The first section is rounded up by a provocative essay by Waiel Awwad exploring the roots of terrorism as an industry and its global expansion. He makes the case that the turmoil in the Middle East has existed for decades. Its roots lie beyond the immediate present. It has merely been exacerbated with the discovery of oil and gas. The region has since been subjected to division, internal fighting, military intervention and regime changes. Given the global interventionist origins of the scourge of terrorism, he argues, the response must also necessarily be multifaceted and diverse. His chapter attempts to examine the best way to do so by raising certain fundamental questions regarding the nature and implications of terrorism today and what lessons Asia can learn to tackle this menace.

The next section examining the means and drivers fuelling the resurgence of extremism begins with a special insight from television journalist Baker Atyani. He recounts his own experience as a hostage held for 18 months by the Abu Sayyaf Group (ASG) in southern Philippines to throw light on the issue of hostage taking as tool used of terrorism and methodology of negotiations. Taking the issue of terror finance further, Atul Goel, a serving officer from the Indian Police Service, writes comprehensively on the challenges faced by India, especially countering terror finance in Kashmir. He delineates an outline of the sources, transfers, and distribution mechanisms that are used to propogate and proliferate terrorism within the region. South Asia expert, Professor Christine Fair, in her seminal chapter on 'Women And Support for Terrorism in Pakistan', argues that gender is an extremely important axis in studies regarding terrorism. While conflict related sexual violence and other such issues are studied to a great extent, what gets invisibilised are the female support systems that allow for the proliferation of terrorist activities. In her empirical analysis, she attempts to conduct a detailed study of these structural foundations and engage with the reasons why ideological support for the phenomenon is prevalent. The chapter examines the various reasons for support such as economic incentives, piety and religious beliefs, the presence or absence of democracy, sectarian orientations and gender; in order to develop a holistic image of how the network of global terrorism has come about and the way the cogs work together to proliferate the mechanism at every level. This section then ends with a powerful narrative from Lamya Haji Bashar, who is a Yazidi human rights activist and a survivor from the Daesh camps. Her story raises awareness about the experiences of women in Da'esh held territories. She contextualises her experience with an aim to help efforts develop a holistic and effective de-radicalisation narratives to battle Daesh ideology.

In the third section of this book, authors focus on the role of technology as a driver of terrorism. In her chapter titled 'Breaking the ISIS Brand: Trajectories into and out of Terrorism and the Social Media Recruitment of ISIS', Anne Speckhard attempts to examine the various mediums that have been used by the ISIS thus far to proselytize its audience and proliferate its message. She delineates the various demographics that the groups target and the steps involved in shepherding their believers. Speckhard argues that longer ISIS goes unchallenged virtually, the more potent the threat becomes and offers to shed light on ways to frame effective counter-narratives. Journalist Saikat Datta in his chapter on technology and intelligence in countering terrorism makes a case that while challenges posed by technology are new, the answers to countering them lie in traditional means and not in an omnipresent surveillance regime. Coordination among multiple stakeholders is key to ensuring an intuitive approach. The third perspective in this section takes this conversation further looking at India's experiences in dealing with Online Radicalisation. Sanjeev Singh, a senior officer with the Indian Police Service, draws from his experience to infer on how modern radicalisation not only includes proselytisation through digital platforms, but technology is also a key component in strategisation, information gathering, target selection and operational execution by terrorist groups. In the presence of growing challenges, technologist Manjula Sridhar's perspective offers a way forward. In her chapter titled 'Tackling Malicious Profiling Online' she demonstrates the utility of something as simple as categorising gathered social media data on the basis of fake versus real accounts. She uses this model as an example to reinforce and explain the various ways in which data can be used for aiding securitisation efforts and building capacity against threats and doomsday attacks.

In the next section the focus shifts from global norms and trends to more regional perspectives. In a special insight, Mustafa El Sagezli, recounts his experiences of countering terrorism in the Maghreb and its implications for global security, especially in the case of former foreign fighters. He traces the roots of conflicts back to complex inherited histories of colonial resentment and unbalanced economic power distribution. Sagzeli argues that for a counter strategy to be effective, engagement with the dispossessed sections of society that are forced to turn to terrorism due to a lack of basic resources would be a pre-requisite. The Maghreb region has witnessed the burgeoning of several extremist movements because the civil order of the region was disrupted through military interventionism. It is therefore essential to first understand the paths that have led to the current situation before evolving a strategy that might be able to counter it through collective/collaborative effort. Frank Ledwidge offers a scathing critique of NATO's approach to 'the war on terror' and explains why he thinks it was a strategic failure. The approach taken in Afghanistan may be seen as an example that can be applied to the West's effort in Western Asia as a whole. Bereft of historical or political awareness and beguiled by an internal narrative of proficiency in 'counterinsurgency', the US and particularly the UK entered an area of which they had little understanding; they elected to fight a military campaign against a political problem. In so doing they failed either to engage regional powers constructively, or indeed set a sensible and achievable political strategy. This chapter attempts to highlight and outline the various ways in which the West failed in the region and how that can be avoided in the future. In the final chapter in this section, Eitan Shamir argues that the option of a military raid is becoming more relevant in the contemporary strategic environment. The raids discussed here are military operations that are conducted in order to weaken and/or deter a non-state actor, at least temporarily. In the absence of diplomatic and economic leverage, the aim is to limit the actor's ability to harm others.

Section four brings together counter-terrorism perspectives from South Asia and South East Asia. Lt. Gen. Chowdhury Hasan Sarwardy from Bangladesh, examines the Bangladeshi landscape and attempts to determining the varying factors that have gone into the current resurgence of terrorism. The author presents varying motivations and methodologies that are used to wreak havoc and destabilise civil order within the region. General Daya Ratnayake writes his perspective on the Sri Lankan defeat of terrorism and lessons that can be drawn from his country's experience. Through this chapter, the author provides a brief overview of the political turmoil, the ideological variations, the conflict and the eventual resolution in the hopes of developing a set of workable methods aimed at securitising the region. In a provocative chapter titled 'A 9/11 for South Asia?', Pakistan specialist and commentator, Ayesha Siddiqa argues that the conflation between religion and politics is a key issue that will continue to crop up repeatedly over the years. The continuation of such threats can be attributed to the fact that states continue to see non-state actors and violence as a policy tool and have no vision for the region to come together to fight the menace. She surmises, that until this blind sight is corrected there can be no evolution of a regional security document or healthier security practices. Professor Kumar Ramakrishna rounds up this section, with his chapter that discusses the ISIS threat to Southeast Asia by considering the aspect of returning foreign fighters; organised indigenous militant networks that are coordinating operations with ISIS as well as self-radicalised lone wolves. He attempts to examine whether or not law enforcement measures targeting the physical threat of ISIS are necessary and adequate and are doing enough to counter the ideological threat that ISIS poses.

The final section on the book focuses on the issue of developing counter narratives which are effective and adaptive to the prevalent discourse. Lt. Gen. Syed Ata Hasnain a veteran military officer from India submits his insights on the need to craft a new narrative for Kashmir. He argues that it is necessary to understand the narrative emerging from the region in greater detail in order to build a counter narrative that would be able to achieve emotional resonance. Adil Rasheed's chapter on deconstructing Jihadist narratives provides insight into not only what drives the extremist ideology but also the various processes through which it recreates and reproduces itself. In this chapter he provides a historical as well as theoretical overview of what drives such extremism and how it can be eradicated for good. The last word comes from Mr S.M. Sahai, a senior practitioner with the Indian Police Service, who attempts to demystify Islam in the context of Kashmir. He argues that most misapprehensions and misunderstandings regarding Islam as a religion stem from the false belief that the religion itself is extremist which flawed perception is. This misnomer needs to be countered by providing historical context to the debate. He documents the various ways in which radicalism permeated the Kashmiri landscape and how it is a recent phenomenon. He also posits a revival movement of Sufism in Kashmir as an alternate way of engaging with the sociocultural environment of the region and in the process reducing resentment induced violence.

It is hoped that these wide-ranging perspectives add value to the evolving debates on countering terrorism and resonate with readers of the volume.

NOTES

1 Ben Saul; The Legal Response of the League of Nations to Terrorism, Journal of International Criminal Justice, Vol. 4, No. 1, 1 March 2006, pages 78–102, available at https://doi.org/ 10.1093/jicj/mqi096

2 Ibid.

3 Asoke Mukerji, 'Extradite or Prosecute: Why the Counter-Terrorist Principle India is Pushing is So Crucial' The Wire, 4 June 2016, available at https://thewire.in/world/extradite-or-prosecute-negotiating-the-comprehensive-convention-on-international-terrorism-at-the-un /, accessed on 3 January 2018. Ambassador (Retd.) Asoke Mukerji was India's permanent representative to the United Nations in New York.

4 Ibid.

5 For more details see 'International legal instruments', United Nations Office of Counter Terrorism, available at https://www.un.org/counterterrorism/ctitf/en/international-legal-instruments, accessed on 3 January 2018.

6 Javier Ruperez, 'The United Nations In The Fight Against Terrorism', un.org, January 2006,

available at https://www.un.org/sc/ctc/wp-content/uploads/2017/01/2006_01_26_cted_lecture.pdf, accessed on 3 January 2018. Ruperez had served as Executive Director Counter-Terrorism Committee, United Nations.

7   Ibid.

8   See note 6.

9   Ibid.

10 Asoke Mukerji (2016), See note 2.

11 Javier Ruperez (2006), See note 6.

12 The Global Regime for Terrorism, 31 August 2011, Council on Foreign Relations Report, available at https://www.cfr.org/report/global-regime-terrorism, accessed on 3 March 2017.

13 Javier Ruperez (2006), see note 6.

14 For more see note 12.

15 Council on Foreign Relations Report (2011) See note 12

16 Ibid.

17 For more see https://www.un.org/en/counterterrorism/ , accessed on 22 July 2018.

18 Council of Foreign Relations Report (2011), see note 12

19 Ibid.

20 Ibid.

21 Ibid.

22 Ibid.

23 Ibid.

24 Ibid.

25 Eric Rosand, Alistair Millar, Jason Ipe, and Michael Healey (October 2008) 'The UN Global Counter-Terrorism Strategy and Regional and Subregional Bodies: Strengthening a Critical Partnership' Report by Center on Global Counterterrorism Cooperation, available at https://www.globalcenter.org/wp-content/uploads/2008/10/strengthening_a_critical_partnership.pdf, accessed on 3 March 2017.

26 Ibid.

27 For more see 'How To Put an End to Terrorism as a Card in the Games Nations Play', Text of Foreign Secretary S Jaishankar's address at the counter-terrorism conference in Jaipur on 3 February 2017, reproduced by *The Wire*, available at https://thewire.in/20749/how-to-put-an-end-to-terrorism-as-a-card-in-the-games-nations-play/, accessed on 3 March 2017.

28 Ibid.

29 Ibid.

30 Ibid.

31 Ibid.

32 Asoke Mukerji (2016), see note 2.

33 Ibid.

34 Ibid.

35 Suhasini Haidar, 'Delhi hopes UN will push global terror convention', *The Hindu*, 3 July 2016, available at https://www.thehindu.com/news/national/Delhi-hopes-UN-will-push-global-terror-convention/article14467324.ece, accessed on 3 March 2017.

36 Ibid.

37 Ibid.

38 Permanent Mission of India to the United Nations, "India and the United Nations - Counter-Terrorism," Permanent Mission of India to the United Nations, New York, available at https://www.pminewyork.org/pages.php?id=1987, accessed on 3 March 2017.

39   Ibid.

40   Hardeep S. Puri, "Opening Statement by Ambassador H.S. Puri, Chairman" (speech transcript, Counter-Terrorism Committee, Strasbourg, France, 19 April 2011), available at https://www.pminewyork.gov.in/pdf/uploadpdf/12515ind1848.pdf, accessed on 3 March 2017.

41   See note 38.

42   Ibid.

43   Text of the PM's Statement at the United Nations General Assembly, 27 September 2014, available at https://www.narendramodi.in/text-of-the-pms-statement-at-the-united-nations-general-assembly-6660, accessed on 3 March 2017.

44   English rendering of Speech by External Affairs Minister at the General Assembly of the United Nations - The UN at 70: A Time for Action, 1 October, 2015, available at https://www.mea.gov.in/Speeches-Statements.htm?dtl/25878/English_rendering_of_Speech_by_External_Affairs_Minister_at_the_General_Assembly_of_the_United_Nations__The_UN _at_ 70_A_ Time_ for_Action, accessed on 3 March 2017.

45   Statement by External Affairs Minister at the General Debate of the 72nd Session of the United Nations General Assembly, New York, 23 September, 2017, available at https://www.mea.gov.in/Speeches-Statements.htm?dtl/28978/Statement+by+ External+ Affairs+ Minister+ at+the+General+Debate+of+the+72nd+Session+of+the+United+Nations+General+Assembly+New+York+September+23+2017, accessed on 22 July 2018.

46   Suhasini Haidar, 'Delhi hopes UN will push global terror convention', *The Hindu*, 3 July 2016, available at https://www.thehindu.com/news/national/Delhi-hopes-UN-will-push-global-terror-convention/article14467324.ece, accessed on 3 March 2017.

47   Dipanjan Roy Chaudhary, 'India to garner support for anti-terror initiative CCIT at BRICS', *The Economic Times*, 12 July 2018 available at https://economictimes.indiatimes.com/news/defence/india-to-garner-support-for anti-terror-initiative-ccit-at-brics/articleshow/54859024.cms, accessed on 22 July 2018.

48   Ministry of External Affairs of India, Annual Report: 2015–2016, pp 186, 1 October 2016, available at http://www.mea.gov.in/Uploads/PublicationDocs/26525_26525_External_Affairs_English_AR_2015-16_Final_compressed.pdf., and Ministry of External Affairs of India, Annual Report: 2017–2018, p. 202, 2 March 2018, available at http://www.mea.gov.in/Uploads/PublicationDocs/29788_MEA-AR-2017-18-03-02-2018.pdf, accessed on 22 July 2018.

49   Ibid.

50   See note 44.

51   Question No.1765 Comprehensive Convention On International Terrorism, 26 July 2017, Lok Sabha, available at https://fsi.mea.gov.in/lok-sabha.htm?dtl/28724/QUESTION+ NO 1765+COMPREHENSIVE+CONVENTION+ON+INTERNATIONAL+TERRORISM, accessed on 22 July 2018

52   Asoke Mukerji (2016), see note 2.

53   Ibid.

54   For more see 'How To Put an End to Terrorism as a Card in the Games Nations Play', Text of Foreign Secretary S Jaishankar's address at the counter-terrorism conference in Jaipur on 3 February 2017, reproduced by *The Wire*, available at https://thewire.in/20749/how-to-put-an-end-to-terrorism-as-a-card-in-the-games-nations-play/, accessed on 3 March 2017

55   Ibid.

56   Editors note: The views in the chapters are of the authors and do not represent those of the editor of the volume or the Institute.

SECTION ONE

Norms and the Global War on Terror: Challenges for Asia

Special Insight I
Keynote Address

H.E. Mhd. Hanif Atmar
National Security Adviser of Afghanistan (2014–2018)

Security and counter-terrorism are some of the most definitive challenges of our time. Let me congratulate Ambassador Prasad, his colleagues and the Indian government for a genuine and effective forum—for the South Asian region as well as the global community—to hold honest and open discussions about the collective threats faced by our nations, in order to determine the ways in which we can come together to neutralise these threats. It is all the more important that this is held in India because of its international credentials with regard to respect for norms. This gives us a level of comfort to hold these discussions in good faith and with the understanding that they will be translated into good policies. I shall also take this opportunity to thank India, its people and its government for their strong friendship, generous support and reliable partnership with Afghanistan. In 2016, the Afghanistan President visited and thanked every Indian for his/her one dollar contribution to Afghanistan. I shall do the same as a billion dollars from India as a contribution to Afghanistan is extremely important. It represents the goodwill of a nation that honours friendship and values solidarity with a nation like Afghanistan that has been the front-line country against our common enemies and threats. So, thank you for all of that.

I shall use this opportunity to bring up the current state of affairs in Afghanistan and the ways in which the scourge of terrorism has affected the country. However, before I do that, the first question that I would like to answer is: why does Afghanistan matter? There are several reasons why the situation in Afghanistan is often at the centre of most discussions on counter-terrorism. First of all, we share a region with Pakistan and other neighbouring countries that, collaboratively, has had the highest concentration of organised terrorists compared to any other region in the world. According to the statistics, 20 out of 98 United States (US)-

designated terrorist organisations are operating out of this region. Not all these violent elements are operating with the intention of attacking Afghanistan alone; they have goals beyond Afghanistan. But the region becomes important for them as it is seen as a breeding ground, or a sanctuary. This strategic geographic region, in fact, gave them a platform from where they could launch the 9/11 attacks. For that reason, you have the highest concentration of the world's most lethal terrorist organisations within this region, and therefore it is central to any discussion regarding countering terrorism successfully. The second question that emerges is: what enables groups to be there and survive? It is not merely the geographical control but also socio-political control that supports their nefarious purposes. The region has provided sanctuary for them. It is the symbiotic relation that they have developed with state and non-state actors, as well as the critical support and enabling infrastructure that they enjoy, that has allowed them to spread their roots so successfully.

Success against terrorism in Afghanistan is vitally important for the security of the region and global community. Unfortunately, the reverse is also true. Failure in Afghanistan is the failure of the region, and the global community, in their efforts to secure their nations. There are still many lessons to be learnt from Afghanistan, as also several experiences that can be drawn. Without delving into an exhaustive list of such lessons, one key point I would like to highlight is that we as a region have a common enemy now. But unfortunately, we do not have a common strategy to defeat it. In the context of developing a comprehensive strategy, I would like to flag four key points.

First, it is important to remember that terrorism is morphing and adapting in this region, to pursue its goals beyond Afghanistan. Since 9/11, these organisations have established a distinctive ecology, system and industry. We are no longer talking about lone wolf or a blindly violent terrorist organisation. There is a symbiotic nexus of three critical actors: first, violent extremists; second, criminal economics; and third, state sponsorship of terrorism. These three nodal points have emboldened the enemies of humanity that have come together to threaten the security of every nation in this region, and by extension the world community. In order to successfully fight them, it is important to first analyse how their strategies play out in Afghanistan. I shall do this by first focusing on the violent groups. There are four groups of extremist, terrorist organizations that we continue to fight. Group one includes the Afghan terrorists, including the Taliban, the Haqqani network and the Hezbi Islami, with whom we were successfully able to negotiate a peace agreement. The second group consists of Pakistani terrorist organisations, including the Lashkar-e-Taiba (LeT), Jaish-e-Mohammad (JeM) and Tehrik-e-Taliban Pakistan (TTP). The third group of such networks is regional and includes the so-called Islamic Movement of Uzbekistan (IMU) and the East Turkestan Islamic Movement (ETIM) of China and Sorolla and Generolla. Finally, the fourth group is the one that is very well known and talked about, including al-Qaeda and Daesh. What is important about these groups is that they have two sets of relations that are symbiotic. First, among themselves—they need each other. For example, outside terrorists need Afghani terrorists in order to be able to come to Afghanistan and, conversely, Afghan terrorists need them, for finance, technology and training. But there are two further sets of relationships. One, with rogue state elements, that provide them sanctuaries; and second, with criminal economic networks, including drugs. Before building counter-strategies, it is important to examine whether the terrorists' war is about politics, or economics or a combination of both. The drug industry and criminal economy produces such a tremendous amount of resources that they can easily be used to finance both state and non-state actors to pursue terrorist goals. And there is also a personal accountability issue here. Operators involved in the drug industry hardly listen to the policymakers. And these sorts of relationships actually make it possible for them to sustain their operations.

Given these facts, I would like to dispel three important myths that are commonly held about terrorism and the war in Afghanistan. The first myth concerns those who argue that the war in Afghanistan is a civil war. It is not. It is a drug war, it is a violent terrorist war and it is, unfortunately, an undeclared state-to-state war. A combination of all of this can easily be demonstrated by the multiplicity of the actors on the ground sustaining this war. The second myth pertains to those who believe that the distinction between good and bad terrorists will bring them security and will enable them to pursue their goals without being affected themselves. This is a flawed perception and making such distinctions can actually change a perpetrator to a victim as well, because such terrorist organisations are capable of morphing themselves into Frankenstein monsters that will come after their own masters. The third myth is associating such terrorism with Islam. It is absolutely untrue. Let me offer three reasons as to why such narratives are unhelpful. First, technically, associating terrorism with Islam is wrong because it will deprive us of the true understanding of what terrorism is and what it stands for. It is misleading. Second, ethically, it is inappropriate to associate terrorism with Islam because it fails to understand or appreciate the sacrifices that Muslims are making in order to defeat terrorism and the suffering that Muslims have faced at the hands of and because of terrorists. No Muslim nation is losing more innocent lives to terrorism than Afghanistan. But collectively, the Muslim world is losing more people to terrorism than any other civilisation. Third, politically, associating terrorism with Islam is unwise because this will lead to the loss of a natural ally.

Afghanistan is a good case in point. Our friendship with the US, with North Atlantic Treaty Organization (NATO), with India and with the rest of the Muslim world, to fight terrorism, our common enemy, is indeed a testament to the fact that Muslims are reliable partners in defeating extremist ideologies that have nothing to do with Islam. This understanding is important for shaping policies. Through effective dialogue, policies can contribute to an environment in which sound judgement is exercised to identify threats and build appropriate and effective strategies. With this understanding, we would be in a much better place to shape both our counter-terrorism strategies and peace and reconciliation efforts.

This brings me to the second point that I would like to make. Despite the international investment in counter-terrorism, terrorism is growing in terms of capabilities and presence in the Afghan-Pakistan region as these organisations have sanctuaries, financing, recruitment, training and equipment facilities. In Afghanistan, we estimate their number between 40,000–45,000 terrorist soldiers, all of whom have been deployed in the region. One-fourth of them are foreigners. They are not from the region, which makes it extremely difficult for us to decide who to make peace with and who to fight. We cannot make peace with these foreigners. They are not Afghanis, and we will have to think of a different strategy together because these foreigners are coming not just from the countries in the region but also from the rest of the world. There has been a displacement effect. The operation by the Pakistani Army called Zarb-e-Azb and the pressures on Islamic State of Iraq and Syria (ISIS), Daesh, al-Qaeda elsewhere in the Middle East have led to a sort of displacement effect. That is why you have such a high concentration of these terrorist organisations in Afghanistan.

As I said earlier, these networks have their individual goals to pursue. However, they have one thing in common and that is the destruction of the state in Afghanistan in order to establish a sanctuary. But upon reflection, if one examines the ways in which these networks function, there is hardly any country in this region that does not have an enemy among them. Al-Qaeda and Daesh will become enemies of humanity and not just the West. It is argued that LeT and JeM are only threats to India; however, that is not true either. Actors such as IMU, ETIM are planning to threaten China, Russia and Central Asia. Further, while there are also Pakistan-based terrorist networks threatening Afghanistan as well as the world, conversely TTP and its splinter groups are actually waging violence in Pakistan against innocent people. Given these statistics, one thing we all need to acknowledge is that the division of good and bad terrorists is a false one. We do not have any friends among them. If anything, every one of us has an enemy in them. It is important for our common understanding and common policy. For Afghanistan, this understanding has come at an extremely high cost. Over the past 14 months, we have lost over 10,500 men and women, 25 per cent of them civilians. Every day we are losing 28 Afghans to terrorism on an average. If you combine it with the wounded, every day we are losing 81 people on an average. It is a very high cost. Despite that high cost, we are still holding our ground.

While we are thankful to the US, our NATO partners, India, and our other regional partners, including China, Russia and Iran, for their continuous support to this noble struggle, there is still a long way to go towards establishing world peace. Some would argue that we have a stalemate as our president responded. Yes, we do, but that being said, this stalemate has emerged with one-tenth of the international soldiers that we had between 2009 and 2014.

The third point I would like to make is that the inadequacy of regional response to terrorism is actually making the challenge worse. Our regional response is inadequate at best. Why? Because over the past two years, we have engaged all our regional partners and unfortunately, much to our disappointment, we are seeing a continued breakdown of regional consensus over terrorism. There are varying reasons for this. Some states cite rivalries, disputes and incompatible differences with other global actors and try to translate that into their policies in Afghanistan and the region. But frankly speaking, there is no justification for such behaviour. At the end of the day, the longer terrorism remains unstopped, the more each and every one of us has to lose.

The question that emerges, therefore, is what are the issues that are preventing consensus formation? The first one is that we all decided since 9/11 that there should not be a distinction between good and bad terrorists. They are all terrorists, they are all bad. But unfortunately, recently, much to our disappointment, there are actors who are trying to justify that maybe some terrorist organisations can be partners against others. And normally these partnerships tend to be with the Afghan Taliban and the Haqqani network or the LeT and the JeM. When we speak to collaborators and regional partners about these issues, we have to constantly bring up the fact that there is no empirical evidence that the Taliban are the enemies of Daesh. Terrorist organisations are mutating in form. The majority of Daesh in Afghanistan today are either TTP or Afghan Taliban. It is also important to remember that anything that is given to them will be used against all of us collectively, political differences notwithstanding. And who are we to you, a friend or an enemy? We consider ourselves a friend. The breakdown of the consensus is to the detriment of not just Afghanistan but the entire region.

Second breakdown in that consensus is due to the centrality of state-to-state relations for counter-terrorism and cooperation. There are actors in the region who are trying to use non-state actors in pursuit of their national security interests. That is wrong. There is no substitute to effective state-to-state cooperation. Finally, the third problem emerges when states decide that they want to have security for themselves no matter what happens to their allies. This is also wrong. In a globalised world, one can either be collectively secured or we can be collectively insecure.

The fourth and final point relates to the lesson that I suggested right at the beginning that, from Afghanistan's perspective, what we have learnt painfully is that we, as South Asia, Central Asia, South East Asia and the global community, all have a common enemy. What we do not have is a common strategy to defeat it. And fortunately or unfortunately, collaboration is the only way to defeat that enemy.

I am not going to provide an exhaustive list of elements of how that strategy should be shaped and what it should contain. But I will offer a few key points which need to be considered in developing such a strategy. First, it is going to be a generational challenge. We cannot defeat terrorism in a year or two, or even in 10 years, by planning only for a year at a time. If the fight is for decades, we need to plan for decades. That enemy is not going to go away that soon. Second, considering the experience within the region, there needs to be action at four levels: global, Islamic world, regional and national. And we have to be able to coordinate our diplomatic, security, political and developmental assets in order to have action at four levels. What we should aim for is to develop a strategy at four levels. The first objective should be to end state sponsorship of terrorism. There is no other way to defeat terrorism unless we end its sponsorship. There are states that support terrorism and there are elements within states that do the same. We often hear from the international community that it is difficult to designate a state response against terrorism because there are many implications. It is rather disappointing that we do not have the courage and determination to set up an effective response. Also, even if we do not have that courage to designate a state, it is still important to highlight individuals that are sponsoring terrorism and hiding behind the states. International accountability will have to do this. It is also important to identify and prevent individuals and states from supporting terrorism, no matter which states they are working for.

Second, it has to be a coordinated effort of the intelligentsia, military and diplomatic parties to remove sanctuaries and the support infrastructure, including financing, training, recruitment and equipment. The third level is national action. We agree with those who believe that in addition to doing things about terrorist organisations, we also need to address the internal dynamics of terrorism itself, that is, the elements that provide a fertile ground for terrorism. There are three things that matter the most: improving governance; addressing poverty; and improving educational systems, among the many other priorities. These will have immediate and decisive impact on terrorism. Our current engagement against terrorism, with the US and the NATO, will definitely require additional regional help. From our perspective, Afghan peace and reconciliation will be the most effective counter-terrorism strategy in the region and beyond the region. If you remove the Afghani terrorist elements away from the regional and global terrorists, they will not have sanctuary in the region, which will immediately impede regional and global terrorism.

1

Developing a Common Denominator to Fight Terrorism in Asia

Maj. Gen. Mahmud Ali Durrani (Retd.)

Within the broad subject of 'Norms and the Global War on Terror', this chapter is an attempt to focus on what I consider the foundation for a regional counter-terrorism (CT) strategy. In practical terms, this necessitates the construction of a common CT template. For the purposes of this chapter, I will attempt to define a common CT template, which will include an important actionable point, that I term a minimum denominator. My common minimum denominator is based on my personal CT experience within Pakistan and hopefully, will also reflect the views of my Indian interlocutors. The inspiration for my chapter can be traced to the concept note prepared by the editor of the volume for the Asian Security Conference deliberations.

It is surprising that in spite of this long ongoing war on terror, the world has been unable to formulate a definition of what constitutes terror or terrorism. It is time that we, at least at the regional level, begin developing a clear understanding of terrorism. Every nation has its own conception of what constitutes terrorism and this definition is often influenced by the nation's geopolitical reality. The United States (US) has defined terrorism under the Federal Criminal Code as:

> ...activities that involve violent...or life-threatening acts...that are a violation of the criminal laws of the United States or of any State and...appear to be intended to intimidate or coerce a civilian population; to influence the policy of a government by intimidation or coercion; or affect the conduct of a government by mass destruction, assassination, or kidnapping....[1]

The US Army manual defines terrorism as the "calculated use of unlawful violence or threat of unlawful violence to inculcate fear. It is intended to coerce or intimidate governments or societies to attain political, religious, or ideological goals."[2]

While I have not defined terrorism thus far, in my opinion the essential elements that constitute a terrorist act are:

1. The use of sudden violence against unsuspecting individuals or groups to strike fear and helplessness in an essentially civilian population.
2. The use of unlawful force for the purposes of striking terror and fear. Violence, therefore, becomes the primary instrument of the terrorist.
3. The coercion of groups of individuals and governments with the objective of cornering the latter into following the terrorists' agenda.
4. The proliferation of political, ideological or religious goals that terrorist groups are unable to undertake through legitimate means.

Today, terrorism has become a household word because no country has been spared from this threat. Of all the forms of terrorism that are prevalent currently, terrorism conducted in the name of religion is the most vicious version, and also the most prevalent form.

Terrorism is, therefore, a serious global threat that needs to be defeated by a well-considered strategy at the national, regional and international levels. For example, the terrorist attack in Mumbai on 26 November 2008, carried out by a terrorist group based in Pakistan, was a classic transborder terrorist event. Unfortunately, mistrust overruled common sense.

While Pakistan has constantly been blamed for supporting terrorism, the flipside of the issue is that Pakistan itself continues to suffer the most from the scourge, both in terms of foreign and domestic perpetrators of terrorism. While there have been sporadic terrorist attacks in Pakistan over the last few decades, the well-organised and indiscriminate terrorist attacks spiked post-9/11. This was essentially due to the flow of Taliban out of Afghanistan and into Pakistan's tribal territories[3] in the wake of the US-led bombing attacks in Afghanistan.[4] The arrival of the Taliban into the Pakistani mainland resulted in the killing of over 90 tribal leaders known as *Malik*s and helped establish their writ based on coercion and terror.[5]

Aside from the influx of the Taliban from Afghanistan, other contributory factors that have fuelled terrorism in Pakistan are: poverty, a deficient education system, weak and corrupt police and a cumbersome legal system. This is in addition to the presence of strong politico-religious parties, with a very narrow interpretation of Islam.

The Pakistan Army has been battling terrorists since 2004, especially in tribal areas. We have suffered large-scale casualties, both of innocent civilians and law enforcement personnel, across Pakistan. According to our internal assessment, the total number of casualties since 2003 have been approximately 81,000. A more realistic estimate of the total casualties would be around 60,000: 50 per cent of these casualties were civilians; 40 per cent were terrorists; and the remaining were security personnel.[6]

After the gruesome terrorist attack on a school in Peshawar on 16 December 2014, which killed 141 people[7]—mostly children—the political leadership finally got together and agreed on a 20-point National Action Plan[8] aimed at defeating terrorism. However, I believe that a lot of work still has to be done to make the action plan a success. Aside from the various actions spelled out in the plan, it is also important for Pakistan to develop a counter-narrative to oppose the narrative of Islam being preached and followed by the Taliban and its supporters. Besides this joint strategy, there is also a need to develop dedicated multinational organisations at the regional level and beyond, in order to effectively coordinate and fight religious extremism and militancy.

The fundamental challenges to fighting terrorism, especially in South Asia, are the existing differences between various nations and the presence of serious mistrust due to the ongoing conflicts. Take the example of India and Pakistan. It is well known that violence across the Line of Control (LoC) in Kashmir has escalated in the recent past. The Pakistani establishment, its media and public place the blame for this squarely on the Indian establishment, especially on the Research and Analysis Wing (RAW). In India, the situation is reversed, with the establishment, the media and public being convinced that it is the Pakistani military and the infamous Inter-Services Intelligence (ISI) agency who are the real culprits. I am convinced that violence along the LoC does not help either country and is a total waste of men and material. Furthermore, while senior leaders of both the countries privately agree with these facts, they do not acknowledge these facts publicly and have failed to arrest this escalation thus far.

In the spirit of this conference, my primary recommendation is to focus on the essential dos and don'ts in the form or a common denominator on which we all agree as the basis of our CT policy. The starting point will be to agree on a definition of what actually constitutes terrorism.

Essential Elements of a Common Denominator to Fight Terrorism

I believe that the following points can be used to form a common denominator for fighting terrorism. I am confident that these points are non-controversial and can be agreed to by all nations.

1. Extremism, especially religious extremism, should be discouraged by all nations.

2. States with religious majorities should discourage such majorities from legislating extreme interpretations of religion that work to the detriment of religious minorities, especially under the umbrella of democracy.

3. Terrorism in any form, irrespective of its objective, should be forcefully condemned and banned.

4. Other than the state, no group or entity within a nation should be allowed to declare a war on any other nation.

5. Each nation should make sure that its territory is not used by any terrorist or terrorist group to attack a second nation.

6. Each territorial region and sub-region should develop counter-terrorist mechanisms in order to ensure assistance in a timely fashion, with the aim of defusing and defeating terrorism. This case particularly holds true for transborder terrorism, where intelligence agencies play a major role in providing intelligence in assisting each other.

7. Resolving existing territorial disputes between nations through dialogue will help defuse terrorism and should be pursued with vigour.

It is essential that each nation that is threatened by terrorism develops a national action plan or a national strategy aimed at fighting terrorism. While developing a plan is an important first step, the state must also have the courage and conviction necessary to implement such a plan.

I have already mentioned the factors that have contributed to the growth of terrorism in Pakistan. Unfortunately, most nations in Asia, particularly South Asia, suffer from certain common problems that must be addressed urgently:

1. *High levels of illiteracy or inadequate education*: An insufficient number of schools and a distorted education system is the norm in many Asian countries. While a very small percentage of students attend madrasas, their role in projecting very narrow interpretations of religion is tremendously significant. Today, some nations are in the process of rewriting their history, which will strike at the very heart of their secular credentials. Such misguided nationalism promotes bigotry.

2. *Poor judicial practices and an inefficient police force*: The lack of a strong legal system is a major cause of frustration amongst the masses who, at times, are forced to take the law into their own hand and this pushes them into the lap of the extreme right.

3. *Poverty and an unfair distribution of wealth*: The socio-economic realities of daily existence cannot be negated, especially in areas where the gap between the rich and the poor is wide and unfair. Places like these become

hotbeds for recruitment and terrorist organisations have a field day in finding recruits.

In conclusion, I would like to reinforce certain key points regarding the development of collaborative CT strategies. First, there is a need to come to an agreement regarding a globally applicable definition of terrorism. Vagueness and a lack of clarity has hindered the objective to rid the world of the scourge thus far. Second, the socio-economic factors that lead to the growth of terrorism need to be rooted out. This is particularly relevant for developing countries that suffer from high levels of poverty, illiteracy, flawed systems of justice, social inequality and religious extremism. Finally, nations need to come together to develop a counter-narrative and counter-strategy against terrorism by coming to terms with common denominators and basic conceptions that hold true in every context. If these measures are taken, then the world will be a step closer towards eradicating this increasingly universal twenty-first century epidemic.

NOTES

1   Legal Information Institute, '18 U.S. Code § 2331—Definitions', 1992, available at https://www.law.cornell.edu/uscode/text/, accessed on 25 August 2017.
2   The US Army, *Field Manual No. FM 3-0*, 14 June 2001, Chapter 9–37.
3   The Federally Administered Tribal Areas (FATA) is a semi-autonomous tribal region in north-western Pakistan, consisting of seven tribal agencies (districts) and six frontier regions, that is directly governed by Pakistan's federal government through a special set of laws.
4   Based on author's own assessment and experience in official service.
5   Ibid
6   Ibid.
7   *BBC*, 'Pakistan Taliban: Peshawar School Attack Leaves 141 Dead', 2014, available at http://www.bbc.com/news/world-asia-30491435, accessed on 12 September 2017.
8   The National Action Plan was established in January 2015, following the Peshawar attack. The plan provided a framework for the Twenty-first Amendment to the Constitution of Pakistan, which established speedy trial military courts for offences relating to terrorism.

2

Geopolitics of Islamic Jihad
The Islamic State: Roots, Savagery and Future*

Abdel Bari Atwan

If we want to know how dangerous the Islamic State of Iraq and Syria (ISIS) is, then we must take a quick look at its allies and adversaries. The ISIS has managed to antagonise more than a hundred countries, including two superpowers, the United States (US) and Russia, middle states such as France, Britain and Germany, as well as key regional states like Saudi Arabia, Iran and Turkey. Their supporters, on the other hand, are scarce. Not one country has openly declared its support for this "State". However, some regional countries, such as Turkey, Saudi Arabia and Qatar, believe (out of sectarian reasons) that the ISIS is a "Sunni" card against the Shiite axis led by Iran. The latter comprises Syria, almost half of Iraq and Hezbollah in Lebanon. This is the first time since the Second World War when the two great powers, the US and Russia, have met on the same ground against a common enemy, which is the Islamic State, or "ISIL" as some prefer to say, and both send fighter jets, drones, and helicopters, in addition to other jets from European and Arab countries.

What Makes the ISIS Different

The ISIS differs from other terrorist organisations—especially its parent organisation, al-Qaeda—in some major ways, which are summarised as follows:

1. First of all, it made itself financially self-sufficient. This is due to its takeover of more than 13 oilfields in eastern Syria and several natural gas

---

*This chapter was written and presented in March 2017, based on the author's previously published work. There have been several changes since then, including the reduction of physical ISIS territory and military defeat. This chapter attempts to provide an overview into the functioning of ISIS as an organisation.

fields, in addition to a phosphate field near Palmyra. Through these takeovers, the ISIS managed to generate a daily income of nearly US$ three million by selling crude oil or oil refined in primitive refineries throughout 2014. However, this income declined in 2015 due to the airstrikes conducted near these fields and the refineries associated with them. Additionally, restrictions were also imposed on exports to neighbouring countries, especially Kurdistan in northern Iraq, Turkey and the Syrian regime. These exports relied on a network of mafia and middlemen, who engaged in the illegitimate business of selling a barrel of oil in the international market for half its price or sometimes even less. The ISIS's capture of Mosul in the summer of 2014 was another key event that served as a source of finance for the outfit. The capture led to ISIS obtaining half a billion dollars from the reserves of the Iraqi Central Bank's branch and other banks. Trade of Syrian and Iraqi museum antiquities was also one of the major sources of their income, in addition to taxes imposed by the state on their "citizens", which are presently estimated to be around US$ 900 million.[1]

2. Second, the ISIS also enjoyed self-sufficiency in terms of armament and ammunition. It had captured stocks of the Iraqi Army in Mosul, Ramadi, Tikrit and Biji. These areas contained advanced American weapons, including artillery, rockets, ammunition and more than 1,700 tanks and armoured vehicles. The ISIS also took over Russian weapons from the stocks left behind by the Syrian Army after the fall of several cities like Raqqa, Deir Azzor, Izaz and parts of Aleppo and Homs.

3. Third, the ISIS is almost the only organisation that stayed on its land amongst its "citizens". It required no sanctuary in another country the way al-Qaeda had to—the latter first established itself in Sudan, and then became the Taliban's guest in Afghanistan. This establishment in its own country allowed the ISIS to function under lesser restrictions, thereby ensuring greater autonomy over its decisions. Furthermore, it also secured sovereignty over its land to a great extent.

Though the ISIS differs from traditional terrorist organisations in the above-mentioned ways, it is also necessary to examine what the ISIS is in the first place. Several people argue that the ISIS is neither a state nor Islamic. However, if we look at how the international law defines a state, we can see that the ISIS can roughly be placed under that definition as a "State". It has a flag, a government, administrations, an army of 100,000 fighters, its own currency (the gold dinar), a television station (*Al-Tawheed*), a radio station (*Al-Bayan*), an official magazine

(*Dabiq*), an advanced media network (Al-Forqan, Al-Hayat, Al-Itisam), in addition to police, intelligence and women police agencies. As for its Islamic identity, it has adopted the Wahhabi doctrine as the official doctrine of the state. These fundamental elements aside, there are still several groups that consider the ISIS blasphemous and similar to the Kharijites movement.[2]

Despite the varying opinions regarding the legal status of the ISIS, it can be defined as a "de facto state." The ISIS represents a new phenomenon in the current world scene and the Middle East in particular. For example, there are other asymmetric "states" such as the "Emirate of Hamas" in the Gaza Strip, the "Emirate of Hezbollah" in southern Lebanon, the Kurdistan region in Iraq, the Boko Haram Emirate in northern Nigeria etc. However, the ISIS can be distinguished from the rest of these by its absolute control over its borders, the immense area under its control, the flow of two rivers in its land (Tigris and Euphrates) and the security it enjoys in comparison with its unsettled neighbours.

Socio-political Causes that Led to its Emergence

In order to better understand the ISIS phenomenon, and the reasons underlying its emergence and resurgence, there are seven keywords that we need to look at closely. These keywords will help provide insight into the group's psychology in a scientific and objective manner because they summarise the establishment, rise, expansion and the extent of the strength of the ISIS, and the danger it poses not just for the Middle East but rather for the whole world.

1. *Humiliation*: For half a century, the Arab people have been living a state of dual humiliation: from their rulers on the one hand; and Western colonialism on the other. Furthermore, frequent defeats due to Israeli aggression have also served to reduce the status of the average citizen. The ruling regimes' repression, that often manifests through toxic political practices such as dictatorship, tyranny and human rights violations, has served to push Arab citizens to the brink. The absence of political and democratic freedom and freedom of speech have further catalysed their will to revolt.

2. *Frustration*: There are generations of Arab citizens who have been living in frustration, lack of hope and despair. There are almost 100 million unemployed people,[3] which make up almost a quarter of the population of the Arab world. These figures include both partial and total unemployment. Furthermore, even those who are employed have unproductive and routine jobs. The region suffers from disguised unemployment in the absence of work and low production values in most sectors.

3. *Marginalisation*: Perhaps the marginalisation of Sunnis in Iraq after the American invasion, in the name of de-Baathification, played a major role in motivating the dispossessed to seek revenge and thereby increased public support for the ISIS.

4. *Western military intervention*: The intervention of Western military powers that targeted several countries like Iraq, Libya, Somalia, Afghanistan, and even the indirect intervention in Syria, led to the collapse of governments and institutions and created failed states plagued by bloody anarchy. This created a security vacuum that was filled by fundamentalist Islamic groups like al-Qaeda and the ISIS, in addition to other groups like Ansar Al-Sharia in Libya, Ansar Bait Al-Maqdis in Sinai, Youth and Islamic Courts in Somalia, Taliban in Afghanistan and more than a thousand Islamic factions in Syria.

5. *Absence of good governance*: The intervention and disruption of governance mechanism in most, if not all, Middle Eastern countries was another major catalyst for the rise of the ISIS. The tyranny of the ruling regimes, coupled with the spread of corruption, favouritism and the minorities' monopoly of both power and wealth, dispossessed the locals. Furthermore, preventing the vast majority from taking part in the decision-making process and the lack of state institutions led to a breakdown of civil society mechanisms. This breakdown was also accompanied by a lack of the separation of powers, an independent and fair judiciary and political and financial accountability. In the absence of checks and balances, the citizens had no refuge.

6. *Underestimation*: There is complete unawareness regarding the concept of "estimating the situation" on most levels, be it political, social or economic. There is a lack of understanding of how deep the ideological roots of the ISIS have infiltrated the region. People's surprise at the unmitigated growth of the ISIS, and the striking power it has achieved, stems from a lack of awareness regarding the geopolitical realities of the region. This confusion regarding the roots and the means to quell it in the decision-making headquarters in the West and East has manifested in disorderly half-hearted action that has deterred the menace but not weeded it out. At the beginning of the Syrian crisis, the Gulf states and other Western countries focused their efforts on one goal, which was to topple the ruling regime, utilising billions of dollars and thousands of fighters. They thought the fall would be quick and that this was the ideal method to establish Western notions of "progressive democracy" in the region. Large portions of the money and weapons exchanged reached the

ISIS and its sibling, Al-Nusra Front, and other extremist groups instead. Several mujahideen flocked to these groups through Turkish territories with the support and encouragement of the authorities there, who turned a blind eye to the situation.

7. *Social media*: The rise of social networking sites like Twitter, Facebook, WhatsApp, Skype, YouTube and others has also served to proliferate and disseminate the message much quicker. While the ISIS is purportedly fighting the corruptive influences and ideological dominance of the West, it has certainly benefited the most from these inventions. The social media has been used most effectively by it as a proselytising tool whose services are used to recruit thousands of jihadists to the cause through the spread of ideology and literature. The outreach has been enormous as these means are being used to appeal to more than a billion-and-a-half Muslims around the world for recruitment, as well as for terrorising enemies.

The media is not just limited to social networking sites (SNS) and social media platforms. The ISIS has also invested heavily in creating featured documentaries aimed at spreading its message across the world. It possesses an advanced network, run by Ahmed Abu Samra. Samra is a Syrian who was born in Paris to a father who was a doctor. He later moved to the state of Massachusetts in the US, where he obtained his bachelor's degree in information technology. He carried his expertise to his new headquarters in Raqqa, and was able to mobilise tens of his colleagues and other qualified people in this arena. There are specific units that are designed to produce documentaries and proliferate propaganda. These documentaries are meant to compete with Western documentaries and the technology used is often superior to the kind found in Hollywood. Additionally, there is also an electronic army made up of hundreds of people inside and outside the territory of the state. The organisation has more than 50,000 accounts on Twitter that tweet more than 100,000 tweets per day.[4] This is in addition to tens of thousands of pages on Facebook and thousands of WhatsApp accounts that are also invested in spreading the message as efficiently as possible. A good comparison to examine how SNS have really boosted the proliferation of the ISIS' message is al-Qaeda's attempts at ideological proselytisation. Sheikh Osama bin Laden was less fortunate than his protégé, Abu Bakr Al-Baghdadi, as he used to sit in a secret room in front of a camera for several hours to record a "video" of his sermons, and then send it to an influential person at the *Al-Jazeera* channel. Here, the channel reduced his speech more or less to a quarter of an hour, and then broadcast what it chose, neglecting most of the sermon, if not all. The lack of control over what parts of the message got broadcasted, and in what light, took away the narrative power from the al-Qaeda. The ISIS has not faced such issues and with the click of a button, the organisation can reach more than 200 countries around the world.

Historical Context and External Factors that Led to the Rise of the ISIS

While the US did not establish the ISIS, however it did create the public support the group received. When if first besieged Iraq and starved 26 million of its citizens through brutal sanctions in retaliation for Iraq's occupation of Kuwait, it provided the first seeds of resentment and rebellion in the Arab groups. This is particularly galling as the occupation has since been considered merely a trap aimed at destroying Iraq enough for its eventual occupation in 2003. Paul Bremer, the American military governor of Iraq, in my opinion, committed two major mistakes that have haunted the region and turned it into the chaotic mess that it is: the first was establishing the ruling council in Iraq based on quotas and sectarianism; and the second was dismantling the Iraqi Army, security/civil institutions and the Republican Guard. This threw more than a million Iraqi officers and soldiers into the streets. They were humiliated, marginalised and left without jobs, salaries or pensions. These dispossessed and disenfranchised masses then became the kernel fanning the flames of the ISIS. The sectarian policies of Nuri Al-Maliki, former Iraqi prime minister, further served to place the final nail on the coffin of civil society in the region.

Saddam Hussein, the late Iraqi president, had realised that the US' primary motive was to topple and replace his regime. This conviction was strengthened when two no-fly zones were enforced in north and south Iraq. He started preparations aimed at resisting the invading forces and launched the "Faith Campaign" by closing night clubs, prohibiting alcohol and writing *Allahu Akbar* (Allah is the greatest) on the Iraqi flag with his blood. The true seeds of the ISIS emerged in the Abu Ghraib prison, where the torture of Iraqi resistance fighters occurred. These prisoners included officers and soldiers of the army, the Republican Guard, and Iraqi security forces. The tortures were committed by the American forces here, and in Buka, another prison near Basra. In the latter, a meeting between Abu Bakr Al-Baghdadi and an elite group of those officers and soldiers took place. Baghdadi, who held a PhD in Islamic sharia, gave religious lectures at night. He spent more than a year in a cell on the charge of extremism and incitement of resisting the occupation.

Abu Bakr Al-Baghdadi joined the Tawhid and Jihad movement, which was established by Abu Mosab Al-Zirqawi in 1999. This movement was engaged in resisting American occupation as a resistance branch of the al-Qaeda. He later became a member, and eventually the head, of the Mujahideen Shura Council. Ultimately, he rose to the position of the head of the ISIS in Anbar. He chose to declare the Islamic caliphate in Ramadan in 2014 from the platform of the Great Mosque of Al-Nouri in Mosul. The time and place were particularly significant because he realised the significance of this act of resistance and the symbolic association it would hold for millions of Muslims. Symbolism was a crucial part of Baghdadi's strategy and long-term aspirations. It was no accident that he added the two words, "Al-Husni" and "Al-Qorashi", to his name to emphasise that he belongs to "Al Al-Bait".[5] Symbolism also played a major role in choosing Raqqa as a temporary capital for the ISIS as it was the summer capital for the Abbasid caliph, Harun Al-Rashid.[6]

One of the most prominent misconceptions regarding the ISIS is the common belief that the group consists of "amateur" fighters, with shabby beards and loose slacks, who know nothing except murder and slaughter. Despite the fact that this state has relied on savagery, gruesome executions, beheadings and stoning adulterers, these acts have not been committed in a void of gratuitous violence. These have been calculated acts, aimed at either terrorising the enemies and forcing them to flee the savagery or recruiting religious allies. The success of this policy of projection of cruelty was visible when more than 30,000 Iraqi soldiers stationed in Mosul fled in civilian clothes, leaving behind their weapons, once the word spread that the ISIS fighters were approaching the city. The fact of the matter is that the hard kernel of the ISIS comprises colonels and major generals from the Iraqi Army and Republican Guard who are leading from behind. These veterans are well versed in military and strategic statecraft and use their wartime experiences to efficiently oppose, resist and intimidate their enemies. It is this expertise and power that has enabled the ISIS to take over cities through well-executed military plans. If this expertise did not exist, the ISIS would also have been unable to establish government institutions and administer their diktats in a modern manner, aimed at providing services for protectorate. The ISIS is distinguished from other fundamentalist jihadist movements like al-Qaeda by: its public adoption of the Wahhabi doctrine; its strict implementation of Islamic sharia law/fatwas; and the incorporation of advisory opinions of Sheikh Ibn Taimiah, who is the religious reference for all those who follow the Islamic jihadist approach. This is how it has managed to attract tens of thousands of youth, from all parts of the world, by selling them the idea of jihad under the banner of a "true" Islamic state as described in its literature.

In order to oppose this rising militancy, the US formed a coalition of 60 countries to fight the ISIS. The coalition's fighter jets have made more than 6,000 sorties so far, while Russian fighter jets made around 2,000 sorties and airstrikes in a matter of a few weeks. However, the ISIS, even if wiped out militarily, will pose an ideational challenge, that the international community will have to fight the long war with.

Shifting Strategy and International Responses

The terrorist attacks that struck Paris in November 2016 may be an indication of a change of strategy by the ISIS. The latter might be moving towards the strategy of "consolidation": capturing land and reinforcing control over it in order to capture new land from Western powers, that is, the "distant enemy". Perhaps this change is a reaction to the military pressure and airstrikes the group has been exposed to, that might have led to it losing some territories in the recent months like Tikrit, Biji and the Sinjar Mountain. The expansion theory adopted by the ISIS is primarily based on expanding its reach in neighbouring Iraq and Syria, and then reaching Saudi Arabia and the two cities of Mecca and Medina in particular.

However, the build-ups and coalitions formed to oppose it and prevent it from expanding have forced it to reconsider its global expansionist tendencies. Therefore, it has spread its roots regionally by opening branches in many places, such as the "Sinai Mandate" in Egypt, Darna, Sirt, the Jafra Mandate in Libya, and other mandates in Somalia, Afghanistan and Pakistan, over and above the Boko Haram Mandate in north-eastern Nigeria. After the escalation of the ISIS danger and the failure of the airstrikes to destroy it, the Western countries started to change their policies and have, therefore, moved closer to the Russian position that calls for Assad to stay in power and to use his army, which has become experienced in urban and guerilla warfare after fighting the armed opposition. The plan is to use this army to confront and control the ISIS on the ground.

It is difficult to predict the fate of the ISIS and its ability to survive and persist under congestion of fighter jets in the skies of the region. However, it can be said that eliminating it will be uneasy and dangerous because the military solution by itself cannot achieve this goal if it is not part of a strategy of complex objectives. One of the most important of these objectives is to dismantle the public support which provides strength and continuity to the ISIS, through well-thought-out political solutions that meet the needs of this public in justice, equality and partnership in governance, away from sectarian quotas and by building up a unifying identity that is based on true cohabitation, cancelling all manifestations of exclusion and marginalisation and stopping all forms of Western military intervention.

Enemies of the ISIS make up an international force which is politically, militarily and economically the greatest. Therefore, the defeat of ISIS is feasible. However, what are the alternatives for the people of this region after this defeat is achieved and this state with its danger is eliminated? Western powers are experts in destroying rather than building up. What happened in Libya, Iraq, Yemen, in addition to what's happening now in Syria are explicit examples. There is always a Plan A to change regimes, but there is never a Plan B for what comes after this change. For that reason, danger persists and Islamic groups propagate as an extension to groups that have disappeared or establish new organisations with new names.

NOTES

1   For more see Matthew Rosenberg, Nicholas Kulish and Steven Lee Myers 'Predatory Islamic State Wrings Money From Those It Rules', *The New York Times*, 29 November 2015.

2   *Editor' note*: according to the Oxford Bibliographies, The Kharijites (Arabic: khawarij; sing. khariji) were the first identifiable sect of Islam. Their identity emerged as followers of Muhammad attempted to determine the extent to which one could deviate from ideal norms of behaviour and still be called Muslim. The extreme Kharijite position was that Muslims who commit grave sins effectively reject their religion, entering the ranks of apostates, and therefore deserve capital punishment. This position was considered excessively restrictive by the majority of Muslims, as well as by moderate Kharijites, who held that a professed Muslim could not be declared an unbeliever (kaffir). The Kharijites believed it was forbidden to live among those who did not share their views, thus acquiring the name by which they are known in mainstream Islamic historiography—khawarij means "seceders" or "those who exit the community." Radical Kharijites, on the other hand, declared those who disagreed with their position to be apostates, and they launched periodic military attacks against mainstream Muslim centres until they ceased to be a military threat in the late eighth century CE. The Kharijites were also known as Haruriyah (from Harura, the site of one of one of their main camps in Iraq), and more genericaly as *ghulat* (extremists). For more see: http://www.oxfordbibliographies.com/view/document/ obo-9780195390155/obo-9780195390155-0047.xml, accessed on 22 July 2018.

3   Based on author's research survey on figures available as of 2017.

4   Based on author's research up to March 2017 (figures subject to change, given nature of SNS)

5   The reason for this addition is because he believes that the caliph should be a Sunni Arab who is a descendant of the Prophet.

6   According to the Oxford Bibliography, the Abbasid dynasty ruled the central and eastern Islamic lands, at least nominally, and headed the Sunni Muslim community for five centuries from its capital Baghdad. The Abbasid claim to the caliphate was based on kinship with the Prophet through his uncle al-'Abbas (hence the name). For that reason they restored a truly Muslim government. The first Abbasid caliph, Abu al-'Abbas al-Saffah, replaced the Umayyad Marwan II in 132AH/749 CE; the surviving members of the Umayyad family fled to al-Andalus, where they ruled the Islamic West for the next six centuries. The last Abbasid caliph, Abu Ahmad al-Musta'sim, was killed during the Mongol sack of Baghdad in 656 AH/1258 CE. By that time the political significance of the Abbasids had long been greatly reduced. The caliph, while retaining his religious authority, had lost a large part of his political and military

influence. The caesura between the periods of prosperity and decadence is conventionally identified with the appointment of the military governor of Wasimt, Ibn Ra'iq, to the newly minted office of amir al-umara' (chief commander) in 324 AH/936 CE, which made him the de facto ruler in Baghdad. Some of the most famous caliphs in history, such as Harun al-Rashid and al-Ma'mun, were Abbasids, and their times are considered the golden age of the Muslim Empire. The foundations of practices that survived into later times were laid down under the Abbasids, for instance, armies made up of slave soldiers (mamluk) and standard administrative practices. For more see : http://www.oxfordbibliographies.com/view/document/obo-9780195390155/obo-9780195390155-0218.xml, accessed on 22 July 2018.

3

Invisible Jihad
Challenges for India and Asia

Praveen Swami

This little, we know: the two young men appeared inside the church, one sunny spring morning, a little after mass had begun, and attacked the congregation with cutlasses. Guards were called out, but before they could arrive, Lizardo Evans, one of the worshippers, lay dead on the church floor. Many others were injured. From the small church of Saint—Etienne-du-Rouvray near Rouen, to Wuerzburg in Germany or Orlando in the United States, and a dozen other places across the world, the script has been much the same. Each of these attacks, we know, were carried out in the name of God, and his regent on earth, the so-called Caliph of the Islamic State. In all these cases, though, there is one important thing that we do not know: exactly what went on in the minds of the attackers, in the hours and weeks before they went to what they must have known was a certain death.

Except, the attack on the church that sunny spring day took place not this year, nor the last, but in March, 1764, at the Portuguese colonial fort of Darmpatnam, on the Malabar coast. Like the United States special forces who killed Osama Bin Laden, so many centuries later, the guards at the Darmapatnam church wanted to erase the killers from history. A contemporary bureaucrat recorded:

> The bodies of the above Moors were immediately ordered to be thrown in the sea as an example to deter others from the like attempts in future and to prevent any religious [*illegible*] being got of them, that they may not be worshipped as saints as is the practice by their cast[e] by all who murder a Christian.[1]

Two and a half centuries on, as Indians contemplate the rise of the Islamic State, the story of the suicide-attackers of Darmapatnam helps illuminate our understanding of just what the macabre theatre of death it has unleashed actually means. Though jihadist violence seems to have exploded around us in the last few years, it in fact has deep roots in India's political landscape. The Darmapatnam suicide-attackers were driven by a particular understanding of Islam, much as today's jihadists are. The fact is, however, that their response was only one of many different responses by Muslims on the Malabar coast to a new situation they found themselves confronted with. In other words, the Darmapatnam suicide attackers were agents of politics—not just god.

For us today, this history is vitally important. It helps us place in context the activities of Indian jihadists, growing numbers of whom are now headed to the Islamic State and hope one day to return to initiate an Islamist insurgency at home. The dozens— perhaps hundreds—of young men who are, or have been, involved in jihadist groups aren't just religious bigots, though some undoubtedly are just that. They aren't just victims of religious discrimination out for vengeance either, though that's true of many, too. Nor can they be simply dismissed as crazed nihilists, though some, without doubt, would benefit from psychiatric care. For as long as we persist in seeing Indian jihadists through the lenses of cliché and ignorance, both our cultural responses and our strategic ones are fated to fail.

Beginnings

From the window of his apartment, Ejaz Badruddin Majeed stared out over the grimy suburban heights of Kalyan, willing himself, it seemed to me, to see past the oceans and the deserts, all the way to Iraq. "He had asked me for a motorcycle and I said, no, not just yet", said the quiet, greying homeopathic doctor, "He didn't say anything, but perhaps that's why he went away". His son had left a letter, though, that suggested otherwise. The letter had a passage from the Quran: "fighting has been enjoined upon you, though it is hateful to you".[2] He explained to his mother that the angel of death would ask why he didn't migrate to Allah's land to fulfil that command.

"May we all meet in paradise", the letter concluded.

I had met Ejaz Majeed in August, 2014, to report on the stories of the first four Indian men known to have joined the Islamic State:

> Ejaz Majeed's son, Areeb Majeed, Fahad Tanvir Sheikh, Aman Naim Tandel and Shaheem Farooq Tanki—all young men in their twenties, from secularised families, and with no known past involvement in radical Islamist politics.

Through the next year, I was to see other, similar farewell notes— the maudlin literature generated by Indian jihadists leaving for battlefields in Iraq and Syria.

These texts were populated, almost without exception, with religious clichés drawn from the internet; the reading of the online Islamist was not a rich one.

Literature, which unlike religious texts drives thinking and hence doubt, was among the jihad's enemies. In 2013, at about the same time the Thane jihadists had begun plotting their journey, Jabhat al-Nusra, al-Qaeda's affiliate in Syria, had demolished an iconic statue of Abu'l Ala al-Ma'arri. The tenth century Arab poet's work in many senses anticipated that of Dante Alligheri. Trenchently sceptical, al-Ma'arri's political views were contentious, but his work forms a core part of the classical cannon.

In his masterwork, *The Epistle of Forgiveness*, al-Ma'arri has the poet-protagonist, engaged in a sardonic tour of the afterlife, attempting to wheedle his way into Paradise by composing flattering verses to its porter-angel. He is eventually allowed entry through the intercession of Muhammad's daughter, Fatimah—and secures a houri only to discover that:

> … the girl, though beautiful, is rather skinny. He raises his head, and instantly she has a behind that rivals the hills of 'Alij, the dunes of al-Dahna, and the sands of Yabrin and the Banu Sa'd. Awed by the omnipotence of the Kind of Knowing God, he says, "Thou who givest rays to the shining sun, Thou who fulfillest the desires of everyone, Thou whose awe-inspiring deeds make us feel impotent and summon to wisdom the ignorant: I ask Thee to reduce the bum of this damsel…."[3]

The evidence makes clear that while the four men were of a fringe —India has sent far fewer jihadists to the Islamic State and al-Qaeda than neighbouring countries like Pakistan, China or even Maldives—they weren't alone. India's intelligence services estimate perhaps 100 citizens have travelled to West Asia for jihad; there is no firm count, though, because many suspects were living in the diaspora.

There is, more disturbing, a string of cases piling up within India, of plots alleged to have been inspired by the Islamic State: cells have been discovered in Delhi, Rajasthan, Maharashtra and Andhra Pradesh and Kerala, plotting violence against their homeland. In spite of its savage reputation—or, perhaps, because of it—the Islamic State and al-Qaeda have even acquired a certain utopian lure: in July 2016, entire families from Kerala upped and moved to Syria, seeking an Islamic lifestyle.

In the years since I met the Thane jihadists' families, the numbers have multiplied: 67 Indian citizens are facing trial for Islamic State-related plots within the country, and another 62 have left to join it either in Syria or Afghanistan, 21 of them with their families, including infant children.

Estimates I have collated from official press-releases on these arrested individuals show that 68 percent come from families that can be described as middle class; 68 percent had graduate or post graduate degrees, mainly in engineering; while only 11 percent had a religious education. In interviews, about half have cited global causes as their inspiration; another half say Indian issues related to communalism, ranging from riots to compulsary yoga, accounted for their radicalisation. Their is, to the best of my knowledge, no scholarly work on these issues; I take this opportunity to suggest one is needed.

In 2016 the Thane men appeared in a video that made express their linkages with the wider jihadist movement in India. Aman Tandel reappeared, using the pseudonym Abu Amr' al-Hindi vowing to return home "with a sword in hand, to avenge the Babri Masjid, and the killings of Muslims in Kashmir, in Gujarat, and in Muzaffarnagar". He paid homage to his friend from Thane, Shahim Tanki, who is said to have been killed in a bomb attack in Raqqa last year.[4]

Explaining his personal journey, Uttar Pradesh resident Abu Rashid Ahmad says he was forced to leave Mumbai for the Khorasan region, or the Afghanistan-Pakistan borderlands, after the 2008 shootout at Batla House in which Indian Mujahideen commander Atif Amin was killed. This first hijrat, or religious migration, was followed by a second one to Syria, the man recounts. "In India," the man who fled Mumbai says, "we see that it is that it is the cow, the trees, the sun, the moon…that is worshipped. Instead of fighting these things, the Muslims of India trade and maintain social relations with these infidels." He vows, though, to return to avenge atrocities against Muslims in India. "Have you forgotten the train bombings in Mumbai, or the bombings in Ahmedabad, and Surat, and Jaipur and Delhi," he asks.

The video also features several other Indian Mujahideen members whose members are known to have been serving with Islamic State forces after breaking with their Pakistan-based leadership. "To those in the Indian state who wish to understand our actions," says an unidentified jihadist, "I say you have only three options: to accept Islam, to pay jizya, or to prepare to be slaughtered".

Large parts of the video, narrated in Arabic, seek to provide context to the presence of Indian jihadists in the Islamic State—men it describes as jihadists from "Hind wal'Sindh", a usage for India and Pakistan. The video begins with medieval warlord Muhammad Bin Qasim's conquest of the region, saying it laid the foundations for Islamic rule. The British, the narrator states, then handed over control of India to Hindus—people it describes as "cowworshippers" who have been responsible for violence against Muslims in many places, including Mumbai, Gujarat, Assam and Moradabad.

"Hindus are striving to convert you Muslims to their faith, O' sons of Bin Qasim", one recruit says, recounting a string of communal riots. "Is there any other humiliation that you still need to suffer before you will give up chanting that Islam is a religion of peace, and learn from the Prophet, who fought with the sword?"

The video assails mainstream Muslim politicians and clerics for compromising with what the narrator describes as a tyrannical system responsible for massacring Muslims. Images of the Majlis-eIttehad-ul-Muslimeen leader Asaduddin Owaisi and All India United Democratic Front politician Badruddin Ajmal are juxtaposed with dead bodies of victims of communal riots. Indian Muslim politicians are attacked for associating with non-Muslim leaders: one image shows the Congress's Mani Shankar Aiyer embracing a Hindu priest and Muslim cleric.

The most acid invective, though, is reserved for Indian clerics who, the video says, are supporting the forces of kufr against the mujahideen of the Islamic State.

Insisting that armed jihad "in the way of Allah" is an individual religious obligation incumbent on every individual Muslim, the video warns clerics that they will soon meet their reckoning. "Do not listen to those who tell you that Islam is a religion of peace," one jihadist says, his face digitally masked over. "Islam was never a religion of peace for even one day. Islam is a religion of war. The Prophet commanded us to remain at war until the day the rule of Allah is established." The video mocks Muslims protesting against the Islamic State.

The jihadists interviewed also praised the quality of life in the Islamic State. "Here there is shari'a," one says. "Here the hands of thieves are cut off. Here, our religion is safe."

India's Hidden Jihadi History

In 1498, Vasco Da Gama had arrived in the Indian Ocean—and inside a few years, imperial Portugal had established a string of coastal fortresses choking the main sea lanes, at the entrances to the Red Sea, the Malabar Coast, the Straits of Malacca, and the southern Chinese coast. Their most valuable prize was Calicut, centre of the world's trade in pepper and other spices prized in Europe. The Portuguese strategy directly undermined the interests of the Muslim merchants who carried spices from the Malabar coast to the Persian Gulf, and then over land to the rest of the world. In 1510, Portugal attempted to conquer Calicut, and succeeded in burning down large parts of the Muslim quarter, including its great mosque, before being repulsed by the raja, and his Hindu troops.

For the next three centuries, a great war raged across the extended region—

not just in Malabar, but all the way to the South China Sea —which would only be settled by British power displacing all others across the Indian Ocean.

The scholar Stephen Dale's work shows how ideas of jihad and *shahadat* [martyrdom] came to define what he calls a cultural ideological "Islamic frontier" along the Malabar coast.[5] The contemporary historian Zayn al-Din al-Ma'bari compiled the *Tuhfat al-Mujahiden fi Ba'd Ahwal al-Purtukaliyyin* [History of the Mujahideen], hoping to "inspire the Faithful to undertake a jihad against the worshippers of the cross". Al-Ma'bari recorded "the evils which the Portuguese inflicted upon the Muslims of Malabar as well as a brief account of the laws and religious merit of the jihad".[6]

In popular culture, too, the Malabar jihadists were venerated: the story of *Kotturpalli Malla* celebrates the martyrdom of the seaman Kunju Marakkar, who abandons his own wedding to rescue a Muslim girl kidnapped by Portuguese sailors. Marakkar is killed, his limbs severed and thrown into the sea. Each place they are washed up, though, witnesses miracles, evidence of divine approval for his acts.

Eighteenth century East India Company records describe fidayeen suicide-squad attacks along the Malabar coast, on occasion targeting religious congregations.[7] For the most part, these were greeted with an incomprehension not dissimilar to that which acts of terrorism. Imperial authorities saw the violence as madness.

There's evidence, too, from this colonial account that the violence by no means had the approval of all Muslims:

> The Several Treacherous actions late Committed by the Malabar Moors at Callicutt as well as at this place [Tellicherry] & Elsewhere & the French Chief having wrote hither, that he had twice Warning given to him to take Care of his Life, have much alarmed the Christians on the Coast in so much that they seldom Stir Out but with Arms for their defence Altho' all Danger Apprehended is from avery small Number of ye Mahomitan Profession who have selected themselves to Murder any Christian when if they Die in the Attempt they are persuaded it is very meritorious and have Adorations paid to their memory by many Enthusiasticks of their faith, which have been performed at the Tomb of him who killed the Sergeant in This Fort in March last and much more at that of him who Afterwards killed the Portuguese Padre at Callicutt altho' the more prudent Part of the Moors deny that such Evil Conformable to their Religion Historian Ayesha Jalal's work has shown that the notion of jihad was important ideological theme elsewhere in India, too, both during the pre-colonial and colonial period.[8] The eighteenth century theological Shah Waliullah, for example, wrote to Muslim rulers and notables

calling for measures against Hindus and followers of the Shia faith. He also wrote to the Afghan warlord Ahmad Shah Abdali, calling on him to invade India.[9] During the great rebellion of 1857, Indian insurgents fighting imperial British troops included among their ranks numbers of self-described jihadis, including at least one regiment of suicide ghazis, who vowed to fight until they met death at the hands of the infidel.[10] While it would, perhaps, be misleading to read this form of jihadi resistance in the context of our times, the fact remains the presence of the ghazis, or Islamic warriors, caused Hindu-Muslim communal friction of a kind that is startlingly modern.[11]

Early in the twentieth century, the jihadi-ghazi tradition acquired a renewed momentum as communal boundaries sharpened. In 1919, Hindu and Muslim leaders agreed to work with one another for the restoration of the Ottoman caliphate—the notional political leadership of the Muslim ummah, or global community. This cause had little support in Turkey. It was, however, seen by India's Congress leadership as a means to incorporate Muslim concerns within its larger anti-Imperial mobilisation agenda.

As things turned out, the Khilafat movement collapsed, strengthening rather than dissolving communal boundaries through its use of pan-Islamic themes. As Yoginder Sikand has noted, the agitation

> … actually helped to further consolidate the sense of distinct Indian Muslim community identity, separate and sharply cut-off from the Hindus. It also enabled the Ullema to establish links with ordinary Muslims all over the country, seeking to rally them under their leadership for the pan-Islamic cause. That this instigating of religious passions would further widen the chasm between Hindus and Muslims was hardly surprising.[12]

In 1921, fired by the pan-Islamic rhetoric of the Khilafat movement and the communal zeal it unleashed, Muslim peasants in the Malabar attacked their British-backed landlords, in the main Hindus. Scores are believed to have died in the violence that followed. From here on, the progress of India's independence movement would be scarred by communal warfare, culminating in the horrors of the Partition of India—and the murderous riots which have periodically erupted afterwards.

Khilafat, of course, was not the sole driving force behind the hardening of communal identities in south Asia. In Jammu and Kashmir, where both Islamist mobilisations and jihadi violence would acquire growing momentum after the first quarter of the last century, it had almost no impact at all. There, as Chitralekha Zutshi has argued, state policies were the principal factor contributing to the "articulation of antagonistic communitarian identities".[13] None the less, it remains a key moment, and the idea of the restoration of the caliphate a central concern for modern jihadi organisations.

In the build up to the Partition of British India, the ideological foundations of the modern jihadist movement in India were laid by the founder of the Jamaat-e-Islami—the largest Islamist political group in both Pakistan and India.

Jihad Fee-Sabilillah [Jihad in the way of God] a 1939 essay by Mawdudi, argues that the pursuit of political power—rather than what he called "a hotchpotch of beliefs, prayers and rituals" — was integral to the practice of the religion.[14]

"Islam," he insisted "is a revolutionary ideology which seeks to alter the social order of the entire world and rebuild it in conformity with its own tenets and ideals."[15] It was therefore imperative for Muslims to "seize the authority of state, for an evil system takes root and flourishes under the patronage of an evil government and a pious cultural order can never be established until the authority of government is wrested from the wicked." Indeed, Mawdudi insisted that the word 'Muslims' referred not to a religious community but to a politically-bound "international revolutionary party".[16]

"The party of the Muslims," Mawdudi concluded, "will inevitably extend the invitation to citizens of other countries to embrace the faith which holds out the promise of true salvation and genuine welfare. At the same time, if the Muslim Party commands enough resources, it will eliminate un-Islamic governments and establish the power of Islamic government in their place."[17] He concluded: "Hence it is imperative, for reasons both of the general welfare of humanity and for its own self-defence, that the Muslim Party should not be content just with establishing the Islamic system of government in one territory, but should extend its sway as far as possible all around".[18]

It is worth noting, parenthetically, that these ideas resonated in the work of the global jihadist movement. Muslim Brotherhood ideologue Sayyed Qutb's work drew extensively on Mawdudi; he acknowledged the debt liberally.[19] Palestinian jihadist Abdullah Azzam, al-Qaeda leader Osama bin-Laden's ideological mentor and co-founder of arguably the largest terror group in the world, the Lashkar-e-Taiba. In his is incumbent on the Islamic state," he stated, "to send out a group of mujahideen to their neighbouring infidel state. They should present Islam to the leader and his nation. If they refuse to accept Islam, jizyah [a tax] will be imposed upon them and they will become subjects of the Islamic state. If they refuse this second option, the third course of action is jihad to bring the infidel state under Islamic domination."[20]

As the scholar Seyyed Vali Raza Nasr has observed, Mawdudi's position was "closely tied to questions of communal politics and its impact on identity formation, to questions of power in pluralistic societies, and to nationalism."[21] His world view, Nasr notes, was

"informed by the acute despair that gripped the community [Muslim]" in the early decades of the twentieth century. Mawdudi saw the Arya Samaj's religious revivalism as an existential threat, "a proof of the inherent animosity of Hindus towards Islam."

The Making of the Indian Mujahideen

He appeared online in 2015 on the Ansar ul-Tawhid website, his face digitally masked, a laptop to his left, religious books to his right, and a Glock 9mm automatic on his desk, delivering the firstever call by an Indian for Muslims in the country to join the global jihad. "My beloved brothers," he said, his voice woven into images of communal carnage, "what has happened to you that, in the sight of god, you do not fight for helpless children, women and the aged, who are begging their lord for rescue?" He went on: "Rise, like Ahmad Shah Abdali and Muhammad ibn-Qasim, like Syed Ahmad the martyr, like the Prophet and his companions, take the Quran in one hand and the sword in the other, and head to the fields of jihad."[22]

The man behind the mask was Sultan Abdul Kadir Armar, the 39-year-old son of a small businessman from Bhatkal in northern Karnataka, and a soft-spoken cleric trained at the respected Darul Uloom Nadwatul Ulama seminary in Lucknow. A key recruiter for the Indian Mujahideen, Armar joined a rebellion against its leadership, which is believed to have led more than a dozen Indians to camps run by the Tehreek-e-Taliban in Pakistan so far. His brother Shafi Armar is now thought to be in Raqqa, the man who succeeded him as the key guide for Indian nationals seeking jihad training in camps in Syria and in Afghanistan.

The first jihadist group based abroad to be formed by Indians, the Ansar ul-Tawhid believes terrorism will not achieve anything. Their imagination fired by the Islamic State's success against better-equipped and trained forces in Syria, its leaders see themselves as the kernel of a full-bown insurgency in India.

In the online address, the man believed to be Armar exhorts, "Listen to the calls rising from the dust in Iraq and Syria…and migrate to the motherland of jihad, Afghanistan, gather your courage, and teach these Brahmins and worshippers of cows, as well as the whole world of unbelievers, that the Indian Muslim is no coward."

The Ansar ul-Tawhid Twitter feed has put out videotape footage of cadres training in camps on the Pakistan-Afghanistan border. The members it lost in fighting include, Anwer Husain 'Bhatkal', allegedly killed during a raid on an

Afghan border outpost—the first Indian among several known to be training in Afghanistan to be killed.

Like the Armar brothers—one cleric, the other a digital-era media producer—the Ansar ul-Tawhid's membership is diverse. One of the members is Afif Hassan Siddibapa, also known as Afif Jailani, a 41-year-old businessman who left a job in Saudi Arabia and settled in Karachi with his wife and children.

Indians Shanawaz Ahmad, a Unani doctor and the son of a local Samajwadi Party politician in Uttar Pradesh's Azamgarh; Abu Rashid Ahmad, who once worked at an eye hospital in Mumbai; and students Mohammad 'Bada' Sajid and Mirza Shadab Beig are also allegedly linked to the group.

Investigators believe that the Indian Mujahideen itself is an offshoot of al-Isbah, literally meaning "a group in search of truth". It started from Bhatkal in late 2001 as a grouping, including Ahmad Zarar Siddibappa, listening to sermons by cleric Muhammad Shish. Siddibappa, by then better known as Yasin Bhatkal, was arrested in August 2013.

Early in the summer of 2004, a group of young men—in the main, one-time members of SIMI—gathered for a retreat at one of the sprawling villas that line the cheerfully-named Jolly Beach, the pride of small, south Indian fishing town of Bhatkal. They swam, went for hikes into the woods, honed their archery skills, and occasionally indulged in some target practice with an airgun. Local residents recall occasionally hearing small explosions, but say they guessed the men were setting off fireworks. Nothing the men did gave Bhatkal's police cause for concern.

It should have: the young men on Jolly Beach were the core of a jihadist network calling itself the Indian Mujahideen, would carry out a succession of bomb attacks from 2005, in which hundreds were killed and injured. Delhi prosecutors say the principal organiser of the Jolly Beach gathering, Riyaz Ismail Shahbandri—also known as Riyaz Bhatkal—signed a manifesto issued by the Indian Mujahideen after its September, 2008, bomb attacks in New Delhi, along with his brother Iqbal Shahbandri.[23] Documents filed in courts across several Indian states assert the men played a key role in raising cadre, sourcing bomb components, and organising attacks. Both men, Pakistani-American jihadist David Coleman Headley is believed to have told investigators, now run what he called the 'Karachi Project': a Lashkar-e-Taiba operation to train and equip Indian jihadists to carry out a fresh wave of attacks.[24] "We, the Indian Mujahideen, ask Allah, the Almighty to accept from us these 9 explosions", the manifesto had read, "which were planned to be executed in the holy month of Ramadan. We have carried out this attack in the memory of two most eminent Mujahids of

India: Sayyed Ahmed Shaheed and Shah Ismail Shaheed (may Allah bestow His Mercy upon them) who had raised the glorious banner of Jihad against the disbelievers in this very city of Delhi. It is the great hard work and sacrifices of these visionary legends [sic.] that shall always inspire us, Inshallah, to carry on the struggle and fight against the Kufr (disbelief) till our last breath".[25]

Riyaz Shahbandri's father, Ismail Shahbandri, left Bhatkal some three decades ago hoping, just like millions of other Indians, to make his fortune in Mumbai. He set up a successful leathertanning works in the city's Kurla area, and eventually bought an apartment in Kardar Building off the busy Pipe Road—an impossible dream for most migrants to the city. Ismail Shahbandri's prosperity ensured Riyaz Shahbandri was able to study at local English-medium schools, and later study civil engineering at Mumbai's Saboo Siddiqui Engineering College. He married a Bhatkal-area woman, Nashua Ismail, the daughter of an electronics store owner, in 2002. By this time, however, Riyaz Shahbandri's story had begun to diverge significantly from the bourgeois trajectory his businessman father, more likely than not, had mapped for him.

Shafiq Ahmad, Riyaz Shahbandri's brother-in-law to be, had lived in the family's apartment as he pursued his studies—and his work as a Students Islamic Movement of India activist—in Mumbai. Shahbandri began to spend time at SIMI's offices in Mumbai around 2001, at the peak of the organisation's radical phase, spending time with men who would play a key role in the development of the jihadist movement of India. Among them were Abdul Subhan Qureshi and Mohammad Sadiq Israr Sheikh, who co-found the Indian Mujahideen; Ehtesham Siddiqi, who is now being tried for his alleged role in the bombings of the city's suburban train system in July, 2006; and Rahil Sheikh, who recruited dozens of Maharashtra jihadists, most notably for an abortive 2006 terrorist strike in Gujarat, to avenge the anti-Muslim violence which had taken place there four years earlier.

Riyaz Shahbandri's world-view may, in part, have been shaped by his brother, Iqbal Shahbandri. For reasons that are not wholly clear—in part, because the Shahbandri family has declined to be interviewed by media—Iqbal Shahbandri's adult life appears to have taken a rather different course to that of his brother. He studied Unani medicine, a form of traditional healing based on Greek, Arab and Indian practices that has some currency across South Asia. However, his primary interests were religious. Even though he never seems to have been undertaken the rigours of a formal education in theology, Iqbal Bhatkal was an enthusiastic participant in the activities of the Talibghi Jamaat, a neofundamentalist proseletysing order whose annual gatherings at Raiwind in Pakistan are reputed to draw more followers than any Muslim congregation other than the Haj pilgrimage.[26]

Sadiq Israr Sheikh had no conception of that jihadist project when he began attending SIMI's Sunday study meetings at a friend's apartment in 1996. But it was at these meetings that the Indian Mujahideen idea was born, over tea and biscuits.[27]

From his testimony to Mumbai Police investigators, it appears Sheikh was drawn to SIMI's political Islamism by resentments common to millions of lower middle class Mumbai residents. Born in 1978 to working-class parents from the north Indian town of Azamgarh, Sheikh had grown up in the Cheeta Camp housing project. Home to thousands of slum residents who had been evicted to make way for the Bhabha Atomic Research Centre, Cheeta Camp provided the foundations for tens of thousands of families to make the journey to the fringes of India's middle-class. Sheikh's parents were able to give their children a decent home and an education.

But Sheikh's story didn't quite run according to the script his parents had in mind. Having dropped out of high school, he obtained certification as an air-conditioning mechanic. Sheikh could find only ill-paid freelance work, not a regular job. Like many of his contemporaries, felt cheated of the growing economic opportunities emerging around him—and came to believe he was a victim of religious discrimination. Hundreds of Muslims had been killed in communal riots that tore the city apart in 1993, and SIMI gave voice to Sheikh's rage.[28] As the scholar Yoginder Sikand has perceptively noted, SIMI's aggressive polemic gave "its supporters a sense of power and agency which they were denied in their actual lives".[29]

SIMI's language turned increasingly violent as the years rolled by: at a rally held at Mumbai's Bandra Reclamation Ground soon after the al-Qaeda attacks of September 11, it voiced support for Osama bin-Laden and hailed the Taliban's Mullah Omar as a role-model for Muslims. Even this, though, wasn't enough for Sheikh. Early in 2001, he stormed out of a SIMI meeting, complaining that the organisation did nothing other than talk.

In April, 2001, Sheikh ran into a distant relative who helped turn his dreams into reality. Salim Islahi—the son of a Jamaat-e-Islami linked cleric who was expelled from the organisation for his extremism—put Sheikh in touch with Aftab Ansari, a ganglord reputed to have discovered Islamist radicalism while serving prison time in New Delhi along with Jaish-e-Mohammad terrorist Syed Omar Sheikh. Sheikh's lieutenant, Asif Reza Khan, arranged for Sheikh to travel to Pakistan in September, 2001.

Qureshi, like Sheikh, was the son of working-class migrants from north India. However, Qureshi received an elite education— ironically, at the Catholic-run Antonio D'Souza High School. In 1996, he had begun working as a software engineer, specialising in network solutions. Qureshi joined SIMI around the same time. Later, he edited the SIMI-affiliated journal Islamic Movement. In 2001, Qureshi submitted a letter of resignation to his employers, saying he intended to "devote one complete year to pursue religious and spiritual matters". Like Sheikh, he left India to train at a Lashkar camp in Pakistan-administered Jammu and Kashmir.

By the autumn of 2002, spurred on by anti-Muslim violence which had claimed hundreds of lives in the state of Gujarat, dozens of volunteers were joining the Indian Mujahideen network—although they group did not yet have that, or indeed any, name. Many were from Hyderabad for training in the wake of the Gujarat pogrom, among them Abdul Khwaja, who using the alias Amjad now heads a Lashkar-linked, Lahore-based cell operating against India. Others came from Maharashtra. By 2003, Sheikh was himself regularly despatching volunteers from the Azamgarh area for training at Lashkar camps

Within months of their departure, the new recruits executed their first successful strikes. Asad Yazdani, a resident of Hyderabad's Toli Chowki area, helped execute the assassination of the former Gujarat Home Minister, Haren Pandya. Pandya, India's Central Bureau of Investigations later determined, was killed in reprisal for his role in pogrom.[30] In 2005, the network was ready to carry out their first bombings, an attack on a Hindu temple in the north Indian city of Varanasi. Over coming years, the Indian Mujahideen succeeded in staging attacks of ever-increasing intensity, among them the July, 2006, strikes on Mumbai's suburban train system that claimed at least 183 lives.[31]

By 2006, there is evidence that the organisation had begun to develop significant transnational linkages.[32] Kerala-born Sarfaraz Nawaz and Muscat-based entrepreneur Ali Abdul Aziz al-Hooti, authorities in India say, operated a key Lashkar-e-Taiba logistical hub, supporting the terrorist group's operations in India, Pakistan, the United Arab Emirates, Bangladesh—and even the Maldives. For counter-terrorism forces across the region, this is bad news. From its origins in Pakistan's Punjab, the investigation shows, the Lashkar has grown into a truly transnational organisation.[33]

Nawaz began his jihadist journey in 1995, when he was just eighteen years old, when he joined SIMI.[34] Five years later, Nawaz was elected to SIMI's New Delhi-based central committee. His contemporaries included many who later played key roles in building India's jihadist movement—among them, key SIMI ideologue Safdar Nagori, and Peedical Abdul Shibly and Yahya Kamakutty, both successful computer professionals who are now being tried for plotting jihadist operations in southern India.[35]

But like the overwhelming majority of SIMI members Nawaz chose a life of middle-class respectability. He obtained a computer networking qualification from an institute in Kochi, married and found a job in Oman.[36]

It wasn't long, though, before Nawaz was drawn back into the world he appeared to have escaped from. During a visit home in early 2006, he heard Tadiyantavide Nasir—an Islamist political activist who, improbably enough, also served as a preacher with the Noorisha order of Sufi mystics—delivered a speech casting jihad as an imperative of the practice of Islam.[37] Inspired, Nawaz set about making contacts with jihadists in Muscat. Friends from his days in SIMI put him in touch al-Hooti, a successful automobile components dealer who also owned string of internet cafés.

Born to an Indian mother, al-Hooti's radicalisation had been driven by stories of atrocities against Muslims he heard on visits home to Miraj, near Mumbai. Before he turned thirty, Indian investigators say, al-Hooti had had twice trained at Lashkar camps in Pakistan. By 2006, Indian investigators say, al-Hooti had emerged as one of the Lashkar's key organisers in the Gulf. Working with Lashkar intelligence operative Mohammad Jassem, also known by the codename Tehsin, al-Hooti helped send dozens of jihadists to the Lashkar's camps in Pakistan for training.

Many of those men proved themselves to be valuable Lashkar assets. Early in 2007, al-Hooti and Jassem despatched Dubai-based, Indian-origin printing-press mechanic Fahim Arshad Ansari to a Lashkar camp in Pakistan-administered Jammu and Kashmir.[38] Having finished a Daura Ribat covert tradecraft course, Ansari was tasked with carrying out surveillance at several important locations in Mumbai. Footage he generated, Indian prosecutors have said, helped facilitate the training of the Lashkar assault time which targeted Mumbai in November.

Funds generated by al-Hooti are thought to have helped Lashkar commander Faisal Haroun, also known by the code-name Naim, set up Indian ocean networks that eventually enabled the group to target India's western seaboard. Haroun is thought to have crafted the 2006 landing of assault rifles intended to have been used in a terror attack in Gujarat, as well as an abortive 2007 effort to land eight Lashkar fidayeen off Mumbai.[39]

Indeed, al-Hooti and Jassem recruited widely across the India ocean region. Maldives investigators have, for example, learned that the men facilitated the training of Ali Assham—a Malé resident who was forced to suspend jihadist career after losing an eye in a bomb-making accident.

By 2007, Oman authorities say, the pro-western Emirate itself had begun to figure on al-Hooti's list of targets. In June that year, al-Hooti held discussions with Lashkar sympathisers in Oman on the prospect of targeting prominent landmarks in Muscat—among them, a British Broadcasting Corporation office, the Golden Tulip Hotel, and a spa in the upmarket Nizwa area. No final operational plans were made, but Oman authorities found enough evidence to secure a conviction earlier this year.

Most important, from the point of view of Indian investigators, alHooti also provided an interface between the Lashkar to deal with the Indian Mujahideen: a loose cluster of semi-autonomous SIMI linked cells responsible for bombings in a dozen Indian cities since 2005, in which hundreds were killed.

In 2008 Nasir turned to Nawaz to secure funding for the training of a new group of Indian Mujahideen volunteers he had raised from the Indian state of Kerala. Nasir also said he needed cash to pay for a planned bomb attack in the city of Bangalore. Between March and May, 2008, police say, al-Hooti transferred an estimated US$ 2,500 for Nasir's use to a Kerala-based hawala dealer. Lashkar commander 'Rehan', one of al-Hooti's associates, also arranged for Nasir's recruits to train with a jihadist unit operating near the Line of Control Jammu and Kashmir's Kupwara district.

In November, 2007, the networks began using the Indian Mujahideen name, in e-mail manifestos released to the media. In a manifesto released minutes before the Indian Mujahideen group carried out synchronised bombings in three north Indian cities in November, 2007, the ideological basis of SIMI cadre's turn to jihad was expressly spelt out.[40]

Describing the "wounds given by the idol worshippers to the Indian Muslims", the manifesto voiced anger that Hindus had "demolished our Babri Masjid and killed our brothers, children and raped our sisters".[41] The Gujarat pogrom of 2002 had "forced us to take a strong stand against this injustice and all other wounds given by the idol worshippers of India". "Only Islam," it concluded, "has the power to establish a civilised society, and this could only be possible in Islamic rule which could be achieved by only one path: jihad".

But if the ideological resonances and modes of praxis of the Indian Mujahideen are global, the specific conditions in which it operatives are local.

The Pre-Networks of Jihad

They buried Abdul Karim's left hand under an acacia tree in the scraggly forest just outside Tonk, wrapped in a plastic bag along with the remains of the metal tube he'd been trying to turn into a bomb. It was 1986, and just a few months earlier a district judge had ordered the gates of the Babri Masjid opened to Hindu worshippers. In the years to follow, much bloodshed would spread across India, with the Ram Janambhoomi movement exploding every few months into communal killings. From that day in Tonk on, Abdul Karim came to be known as "Tunda", the cripple. He would lead his own war through, as a counterforce to the one unleashed by Hindutva groups.[42]

In the weeks before every 6 December, the anniversary of the demolition of the Babri Masjid, jihadist websites and Twitter accounts linked to a new generation of Indian radicals—of the Indian Mujahideen, al-Qaeda in the Islamic State, of the Islamic State-linked Ansar al-Tauhid—invoke the memory of that event, and vow vengeance.

Born in 1941, on the eve of Independence, the son of a metal casting artisan who grew up in Gali Chhata Lal Mian in Delhi's Daryaganj neighbourhood, Abdul Karim grew up in Pilkhuwa, Ghaziabad. Life was hard for the young Karim: forced to drop out of a missionaryrun school at the age of 11, when his father died, he was put to work making cartwheels for his uncle. He began travelling across northern India, working as a metalworker, a cobbler, a carpenter, barber and bangle-maker.

In 1964, Karim married Zarina Yusuf, the daughter of his uncle's brother. For the next two decades, he had a conventional lower-middle class life, working as a trader in dyed cloth, and bringing up three children, Imran, Rasheeda and Irfan.

The birth of the Ram Janambhoomi movement in 1984, though, generated intense communal strife. Karim responded by discovering religion: he turned to the neo-fundamentalist Ahl-e-Hadis sect for answers to the question why Muslims in India seemed to be passive victims in the face of oppression. The search led him, in 1984, to Ahmedabad, where he began preaching Islam at a small seminary. He got married again, to Mumtaz Rahman, after his first wife refused to accompany him, and fathered a fourth child, Shahid.

He also lived an experience that would transform his worldview: witnessing the 1985 communal riots first hand. In his testimony to police, Karim described how Zafar Rahman, one of his in-laws, and seven other relatives had been burned alive. He talked of shops burned down, a mosque destroyed, and a police force that had joined mobs in attacking Muslims.

For weeks after the riots, Karim discussed the issue with an elderly local cleric, Maulvi Wali Muhammad. He segregated himself to study verses of the Qur'an on jihad. Karim emerged determined to defend his faith. He worked with a local vendor of fireworks to produce low-grade explosives using potash, sugar and sulphuric acid, packed into steel pipes.

Karim wasn't the only one with the same idea. Ever since he'd been a medical student, Jalees Ansari was later to tell police, he'd heard Hindus "branded us traitors and Pakistani agents". From his clinic in a municipal hospital in Mumbai, Ansari read of riot after riot break out—in Moradabad, Meerut, Bhagalpur, and Bhiwandi. He saw what had happened in Bhiwandi first hand, as a volunteer distributing medical supplies.

In 1985, Ansari met the man who would give shape to his ideas—a former Maoist from Karimnagar in Andhra Pradesh, called Azam Ghauri, the fifth of 11 children from an impoverished family, and who too had discovered religion in the Ahl-e-Hadis. The men, along with Ansari, set up an anti-riot vigilante group, the Tanzim Islahul Muslimeen, or Organisation for the Correction of Muslims.

Just a handful of residents of Mumbai's Mominpora slum—in the main people with nothing better to do—were on hand to witness the birth of the modern Islamist jihad in India. In the summer of 1985, inflamed by the wave of communal violence that had ripped apart the industrial town of Bhiwandi, activists of the neoconservative Jamaat Ahl-e-Hadis' ultra-right Ghuraba faction gathered to discuss the need for Muslim reprisal.[43] An obscure West Bengal-based cleric named Abu Masood announced the birth of the Tanzim Islahul Muslimeen [Organisation for the Improvement of Muslims].

Back the late-1980s, the TIM's activities barely merited an entry in the local police station's diaries of daily events. Mimicking the drills of the Rashtriya Swayamsevak Sangh's shakhas, Mohammad Azam Ghauri, Mohammad Tufail Husaini and Abdul Karim paraded their recruits around the grounds of the Young Men's Christian Association. Most of the TIM's membership consisted of young Mominpura residents angered by communal discrimination and violence.

On 6 December 1992, the day Hindu fanatics demolished the Babri Masjid, the TIM decided the time had come to act.[44] Flying the banner of the Mujahideen Islam-e-Hind a year to the day Babri Masjid was demolished—martyred, in the words of the faithful—surgeon turned bomb-maker Jalees Ansari organised a series of 43 bombings in Mumbai and Hyderabad and 7 separate strikes on inter-city trains. While most of the explosions were small, it was demonstration of the group's discipline and skills. Central Bureau of Investigations agents caught up with Ansari just thirteen days before he had been ordered to set off a second series of reprisal bombings, this time scheduled for India's republic day in 1994. It should be noted that these early Indian jihadists had no known connection with the organised crime elements who, under the influence of Pakistan's Inter Services Intelligence Directorate, executed the Mumbai serial bombings of 1993—an operation also carried out as acts of reprisal against the demolition of the Babri Masjid and the communal violence which followed it.[45]

Most major Islamist terror cells in India can trace their roots to TIM's founders. Operating with the logistical support of Pakistanbased organisations like the Lashkar-e-Tayyaba and Jaish-e-Mohammad, the cells have drawn much of their cadre from the Students Islamic Movement of India. Ehtesham Siddiqi, a central figure in organising the 2006 Mumbai serial bombings, was SIMI's general-secretary for Maharashtra. Mohammad Sabahuddin, who carried out a series of attacks in Bangalore and Uttar Pradesh, and went on to become the first Indian Lashkar operative to command Indian nationals, was active in the organisation So, too, were Raziuddin Nasir, the commander of a Hubli cell which was planning attacks on western tourists in Goa.

Despite SIMI's emergence as one of the principal threats to India's internal security, though, neither the history or objectives of its cult of the Kalashnikov are well understood.

SIMI, and the Jihadist Tendency

Like many other south Asian Islamist movements, SIMI's genesis lies in the Jamaat-e-Islami. Established in 1941 by Abul Ala Maududi, the Jamaat-e-Islami went on to emerge as a major political party in Pakistan, fighting for the creation of a Shariah governed state.[46] In post-Partition India, however, the Jamaat gradually transformed itself into a cultural organisation committed to propagating neoconservative Islam amongst Muslims. It set up networks of schools and study circles, devoted to combating growing post-independence influence of communism and socialism. A student wing, the Students Islamic Organisation, was set up in 1956, with its headquarters at Aligarh. As Muslims in north India were battered by communal violence the Jamaat slowly moved away from Maududi's hostility to secularism. It began arguing that the secular state needed to be defended, as the sole alternative was a Hindu-communalist regime.

SIMI was formed in April, 1977, as an effort to revitalise the SIO. Building on the SIO's networks in Uttar Pradesh, SIMI reached out to Jamaat-linked Muslim students' groups in Andhra Pradesh, Bengal, Bihar and Kerala.[47] From the outset, SIMI made clear its belief that the practice of Islam was essentially a political project. In the long term, SIMI sought to re-establish the caliphate, without which it felt the practice of Islam would remain incomplete. Muslims comfortable living in secular societies, its pamphlets warned, were headed to hell. Ideologies other than Islam were condemned as false and sinful.[48]

Mawdudi's writings played a considerable role in shaping SIMI's notion of its historic, vanguard role. As Seyyed Vali Reza Nasr has pointed out, Maududi's reading of the Quran led him to believe that:

> …an important aspect of the Prophet's organisation had been segregating his community from its larger social context. This enabled the Prophet to give his organisation a distinct identity, and permitted the nascent Muslim community to resist dissolution into the larger pagan Arab culture. Instead, they were able to pull the adversary into the ambit of Islam. For Maududi, the Jamaat, much like the Prophetic community, had to be the paragon for Muslim community of India.[49]

Winds from the west gave this project an increasingly hard edge. SIMI's leadership was drawn to Islamist regime of General Mohammad Zia-ul-Haq's in Pakistan, and threw its weight behind the United States-backed mujahideen fighting the Soviet Union and the socialist regime in Afghanistan. It also developed a broad common front with forces of Sunni reaction in west Asia. Sikand has noted:

> SIMI's rhetoric grew combative and vitriolic, insisting that Islam alone was the solution to the problems of not just the Muslims of India, but of all Indians and, indeed, of the whole world.[50]

Interestingly, the Jammu and Kashmir Islami Jamaat-e-Tulba—the student wing of the Jammu and Kashmir Jamaat-e-Islami—was undergoing a similar process of transformation. Formed in 1977, the IJT was to develop transnational linkages with neoconservative Islamist groups and, in much the same manner and much the same time SIMI.

At the outset, the IJT reached out to Saudi Arabia—based neoconservative patronage networks for help. In 1979, the IJT was granted membership of the World Organisation of Muslim Youth, a controversial Saudi—funded body which funded many Islamist groups that later turned to terrorism. The next year, the IJT organised a conference in Srinagar, which was attended by dignitaries from across west Asia, including the Imam of the mosques of Mecca and Medina, Abdullah bin-Sabil.

By the end of the decade, the IJT had formally committed itself an armed struggle against the Indian state. Its president, Sheikh Tajamul Husain—now a mid-ranking leader of the secessionist movement—told journalists in Srinagar that Kashmiris did not consider themselves Indian, and forces stationed there were an "army of occupation".[51] Husain also called for the establishment of an Islamic state, through the medium of a revolution. A year later, in 1981, Husain reiterated his call to followers to evict the Indian "occupation". Many of those who would later acquire central positions in the Hizb ul-Mujahideen, including its supreme commander, Mohammad Yusuf Shah, cut their political teeth in this climate.

Indian authorities do not appear to have been particularly concerned by this turn of event. Jammu and Kashmir's chief minister, Sheikh Mohammad Abdullah, did proscribe a IJT meeting scheduled in 1980, but no serious effort appears to have crack down on SIMI elsewhere in India.

Jamaat leaders in India demonstrated more concerned than the state apparatus, and sought to distance themselves from SIMI. Much of the Jamaat rank-and-file, though, was incensed at what they saw as the organisation's betrayal of Maududi's authentic Islamism. In 1982, the Jamaat formally distanced itself from SIMI, but members of both organisations in practice retained a cordial relationship. Interestingly, while the SIO insists on peaceful means, its ideological agenda is not dissimilar to that of SIMI. One official publication, for example, points to SIO's heritage of Salafi neo-conservatism, saying it represents "Ibn Abdul Wahab's belief, Syed Qutb's smile at the gallows, and Syed Maududi's revolutionary call".[52] Given that Qutb's notion of revolution inspired the assassins of Egyptian president Anwar Sadat—and legions of Islamist terror cells after—the violence implicit in the ideology is evident.

Part of the reason for SIMI's spectacular growth after 1982 lay in precisely this heritage and the support that its material manifestations—Islamists organisations the Kuwait-based World Association of Muslim Youth and the Saudi Arabia-funded International Islamic Federation of Student Organisation—were able to provide.[53] Generous funding from west Asia helped it establish a welter of magazines—Islamic Movement in Urdu, Hindi and English, Iqra in Gujarati, Rupantar in Bengali, Sedi Malar in Tamil and Vivekam in Malayalam—that propagated the idea of an Islamic revolution. SIMI also set up a special wing, the Tehreek Tulba e-Arabiya, to build networks among madrasa students, as well as the Shaheen Force, which targeted children.

Much of SIMI's time was spent on persuading its recruits that Islam alone offered solutions to the challenges of the modern life. In 1982, for example, it organised an anti-immorality week, where supposedly obscene literature was burned. A year later, in an effort to compete with the left in Kerala, SIMI held an anti-capitalism week. Predictably, it held out Islam, rather than socialism, as the solution. SIMI also worked extensively with victims of communal violence, and provided educational services for poor Muslims. It appeared to give young Muslims a sense of purpose and identity, urging them to reject drugs and alcohol.

Was SIMI, then, in essence a Muslim social service organisation, occupying spaces the state had vacated? Yes—but also no. As Irfan Habib, Iqtidar Alam Khan and KP Singh observed in a seminal 1976 essay, the conditions of Muslims were not what Islamists "regarded as their principal grievances".[54] Rather, their objective was to use discrimination as a tool with which to legitimise Islamism. Indeed, Islamists wished for "preservation of Muslim separateness, not the end of Muslim backwardness, as their basic aim".[55]

SIMI's polemic appealed to the growing class of lower-middle class and middle-class urban men who felt cheated of their share of the growing economic opportunities opening up in India. In SIMI's vision, this discrimination was intrinsic to, not an aberration from, the Indian secular-nationalist project. Safdar Nagori, one of SIMI's leading figures, even claimed in one interview that Jawaharlal Nehru, India's first Prime Minister, had wished for all Muslims to embrace the heretical teachings of the Punjabi mystic Ghulam Ahmed Qadiani.[56] No historical substantiation of this claim exists —but it, and others, were used to buttress the claim that the secular state was inherently hostile to what SIMI characterised as normative Islam.

Hit by communal bias and educational backwardness, a wide swathe of disenfranchised young men were drawn to SIMI's attacks on Hindu polytheism, Indian secularism and western decadence. The organisation's claims that there could be no justice for Muslims other than in an Shariah-based order resonated with communities battered by decades of communal violence, often backed by the Indian state. By 2001, SIMI had over 400 Ansar, or full-time workers, and 20,000 Ikhwan, or volunteers.[57] As Yoginder Sikand has perceptively noted, the organisation provided "its supporters a sense of power and agency which they were denied in their actual lives".[58]

It wasn't until 1991, though, that SIMI began directing that sense of agency towards terrorism. Soon after the tragic events of 6 December 1992, and the pogroms which followed it, SIMI president Shahid Badr Falahi demanded that "Muslims organise themselves and stand up to defend the community".[59] Another SIMI leader, Abdul Aziz Salafi, demanded action to show that Muslims "would now refuse to sit low".[60]

Growing numbers of SIMI members responded to their call, making their way to Lashkar, Jaish-e-Mohammad and Harkat ul-Jihad-e-Islami training camps. SIMI leaders continued to insist their organisation itself had nothing to do with terrorism. Its polemic, however, became increasingly bitter. In a 1996 statement, SIMI declared that since democracy and secularism had failed to protect Muslims, the sole option was to struggle for the caliphate.[61] Soon after, it put up posters calling on Muslims to follow the path of Mahmood Ghaznavi, and appealed to god to send down a latter-day avatar of the eleventh-century conqueror to avenge the destruction of mosques in India.[62]

By the time of SIMI's 1999 Aurangabad convention, many of the speeches delivered by delegates were frankly inflammatory. "Islam is our nation, not India," thundered Mohammad Amir Shakeel Ahmad, one of over a dozen SIMI-linked Lashkar operatives arrested in 2005 for smuggling in military-grade explosives and assault rifles for a planned series of attacks in Gujarat. Among those listening to the speech was 1993 bomber Azam Ghauri who, by the accounts of some of those present, was offered the leadership of SIMI.

When 25,000 SIMI delegates met in Mumbai in 2001, at what was to be its last public convention, the organisation for the first time called on its supporters to turn to jihad. Soon after the convention, al-Qaeda carried out its bombings of New York and Washington,

D.C. SIMI activists organised demonstrations in support of al-Qaeda chief Osama bin-Laden, hailing him as a "true mujahid," and celebrating the demolition of the Bamiyan Buddhas by the Taliban regime in Afghanistan.[63]

Writing in 2001, in an article published just after the convention, the commentator Javed Anand recalled seeing stickers pasted "in large numbers in Muslim shops and homes, a thick red 'NO' splashed across the words DEMOCRACY, NATIONALISM, POLYTHEISM. 'ONLY ALLAH!' exclaims SIMI's punch-line".[64]

Home Grown, Foreign-Irrigated

At a February, 2000, Lashkar rally, Saeed's deputy, Abdul Rehman Makki, explained elements of a pan-India jihadist strategy group had planned to move its operations beyond Kashmir, and place pressure on India as a whole.[65] He proclaimed the Lashkar would soon initiate operations in Hyderabad, a city claimed by Pakistan's Islamist right-wing to have been seized illegally by Indian forces from its Muslim monarch in 1948. Hyderabad offers a useful case to examine the enormously complex warp and weft of local communal conflict and the transnational crisis of Islam that together make up the jihad in India.

Like SIMI, the Lashkar and its parent religious group, the Jamaatud-Dawa [Centre for Invitation to the Faith] had from the outset seen the jihad in Jammu and Kashmir as a precursor, a wider civilisation conflict that would "continue until Islam becomes the dominant religion".[66] By the account of the Pakistani journalist Zahid Husain, this world view was rooted in Saeed's experience of Partition:

> The horrors of the partition in 1947, which uprooted his family from their home in Shimla, left a huge imprint on Hafiz Saeed's personality. Millions of people were massacred in the communal violence that followed the creation of the new Muslim state. Thirty-six members of his family were killed while migrating to Pakistan.[67]

For years, the Lashkar had been attempting to build a network across using local Islamists.[68] Perhaps the most successful of the Lashkar's agents was Mohammad Ishtiaq, the son of a shopkeeper from Kala Gujran in Pakistan's Jhelum district. Operating under the alias Salim Junaid, Ishtiaq obtained an Indian passport and even married a local resident, Momina Khatoon. Ishtiaq, however, was arrested before he could do real harm.

In late 1998, responding to desperate pleas from the Lashkar's leadership, Hyderabad resident Mohammad Azam Ghauri returned to India to help rebuild its networks.[69] Ghauri was, who figured earlier in this paper as one of the three co-founders of the Indian jihad, turned to friends in Hyderabad's organised crime cartels for help. In 1999, his long-standing friend, Karachi-based mafioso Dawood Ibrahim Kaksar-linked hit-man Abdul Aziz Sheikh, attempted to assassinate the Shiv Sena leader Milind Vaidya—one of the key figures in organising the post-Babri Masjid communal riots in Mumbai.

Help was also sought, and received, from remnants of the mafia of Mohammad Fasiuddin, which had executed Andhra Pradesh Hindu fundamentalist leaders Papiah Goud and Nanda Raj Goud as retaliation for the 1992 anti-Muslim riots there.

Soon after Makki's speech, Ghauri's new mafia-linked network set off bombs cinema theatres in Karimnagar and Nanded. Eight weeks after these bombings, Ghauri was shot dead by the police.

Jihadi organisations continued to attempt to build new networks in Hyderabad. In August, 2001, the Hyderabad Police arrested one of the most intriguing figures in this effort, an unassuming electrician named Abdul Aziz. While working in Saudi Arabia, Aziz had come into contact with an Islamist recruiter looking for volunteers to join the global jihad. Aziz served in Bosnia in

1994, and then fought alongside Chechen Islamists in 1996. In 1999, Aziz again flew to Tbilisi, in search of a second tour of duty. He was, however, deported. With the help of funds from Hamid Bahajib, a Saudi Arabia-based Lashkar financier who had also paid for Ghauri's work, Aziz returned home to try and initiate a jihad of his own.[70]

Aziz, investigators found, hoped to draw on the resources of the Darsgah Jihad-o-Shahadat, or Institute for Holy War and Martyrdom—an Islamist vigilante group set up in the mid-1980s, at around the same time SIMI was gathering momentum. Although its website claims that the organisation's purpose is "protecting the life and properties of [the] Muslim community," and "preserving the honour and chastity of women," the organisation also candidly states that "Islamic supremacy is our goal".[71]

For the most part, these efforts had only limited successes. But starting from September, 2002, at least fourteen young men from Hyderabad set out on secret journeys to terrorist training camps in Pakistan. A decade earlier, as I shall show later in this paper, the demolition of the Babri Masjid by Hindu fundamentalists had led several recruits from Hyderabad into the lap of the Lashkar. This time around, the hatred generated by the communal pogrom in Gujarat helped Islamist groups reap a fresh harvest.

Mohammad Abdul Shahid's story, and the fluid, cross-organisational networks he built, cast considerable insight into the evolving story of the Indian jihad. Police records show Shahid dropped out of college less than a year after his graduation from the Asafiya High School in Hyderabad. He was amongst the first generation of his inner-city family to have access to a higher education—and grew up in a new home paid for, in part, by remittances from his brothers who found work in West Asia. In the wake of the Gujarat pogrom, Shahid involved himself with SIMI groups in the city. He evidently found political activism alone inadequate, for he soon sought access to terror training camps in Pakistan through a relative—one of India's most wanted men, mafioso Rasool Khan Yakub Khan Pathan.[72]

Better known by the alias Rasool 'Party,' Pathan was a long standing vassal of the Karachi-based mafia of Dawood Ibrahim Kaksar. After the Gujarat riots, Pathan took responsibility for transporting the new wave of jihadi recruits for training. According to the testimony of mafia operative Javed Hamidullah Siddiqui, who was arrested in 2004, Dawood lieutenant Shakeel Ahmad Babu arranged the new recruits' passage on flights through Bangkok and Dhaka.[73] Pathan, who has been wanted by Interpol ever since 1993, was waiting for them on their arrival in Karachi. While some recruits trained with the Lashkar, others were routed on to the Jaish and Harkat: a fluid dispersion of assets across organisational lines not seen before the 2002 pogrom.

Within months of their departure, the new recruits executed their first successful strikes. Asad Yazdani, a resident of Hyderabad's Toli Chowki area, helped execute the assassination of the former Gujarat Home Minister, Haren Pandya. Pandya, a Central Bureau of Investigations inquiry later determined, was killed in reprisal for his role in pogrom.[74]

Although the new recruits had trained with the Lashkar and Jaish, they turned to the Bangladesh-based Harkat for operational support. Founded by Bangladeshi veterans of the anti-Soviet Union jihad in Afghanistan, the Harkat operates at least six camps where several hundred Pakistani, Indian, Thai and Myanmar nationals are known to have trained. Its founder, Mufti Abdul Hannan, spent several years studying at the Dar-ul-Uloom seminary at Deoband, Uttar Pradesh, and developed a large network of contacts among Islamists in India. He also built links with key organised crime figures. Among the group's most high-profile actions in India was the January, 2002, terror attack near the American Centre in Kolkata, executed in collaboration with Dawood-linked mafioso Aftab Ansari.[75]

Most often, Harkat operations involved infrastructure provided by one-time SIMI cadre from India and Bangladesh nationals who executed the actual strike. In 2007, for example, the Delhi Police arrested Yazdani's Bangladeshi bomb-makers, the twin brothers Anishul Murshlin and Muhibbul Muttakin.[76] Both confirmed Yazdani's SIMI links had the June, 2005, bombing of the Delhi-Patna Shramjeevi Express at Jaunpur and October, 2005, suicide bombing of the headquarters of the Andhra Pradesh Police's counter-terrorism Special Task Force. A Bangladeshi national, Mohtasin Billa, had carried out the bombing—the first Harkat operation of its kind.

Yazdani was shot dead in March, 2006, just hours after the bombing of the Sankat Mochan temple in Varanasi—another lethal attack which was traced to the Harkat's Bangladesh-based cells.[77] Shahid then took charge of the organisation.

Both Imperial and post-independence Indian politics watered the soil in which these SIMI-linked networks flourished. Nominally independent of British India, Hyderabad's last Nizam, Mir Osman Ali Khan, administered a system in which religious affiliation was a key source of legitimacy building. Although Muslims made up just 10 percent of his realm's population, they held three-quarters of state jobs. And of the seven major feudal estates, six were controlled by Muslim notables.

During the two decades before independence, Hyderabad saw the growth of two communal movements which Hindu and Muslim elites used to strengthen their position. Speaking for the emerging Hindu industrialist class, the Arya Samaj argued that practices like idol worship had weakened the faith, and thus facilitated centuries of what they characterised as alien rule.

In response to the proseletysation efforts of the Arya Samaj, Muslim elites set up the Majlis-e-Ittehad ul-Muslimeen, or Organisation for the Unity of Muslims. The Arya Samaj, the Majlis was founded on the doctrine that Hyderabad Muslims were its natural hakim kaum, or ruling race. Although much of the Hyderabad Muslim elite was Shia, it was deeply influenced by the work of the nineteenth century revivalist Sayyid Ahmad of Rae Bareilly. Ahmad's influential Sunni-chauvinist work, as Vali Nasr has noted, "identified false Sufism, Shi'ism and errant popular customs as the sources of religious corruption and hence declining Muslim power".[78]

These competing communal movements collided in April, 1938, when the city saw its first communal riots. Besieged by the Congress' demands for democratic elections, and the Arya Samaj religious mobilisation Osman Ali Khan responded to the growing violence by proscribing both. He turned to the Majlis for support. Rizvi now set up the Razakars as a paramilitary sword-arm of the Nizam. Majlis leaders, the scholar Lucien Benichou has recorded, candidly stated that their objective was to "keep the sovereignty of His Exalted Highness intact and to prevent Hindus from establishing supremacy over Muslims".

In 1947, Rizvi unleashed his forces in support of the Nizam's claims to independence. Thousands—both Hindus and Muslims opposed to Osman Ali Khan—were killed before the Indian Army swept into the state in September, 1948. Within five days, Hyderabad capitulated. While the Nizam became the titular head of state, Rizvi was captured and imprisoned. He was finally expelled to Pakistan in 1957.

Despite Rizvi's defeat, Islamists continued to flourish in Hyderabad. The Majlis was reborn in 1957, under the leadership of the affluent cleric and lawyer Abdul Wahid Owaisi, who drafted a new constitution committing it to the Union of India. Sultan Salahuddin Owaisi, his son, took over the organisation 1976. Salahuddin Owaisi's sons, Asaduddin Owaisi and Akbaruddin Owaisi, are in turn now its most visible faces.

Starting from nothing, the Majlis rapidly established itself as the principal spokesperson for old-city Muslims. By 1977–78, the Congress—which had unleashed the Indian Army on the Majlis just three decades earlier—was seeking electoral alliances with it. In 1986, an Majlis-Congress alliance took charge of

Hyderabad's municipal corporation. The Majlis spoke for two distinct constituencies within the old city: a devout traditional elite disinherited by the coming of democratic rule, and an urban underclass which remained economically disenfranchised despite it.

Just how did the party succeed in re-establishing itself so fast?

Ashutosh Varshney has offered this simple explanation: In the 1960s, there were riots in eight out of ten years in Hyderabad. After 1978, the trend towards communal violence took a turn for the worse. Except for the period 1986–89, riots took place virtually every year between 1978 and 1993, often many times in the same year.[79]

Communal parties, not surprisingly, acquired centre-stage. With growing support from Hyderabad Muslims based in west Asia, the Majlis grew into a formidable competitor to the Hindu right.

With the Congress and Majlis locked in political embrace, Hindu nationalist forces were able to represent themselves as the sole credible defenders of Hindu interests. Violence became institutionalised, giving rise to what the historian Paul Brass has described as an "organised riot system".[80] For example, gangs of killers were set up to wage war on behalf of their respective religious communities, operating under political immunities granted by various groups—a phenomenon documented in the psychoanalyst Sudhir Kakkar's book, *The Colors of Violence*.[81] Violence, the historian Javed Alam's work shows on the Majlis shows, acquired growing legitimacy.[82] "The distinction between crime and valor," Varshney has noted, "thus disappeared for a large mass of Muslims and Hindus in the old city of Hyderabad".[83]

Islamist terrorism in Hyderabad represented a breakdown of faith in the Majlis' riot-protection system. Muslim interests, recruits to SIMI were told, could only be defended by integration into the wider the global jihadi movement.

Majlis leaders have, in recent years, found themselves in opposition to the jihadism they once advocated. In a recent interview, Majlis leader Asaduddin Owaisi noted that "these misguided youths call me a kafir".[84] "I am on their hit list," he said. Majlis leaders have continued to use chauvinism, for example by leading protests against a visit by the Bangladeshi author Taslima Nasreen.[85] However, there is no sign that these tactics have succeeded in mitigating the success of SIMI and other jihadi groups outside of the political system drawing new recruits.

Addressing poverty in old-city Hyderabad is often advertised as a solution to the jihad's success. While worthwhile as a policy objective, it may not be a prescription for peace. As Varshney has pointed out:

> Hyderabad Muslims have done much better than their Lucknow counterparts. Their success however has led not to a reduction but an increase in communal tensions, partly through a strengthening of the Majlis. The relative economic betterment of Muslims is not a cause of increased tensions. An absence of symbiotic linkages is. The two communities do not constitute a web of interdependence.[86]

Is Perdition Ahead?

Though jihadist attacks within India have been at a low ebb since 2008, when the Indian Mujahideen cadre fled the country, it takes little to see that there remains a durable threat. In 2016, Pakistan based jihadist groups demonstrated their continued ability to strike targets in India, hitting Gurdaspur, Pathankot and Uri, among other targets. Pakistani-American jihadist David Headley, as I previously mentioned has spoken of what he called the "Karachi Project"—a joint operation involving jihadists, elements in Pakistan's intelligence services, to use Indian nations for further strikes on the country.[87]

Now, there is a further threat: the recruitment and training of Indian jihadists overseas, who could yet turn into the hard core of a future threat. Islamist terror groups understand that acts of violence do not in themselves further the Islamist political agenda, or hasten the disintegration of the Indian state. In 2006, terrorism in India, including its Maoist variant, claimed 2598 lives; traffic accidents a staggering 105,749.[88]

What jihadi groups instead hope is that violence will achieve is sunder Hindu from Muslim, bringing about an apocalyptic religious war. In their imagination, this war will led to the triumph of neoconservative Islam and the re-establishment of the Caliphate. While this enterprise may seem somewhat disconnected from the real world, India's long history of communal hostilities has raised concerns that jihadi violence could act as a catalyst for a holocaust of this kind. It is to this challenge that India's political system must respond.

Broadly, three major challenges lie ahead.

First, funnelling funds towards improving educational access or economic opportunity—the chosen weapons of government counter-radicalisation efforts across the world—should not be seen as a deux ex machina which will solve the problem. Sabahuddin Ahmed, the first Indian to head a Lashkar cell which included Pakistani nationals, lacked neither. His father was a lawyer; his middle-class secularised family included doctors, engineers and multinational firm executives. Yet, Ahmed joined SIMI in the wake of the Gujarat pogrom—as did so many others—and went on to execute both the 2005 attack on the Indian Institute of Science in Bangalore and the 2007 assault on the Central Reserve Police Force's training camp at Rampur.[89]

Instead of purely economic interventions to address the rage of young Muslims, which can at best be palliatives rather than prescriptions for peace, a rigorous commitment to the rule of law is needed. Prime Minister Singh has often voiced a commitment to justice and secularism—he called, soon after taking power, for action to ensure "painful incidents like [the 1984 anti-Sikh massacres] and the Gujarat riots never happen again"—but onground implementation been poor.[90] State governments has, for example, failed to act against housing denial, a major grievance for the middle-class and lower middle-class Muslims who often join Islamist political organisations.[91]

Neither have institutional reforms have been put in place to insulate the police from the political pressures, nor laws reworked to ensure rapid justice for victims. Most important, nothing has been done by mainstream political parties to address the de-facto exclusion of Muslims from political life in highly-communalised states like Gujarat—a phenomenon that cedes political space to Islamists.[92] As such, government policies centred on the rule of law and citizenship are essential to counter jihadist narratives.

Second, the problem of religious chauvinism must be addressed without squeamishness or cant. In at least some senses, growing sensitivity of Indian political parties to Muslim concerns have nourished the religious reaction which forms the firmament from which the jihad has sprung. In late 2007, Bangladeshi author Taslima Nasreen was forced out of the state West Bengal after riots broke out there in protest against her presence.[93] Later, the Bengali-language novelist was compelled to leave India altogether. Uttar Pradesh authorities earlier refused to take legal action against a state minister Haji Yaqoob Qureshi, who announced a Rs. 510 million bounty for the lives of Danish cartoonists who caricatured the Prophet Mohammad.[94] Police in Andhra Pradesh, similarly, were reported to have been restrained from pursuing counter-terrorism investigations for fear it might alienate Muslim voters, provoking a major national newspaper to charge Prime Minister Singh's government with "what can be bluntly called communalisation of internal security".[95]

It is true that Hindu fundamentalists have enjoyed similar legal immunities. Uttar Pradesh, Madhya Pradesh and several cities in Haryana—all governed by different political formations—proscribed a film on the Mughal Emperor Akbar in the wake of protests by Hindu organisations.[96] Maharashtra, a Congress-ruled state, even proscribed scholarly literature on the medieval ruler Shivaji and demanded the extradition of its author.[97] However, even-handed treatment of Muslim and Hindu chauvinism is at some distance from a meaningful campaign to combat communalism.

Third, politicians—Hindu or Muslim, Left or Right—must begin to articulate a coherent ideological response to Islamism. Even as India's political and clerical orders have been maintaining a discreet silence on this question, the reach and influence of Islamism is increasing.

Increasingly, the invisible jihad is drawing numbers of highly educated, successful young Muslims—the class that ought to have abiding an abiding stake in a prosperous India and a globalising world.

Back in 2001, SIMI's Safdar Nagori had proclaimed that he was "very bitter" about India. [98] He voiced the rage of a generation of young men who saw opportunity opening up around them—but also found doors slammed shut in their face because of their faith. Many found in the venom of the Lashkar's Hafiz Mohammad Saeed a manifesto for praxis: "the Hindu is a mean enemy and the proper way to deal with him is the one adopted by our forefathers, who crushed them by force. We need to do the same".[99]

Indian politics, sadly, has done little to strip Nagori's position of legitimacy. It must do so now—or India could face a long and murderous war within.

NOTES

1   Stephen F. Dale, 'The Islamic Frontier in Southwest India: The Shahid as a Cultural Ideal among the Mappillas of Malabar,' *Modern Asian Studies*, Vol. 11, No. 1. (1977), p. 42.

2   The Quran, 2:16 https://quran.com/2/216.

3   Abu'l Ala Al-Ma'arri, *The Epistle of Forgiveness*, trans. Geert Jan Van Gelder and Gregor Schoeler (New York: New York University Press, 2016).

4   Praveen Swami, 'Coming soon to avenge Babri, Muzaffarnagar, Gujarat, Kashmir: IS Video', *The Indian Express* (New Delhi) 25 May 2016, available at http:// indianexpress.com/article/india/india-news-india/avenge-babri-isisvideo-islamic-state-indian-mujahideen-2811574/

5   Stephen F. Dale, 'The Islamic Frontier in Southwest India: The Shahid as a Cultural Ideal among the Mappillas of Malabar,' *Modern Asian Studies*, Vol. 11, No. 1 (1977), pp. 41–55.

6   Zayn al-Din al-Ma'bari, trans. David Lopes *Historia dos Portugueses no Malabar por Zinadim* (Lisbon: Imperensa Nacional, 1989), p. 5, cited in Stephen F. Dale, 'The Islamic Frontier in Southwest India: The Shahid as a Cultural Ideal among the Mappillas of Malabar,' *Modern Asian Studies*, Vol. 11, No. 1 (1977), p. 42.

7   Stephen F. Dale, 'The Islamic Frontier in Southwest India: The Shahid as a Cultural Ideal among the Mappillas of Malabar,' *Modern Asian Studies*, Vol. 11, No. 1 (1977), p. 43.

8   Ayesha Jalal, *Partisans of Allah* (Harvard University Press: Cambridge Massachussets, 2008).

9   Ibid., pp. 52–54.

10   William Dalrymple, *The Last Mughal* (New Delhi: Penguin, 2008), p. 24.

11   Ibid., pp. 294–95.

12   Yoginder Sikand, *The Origins and Development of the Tablighi-Jama'at* (New Delhi: Orient Longman, 2002), p. 31.

13   Chitralekha Zutshi, *Languages of Belonging* (New York: Oxford University Press, 2004), p. 174.

14   Abul Ala Mawdudi, *Jihad Fi'l Sabilillah* translated and edited by Khurshid Ahmad and Huda Khattab (London: UKIM Dawah Centre, 1995), p. 5.

15   Ibid.

16   Ibid.

17   Ibid.

18   Ibid., p. 17

19   *Ma'alim fi'l-Tariq* [Signposts on the Road, or Milestones], (Cairo: Privately published, 1964), p. 166.

20   Abdullah Azzam, *Signs of Allah the Most Merciful, al-Rahman, in the jihad of Afghanistan*, p. 58.

21   Seyyed Vali Reza Nasr, *The Vanguard of the Islamic Revolution* (Berkeley: University of California Press, 1994), pp. 23–24

22   Praveen Swami, 'Kerala man is Islamic State recruiter luring Indian volunteers to Islamic State', *The Indian Express,* 20 October 2016, available at http:// indianexpress.com/article/india/india-news-india/kerala-islamic-staterecruiter-indian-volunteers-afghanistan-isis-mosul-attack-3092431/

23   'Final Form Report Under Section 173, Code of Criminal Procedure in the Court of Kaveri Baweja, Chief Metropolitan Magistrate' (Delhi: Delhi Police Special Cell, November, 2010), p. 54

24   Shishir Gupta, 'ISI, LeT getting Indian jihadis together in Karachi for attac', *The Indian Express,* available at http://www.indianexpress.com/news/ isi-let-getting-indian-jihadis-together-in-karachi-for-attack/573878/0), accessed on 1 February 2010.

25   'Eye for an eye: the Dust Will Never Settle Down', (New Delhi: 'Indian Mujahideen in the Land of Hind', e-mailed to media on 13 September 2008).

26   For background on the Talibhi Jamaat and its belief system, see Yoginder Sikand, *The Origins and Development of the Tablighi Jamaat, 1920-2000,* (New Delhi: Orient Longman, 2002).

27   Praveen Swami, 'Indian Mujahideen chief Sadiq Sheikh's Slumdog Story', *The Hindu* (Chennai), 6 March 2009, available at http:// www.hindu.com/2009/03/06/stories/2009030661701200.htm

28   For a summary of the violence, see Kalpana Sharma, 'Chronicle of a riot foretold', in Sujata Patel and Alice Thorner, eds., Bombay: Metaphor for Modern India (New Delhi: Oxford University Press, 1996), pp. 268–286.

29   Yoginder Sikand, 'Islamist Assertion in Contemporary India: the Students Islamic Movement of India,' (Electronic: Islam Interfaith, 2005).

30   'Life for nine in Haren Pandya murder case,' *The Times of India* (New Delhi), 26 June 2007.

31   Sadiq Sheikh's own role in these bombings remains a source of debate. For an overview of the contention, see 'IM's Sadiq Sheikh let off in 7/11 case', *The Indian Express* (New Delhi), 12 May 2009, available at http:// www.indianexpress.com/story-print/457699/ and Praveen Swami 'Maharashtra ATS moves to resolve 7/11 mystery', *The Hindu* (Chennai), 22 February 2009,

available at http://www.hindu.com/2009/02/22/stories/ 2009022258900800.htm

32 Praveen Swami, 'Mumbai terror trail leads to Muscat', *The Hindu* (Chennai), 28 May 2009, available at http://www.hindu.com/2009/05/28/stories/ 2009052857760100.htm. See also, Praveen Swami, 'How Lashkar funded transnational terror campaign', *The Hindu* (Chennai), 28 May 2009, available at http://www.hindu.com/2009/05/28/stories/ 2009052855481000.htm

33 For a brief overview of the origins of the Lashkar-e-Taiba, see Saeed Shafqat, 'From Official Islam to Islamism: the rise of the Dawat-ul-Irshad and Lashkar-e-Taiba' in Christophe Jaffrelot, ed., *Pakistan: Nationalism Without a Nation?* (London: Zed Books, 2002).

34 For a brief outline of SIMI, see 'Students Islamic Movement of India,' South Asia Terrorism Portal (Online), available at http://www.satp.org/ satporgtp/countries/india/terroristoutfits/ simi.htm. For a full account of the origins and growth of SIMI, see Yoginder Sikand, 'Islamist Assertion in Contemporary India: the Students Islamic Movement of India,' (New Delhi: Islam Interfaith, 2005). For a sympathetic Urdulanguage account, see Sayyed Abdul Bari, *Azad Hindustan Mai Muslim Tanzimey* (New Delhi: Institute of Objective Studies, 2001).

35 For an overview of Indian Mujahideen membership, see B. Raman, 'Terror's new faces', Rediff.com (Online), 19 August 2008, http:// www.rediff.com/news/2008/aug/19raman.htm. For details of Shibly and Kamakutty, see Praveen Swami, 'White-collar jihadists a cause for growing concern', *The Hindu* (Chennai), 7 October 2008, available at http:// www.hindu.com/ 2008/10/07/stories/2008100760451000.htm.

36 Material here and below on the background of Nawaz and al-Hooti was gathered during interviews with Indian police personnel in Hyderabad, Mumbai, and Bangalore, conducted during research for Praveen Swami, 'Mumbai terror trail leads to Muscat', *op. cit.*

37 The Noorisha Sufis purport to oppose terrorism; see 'Terrorists giving a bad name for jihad: Tariqa chief', *Expressbuzz.com* (Online), 3 February 2009, available at http:// www.expressbuzz.com/edition/print.aspx? artid=n0S39dRAqKw=. For details on Nasir, see Praveen Swami, 'The Sufi with the Kalashnikov', *The Hindu* (Chennai), 16 February 2009, <http://www.hindu.com/2009/02/16/stories/2009021653740800.htm>

38 For details on Fahim Ansari's background and operations, see Praveen Swami, 'How the Lashkar planned Mumbai massacre', *The Hindu* (Chennai), 28 February 2009, available at http:// www.hindu.com/2009/02/28/ stories/2009022859381200.htm. Also see Praveen Swami, 'Abortive Lashkar plot holds clues to Mumbai massacre', *The Hindu* (Chennai), available at 8 December 2008, available at http://www.hindu.com/2008/12/08/stories/ 2008120859431000.htm.

39 For details of the Aurangabad case, see Stavan Desai, Anuradha Nagaraj and Sagnik Chowdhury, 'Cops follow Aurangabad arms trail', *The Indian Express* (New Delhi), 16 July 2006. For an account of the Lashkar's use of sea routes into Mumbai, see Praveen Swami, 'Signs of another kind of Line of Control', *The Hindu* (Chennai), 14 May 2007.

40 Thirteen people were killed in the bombings; see Atiq Khan and Praveen Swami, 'Thirteen killed as serial blasts rock Uttar Pradesh', *The Hindu* (Chennai), 24 November 2007. Former SIMI members Mohammad Khalid and Mohammad Tariq were arrested in December, 2007, on charges of executing the attack, while their overall commander, Jammu and Kashmir-based Harkat ul-Jihad-e-Islami operative Bashir Ahmed Mir, was shot dead in January 2008; see Praveen Swami, 'HuJI chief shot dead,' *The Hindu* (Chennai), 26 January 2008.

41 Anonymous, 'Causes Behind Jihad (Holy War) In India'. E-mail to newspaper offices signed by the 'Indian Mujahideen,' 13 November 2007.

42 Praveen Swami, 'Generation of avengers with Babri '92 as motif', *The Indian Express*, 16

December 2015 available at http://indianexpress.com/article/india/ india-others/generation-of-avengers-with-babri-92-as-motif/

43 For a full journalistic account of contemporary communal riots, see MJ Akbar, *Riot After Riot* (New Delhi: Penguin, 1988)

44 'Life sentences for 15 for 1993 serial train blasts,' Rediff.com (Online), 28 February 2004, available at http://us.rediff.com/news/2004/feb/ 28blast.htm

45 For an account of the 1993 terrorist bombings in Mumbai, see S. Hussain Zaidi *Black Friday: The True Story of the Bombay Bomb Blasts* (New Delhi: Penguin, 2002).

46 For a compact account of the Jamaat-e-Islami's role in Pakistani politics during this period, see Hassan Abbas, *Pakistan's Drift Into Extremism* (Armonk: ME Sharpe, 2005), pp. 81–82, 100–101.

47 Sayyed Abdul Bari, *Azad Hindustan Mai Muslim Tanzimey* (New Delhi: Institute of Objective Studies, 2001), p. 291.

48 'Interview with [SIMI President] Shahid Badr Falahi', *Afkar-i Milli* (New Delhi), November 2000, p. 44.

49 Seyyed Vali Reza Nasr, *The Vanguard of the Islamic Revolution* (Berkeley: University of California Press, 1994), p. 9.

50 Yoginder Sikand, 'Islamist Assertion in Contemporary India: the Students Islamic Movement of India,' (Electronic: Islam Interfaith, 2005).

51 Yoginder Sikand, 'The Emergence and Development of the Jama'at-iIslami of Jammu and Kashmir', *Modern Asian Studies*, Vol. 36, No. 3 (July, 2002), p. 737

52 Students Islamic Organisation of India, *25 Years of Redefining Education, Regaining Struggle, Renovating Society* (New Delhi: SIO, 2008), p. 8.

53 'Students Islamic Movement of India,' *South Asia Terrorism Portal*, available at http:// www.satp.org/satporgtp/countries/india/terroristoutfits/ simi.htm).

54 Irfan Habib, Iqtidar Alam Khan and KP Singh, 'Problems of the Muslim Minority in India', *Social Scientist*, Vol. 4, No. 11 (June, 1976), p. 69.

55 Ibid., p. 71.

56 Sayantan Chakravarty, 'Interview: Safdar Nagori,' *India Today* (New Delhi), 2 April 2001.

57 'Students Islamic Movement of India,' *South Asia Terrorism Portal*, available at http:// www.satp.org/satporgtp/countries/india/terroristoutfits/ simi.htm).

58 Yoginder Sikand, 'Islamist Assertion in Contemporary India: the Students Islamic Movement of India,' (Electronic: Islam Interfaith, 2005).

59 Ibid.

60 Ibid.

61 Sayyed Abdul Bari, *Azad Hindustan Mai Muslim Tanzimey* (New Delhi: Institute of Objective Studies, 2001), p. 305.

62 Anita Verma, 'India Urgently Needs a Ghaznavi: SIMI Chief,' *The Asian Age* (New Delhi), 29 March, 2001

63 Yoginder Sikand, *Islamist Assertion in Contemporary India: the Students Islamic Movement of India* (Electronic: Islam Interfaith, 2005).

64 Javed Anand, 'Why be Shy About SIMI?', *Communalism Combat* (Mumbai), October 2001, p. 25.

65 Amit Baruah, 'Militant chiefs warn Musharraf,' *The Hindu* (Chennai), 6 February 2000

66 Zahid Husain, *Frontline Pakistan* (New Delhi: Penguin, 2007), pp. 53.

67 Ibid

68 Praveen Swami, 'The liberation of Hyderabad,' *Frontline* (Chennai), 26 May 2000.

69 Ibid.

70 'ISI agents' plans scuttled,' *The Times of India* (Mumbai), 30 August 2001.

71 'Darsgah Jihad-o-Shahadat: DJC Activities', available at http:// www.djsindia.org/index.htm.

72 'Wanted by CBI: RC.1&2(S)/93.SIU.III,' (New Delhi: Central Bureau of Investigations, 2005).

73 [SECRET] 'Note on interrogation of Javed Hamidullah Siddiqui,' (Ahmedabad: Gujarat Police Headquarters, 2004).

74 'Life for nine in Haren Pandya murder case,' *The Times of India* (New Delhi), 26 June 2007.

75 For a full profile of the organisation, see South Asia Terrorism Portal, 'Harkat ul-Jihad-Islami: Evolution of the Outfit' (New Delhi: Institute of Conflict Management, undated), available at http://www.satp.org/ satporgtp/countries/india/states/jandk/terrorist_outfits/HuJI.htm

76 Devesh K. Pandey, 'Blast suspect was trained at Jaish camp,' *The Hindu* (Chennai), 21 May 2007.

77 Muzammil Jaleel and Siddhartha Sarma, 'Pieces in terror jigsaw, two top Lashkar men shot in UP, Delhi,' *The Indian Express* (New Delhi), 9 March 2006.

78 Vali Nasr, *The Shia Revival: How Conflicts Within Islam Will Shape the Future* (New York and London: W.W. Norton, 2006), pp. 99–100.

79 Ashutosh Varshney, 'Postmodernism, Civic Engagement, and Ethnic Conflict: A Passage to India', *Comparative Politics*, Vol. 30, No. 1. (Oct., 1997, pp. 9–10.

80 Paul Brass, *Riots and Pogroms* (London: McMillan, 1996). Introduction

81 Sudhir Kakkar, *The Colors of Violence* (Chicago: University of Chicago Press, 1996)

82 Javed Alam, 'The Majlis Ittehad-ul-Muslimeen and the Muslims of Hyderabad,' in Gyan Pandey, ed., *Hindus and Others* (Delhi: Oxford University Press, 1993).

83 Ashutosh Varshney, 'Postmodernism, Civic Engagement and Ethnic Conflict: A Passage to India,' *Comparative Politics*, Vol. 30, No. 1. (New York: City University of New York, October, 1997), p. 10.

84 Abhishek Sharan, 'Owaisi sees Bilal's hand,' *The Hindustan Times* (New Delhi), 4 September 2007.

85 Kingshuk Nag, 'Hyderabad Blues,' *The Times of India* (Mumbai), 1 September 2007.

86 Ashutosh Varshney, 'Postmodernism, Civic Engagement and Ethnic Conflict: A Passage to India,' *Comparative Politics*, Vol. 30, No. 1. (New York: City University of New York, October, 1997), p. 14.

87 R Boales, 'Is Pakistan using terror to balance against India's military advantage', available at http://www.isvg.org/follow/blog/2011/07/25/thekarachi-project-is-pakistan-using-terror-to-balance-against-indiasmilitary-advantage/), accessed on 25 July 2011.

88 For data on terrorism fatalities, see South Asia Terrorism Portal, 'India Fatalities', available at http://www.satp.org/satporgtp/countries/india/ database/indiafatalities.htm). For traffic fatalities, see '1,05,749 deaths: India tops road accident record book', *The Indian Express* (New Delhi), 21 March 2008. For details of all Islamist terror attacks in India since 11 September 2002, see South Asia Terrorism Portal, 'Major Islamist Terrorist Attacks in India in the Post-9/11 Period', available at http:// www.satp.org/satporgtp/countries/india/database/ OR_9-11_majorterroristattacks.htm).

89 Praveen Swami, 'Inside the mind of the jihad', *The Hindu* (Chennai), 13 April 2008.

90 Press Trust of India, 'Create Atmosphere Wherein Painful Incidents Don't Happen' *OutlookIndia.com* (Online), 12 June 2004.

91 For example, see Sunanda Mehta, 'Not allowed to sell her flat to a Muslim, Pune woman takes on entire 'society', *The Indian Express* (New Delhi), 2 April 2008.

92 Vidya Subrahmaniam, 'The Muslim question in Gujarat', *The Hindu* (Chennai), 9 October 2007.

93 Kathleen McCaul, 'Condemned to life as an outsider,' *The Guardian* (London), 30 November 2007.

94 Rasheed Kidwai, 'Cartoon minister ruffles clergy', *The Telegraph* (Kolkata), 19 February 2006.

95 Editorial, 'In the blood', *The Indian Express* (New Delhi), 27 August 2007. For details of the police's conduct, see Praveen Swami, 'Intelligence had warned of strikes,' *The Hindu* (Chennai), 27 August 2007.

96 The ban was later struck down by the Supreme Court; see 'SC lifts ban on screening "Jodha-Akbar"', *The Economic Times* (New Delhi), 4 March 2008.

97 Suhas Palshikar, 'Maharashtra-style Moditva', *The Indian Express* (New Delhi), 17 May 2008.

98 Sayantan Chakravarty, 'Interview: Safdar Nagori,' *India Today* (New Delhi), 2 April 2001.

99 Hafiz Mohammad Sayeed, 'No More Dialogue on Kashmir', Markaz Dawa wal'Irshad, available at www.dawacenter.com/magazines/voiceofislam/sept99/editorial.html, accessed on 4 October 1999.

4

Countering Terrorism in the AfPak

Ehsan Monavar

We are currently at war with the most dangerous enemy ever known to mankind. Terrorism is a serious issue globally, as well as a persistent threat to humanity. In Afghanistan, terrorism is combined with the geopolitical great game that has been imposed on the region for decades. In the country, brave Afghan people have suffered and sacrificed tremendously to fight this menace. It is an unambiguous observation that Afghanistan is facing its most difficult time today. Currently, it is embroiled in a war against terror and the community is faced with state-sponsored terrorism outfits that consider the region a mere backyard for strategic depth. While there is assistance from international coalition forces, who have provided 150,000 well-trained and well-equipped soldiers, over and above numerous other resources, the most dangerous threat remains towards the local security forces, who have been fighting the war on terror with limited means and despite continued casualties, under extremely difficult conditions. It is a fact that Afghanistan cannot be left alone to fight this war on terror and regional and global countries need to take steps towards opposing this threat seriously and eradicating it completely. International and regional partners need to come together to extend their full cooperation to support this fight against terror.

Situation on the Ground: A Protracted War

The world forgot about Afghanistan after the withdrawal of the Soviet troops, which led to the country becoming a safe haven for terrorist organisations, eventually culminating in 9/11. Most Afghans have lost family members and friends to the conflict. They continue to suffer and have sacrificed several lives to the war zone over the past four decades. The after-effects of terrorist machinations are not limited to violent frontal attacks, but also take a tremendous hit on the socio-economic and socio-political lives of the people. Terror economies breed illegal trade-offs, such as drug/human trafficking. The illegal drug trade in Afghanistan is not only advancing the hold of the terror outfits in the region but also severely undermining the rule of law. Another key activity that serves as a means to finance and fund terror operations in Afghanistan is illegal mining. Perpetuated illegal mining serves to deprive the Afghan government of legitimate revenues for the development of the country. If the government controlled the land and the resources, it could be redirected towards developing the region and improving the socio-economic status of its people. Legal mining would also contribute to building infrastructural capacity and providing meaningful employment.

On an ideological front, terrorist organisations are also abusing religion in waging an ideological war, thereby destroying an ancient cultural civilisation in order to control territories and population for their geopolitical objectives. The war has exacted a heavy toll on the people, with the world's highest casualty rate attributed to the Afghan security forces.[1] During the course of Operation Umari[2] for example, Taliban made three strikes in Kabul including a recruitment centre at a military school and targeted police buildings. In 2017 Taliban's suicide bombers killed and wounded more than 100 people in the coordinated raid targeting intelligence officials and government workers outside the Afghanistan Parliament.[3] This direct attack on the security forces and the intelligence agencies is a pattern used by the Taliban and demonstrates their unflinching will towards destroying any legal order within the country. The ultimate aim of these radicalised groups is to degrade Afghan capacities and capabilities and weaken state institutions. These instances serve to demonstrate that the Taliban is more than a motley collection of financially deprived and undereducated Afghans. The group is working with coordination towards a dedicated action plan. Furthermore, they now have geopolitical and strategic backing from some countries that have given them sanctuary, and they are also ensuring that the problems the group faced in the aftermath of 9/11 are remedied.[4] The Taliban has thus gained access to the northern provinces of Konar, Baghlan, Kondoz, Balkh, etc., and they are trying to block all entry points to the country except those via Pakistan.[5]

Given that the government is trying to open up more areas for import and export, in order to breathe economic life into the country again, the Taliban is opposing these measures by placing checks and blockades in areas under their control. Currently, the Taliban influence in Afghanistan is burgeoning undeniably as international effort is increasing towards getting the leadership to sit down and negotiate with the Afghan government. This was stressed upon during the six-nation summit in Moscow on 16 February 2017. While responding to the conference, Zabiullah Mujahid, the Taliban spokesperson refused to enter into negotiation and instead upped the ante with more attacks. Some countries suggested that integration of Hezb-e-Islami, led by Gulbuddin Hekmatyar[6] could act as an incentive in a blueprint for Taliban's reintegration into the system. While these concepts are discussed in such forums, there does not seem to be in mind any real possibility of the Taliban entering into fruitful negotiations in accepting the writ of the Afghan Constitution. Furthermore, hostilities between Hikmetyar and the Taliban have also flared up from time to time since, and serve as no guarantee. Interestingly, Abdul Raziq, then police chief of Kandahar urged the group's leadership to return to Afghanistan and not rely on foreign governments. As a result, he was also targeted in the bomb blast in Kandahar that claimed the lives of five United Arab Emirate (UAE) diplomats and the ambassador of UAE to Afghanistan, Juma Mohammed Abdullah Al Kaabi.[7]

Afghan Perception: Role of Pakistan in Abetting Taliban

According to the Afghani perception, the Taliban is a continuing example of Pakistan's attempt to gain strategic depth in Afghanistan and keep Kabul in a weakened state of turmoil so that no credible claim for the reorganisation of the Durand Line is made. Using the mendacious narrative of attempting to establish peace talks, Islamabad constructed the lie about Mullah Omar. The fact that the Taliban is being instrumentalised by Pakistan is evident and it can be seen by the fact that Taliban has a working relationship with the Haqqani network and the Lashkar-e-Taiba (LeT). Sirajuddin Haqqani is now a member of the Taliban. However, he has very little traction with the Afghans, who view Haqqani more as a disruptive interlocutor. The division of terrorist groups into good or bad is another such linguistic ploy often used to harbour and provide sanctuary to terrorists. The Taliban, which fits into Pakistan nomenclature of good terrorists, is closely linked to al-Qaeda's South Asian branch, namely, Al-Qaeda in the Indian Subcontinent, which has a number of Indian mujahideen in the Punjabi Taliban, such as the LeT.

Conclusion

This chapter is thus an attempt to provide an overview of the situation as it exists and evolves. Here, I would like to state that Afghanistan and its people have a right to peaceful existence the way other countries do. It is essential to remember that peace is not the absence of conflict and the world cannot stop at the lack of outright conflict as a resolutionary mechanism. In order to truly maintain peace, there needs to be a collective regional and global effort at ensuring that disruptors of peace are held responsible and brought to justice. We can maintain peace through our strengths, as weakness relies on vice, aggression and violence. We have had historically friendly ties with countries in the region, but some do not collude with global efforts at building a terror-free world. It is necessary to hope that such problem states will come to terms with the true menace of terrorism, realise the gravity of the situation and step up their cooperation in this fight against terror before it spreads like cancer in the region and globally.

In conclusion, terrorism is a major threat to humanity. There is a need to move beyond speech towards action. Afghanistan cannot re-establish its civil order merely by itself. The countries suffering from terrorism across the globe today cannot fight the scourge by themselves. There is a need for increased cooperation and friendship. This does not extend merely to the governments but is also essential at the level of the people. A clear example of this is the inability to develop sustainable connections between the government and the people in Afghanistan. The cancer of terrorism goes and hides in these gaps between the outreach and connections. With the help of governments across the world and the bridging of gaps and distances, if political will is mobilised, terrorism can be eradicated once and for all.

NOTES

1   "Afghanistan's Ghani says 45,000 security personnel killed since 2014", *BBC News*, 25 January 2019, available at https://www.bbc.com/news/world-asia-47005558, accessed on 26 January 2019.

2   This was the Taliban's official name for its 2016 and 2017 offensive.

3   John Bacon, 'More than 100 killed, wounded as terror attacks rock Afghanistan', *USA Today*, 11 January 2017, available at https://www.usatoday.com/story/news/world/2017/01/10/dozens-killed-injured-kabul-terror-attack/96390066/ , accessed on 22 July 2018.

4   The fact that they did not have political or military reach in the northern part of the country which resulted in them crumbling under the Northern Alliance coalition forces.

5   Based on author's assessment as of March 2017.

6   For more see Sune Engel Rasmussen "Kabul welcomes the Afghan warlord who once shelled its citizens", *The Guardian*, 24 October 2017, available at https://www.theguardian.com/world/2017/oct/24/kabul-welcomes-the-afghan-warlord-who-once-shelled-its-citizens, accessed on 22 July 2018.

7   For more see "Five UAE diplomats killed in Afghanistan attack" , *al Jazeera*, 11 January 2017, available at https://www.aljazeera.com/news/2017/01/uae-ambassador-afghanistan-wounded-kandahar-blast-170110172931399.html, accessed on 22 September 2017.

5

Terrorism Industry and its Global Expansion

Waiel Awwad

When Mosul and Raqqa were retaken from the Islamic State of Iraq and Syria (ISIS) through a secret deal by the United States (US)-led coalition, the two ancient cities were razed to the ground. No one knows the whereabouts of the terrorists, or where they went[1]. No real battle took place, and the flattened cities tell a different story about the actual reasons behind the carnage, as well as the whereabouts of all those mercenaries who disappeared. While the details of exactly what happened might not be revealed for decades, it will remain of academic interest nonetheless; and gradually, the horrific nature of the personal and political crimes committed will also be forgotten. However, it is worth mentioning here that, as per intelligence reports and the official records, thousands of them were siphoned to Libya, Yemen, Afghanistan and Commonwealth of Independent States (CIS) countries under the auspices of the US forces.

It seems that the shadow of weapons of mass destruction (WMDs), the democratisation impulse, human rights preservation and the combating of terrorism have all become an excuse for certain nation-states to interfere unapologetically in the internal affairs of independent sovereign states. All these actions and justifications have achieved the goal of fooling the international community and justifying the fighting and occupation of these terrorists and territories by the US and the United Kingdom (UK). Another argument that has been used to justify the action is the need to establish military bases in the Levant, and this has been undertaken swiftly as a "preventive measure". While the US and the West maintain that the figure of mercenaries has been no more than 50,000–60,000, local sources in Syria and Iraq believe the number to be more than 350,000 men, mostly from Saudi Arabia, Kuwait, Tunisia, Turkey, Jordan, Iraq, Palestine,

Libya, Chechen and the European Union (EU).[2] Approximately 40,000[3] of them were killed, but the question that remains is: where did the rest disappear? Who are they and for whom do they work? Are the events that erupted in the Middle East really revolutions by the people against their governments? That, as Hamlet said, is the question.

In a documentary from Raqqa, the *BBC*[i] confirmed that thousands of militants fled from Raqqa under the gaze of the US–British and Kurdish-led coalition forces who controlled the city. Moreover, thousands of civilians were taken hostage by the ISIS, and no one knows their fate. Few mass graves were discovered with many bodies, including those of children and the elderly.

The Plight of the Arab World and the Quest for Security

National and international security has always been the primary concern of nations the world over. This concern is related to the controversial issue of war and peace. Furthermore, this is not a new issue and has been, all through history, the intrinsic nature of man's quest for procuring power, authority, natural resources, self-interest and safety. This quest for power has been fuelled in an anarchic world order, with no supranational power to control such issues. In such a situation, nations strive to ensure security within their borders by mobilising their people and enhancing their economies as necessary tools for power projection and capacity building. These efforts are also undertaken in the international arena through an adjustment of foreign policy to counter threats and preserve their interests—mainly security— by coercive means such as war (promulgated by realist and neo-realist thought) or by collaboration (primarily striking deals with the powerful or among those who share the same concerns). Nations lash out in these ways when they sense threats from others, which drives them to securitise their own environment. The threat perception determines how nations design their security strategies, that is, by building their own military capabilities or striking alliances and coalitions with other nations at the bilateral, regional or international level in order to maintain status quo. However, the strife nations undertake for extreme aggrandisation of power under their security strategies constitutes a threat for other countries and sparks off a chain of fear and insecurity for others. When fear arises, nations have to be always prepared for the worst, which creates a cyclical pattern.

This situation was evident during the eighteenth, nineteenth and early twentieth century multipolar world system, and seems to be on the rise again in today's unipolar world system. Some claimants state that this situation of fear, insecurity and threat has been on the rise in the Middle East, and the ongoing wars have been created and triggered by power drivers attempting to control the

Middle East's natural resources and geostrategic location for transportation. These aims have been followed through with intense effort, which have blinded them to the price that needs to be paid to achieve these goals. But these power drivers need an adversary to gain public support, which in my opinion, is "terrorism", specifically Islamic terrorism, along with democratisation by force and preserving human rights.

Terrorism as a Political Tool

The US has used various doctrines to achieve its objectives in remaining the sole superpower. The Bush administration's National Security Strategy (NSS; 2002)[5] as well as the Obama administration's NSS (2015)[6] both reflect a clear manifestation of how their strategies are designed to work and what they aim to achieve. If contextualised in light of Edward N. Luttwark's observations regarding the construction of security strategies, the Bush strategy ignored the potential friction in war caused by accidents, mistakes, emotion and the unexpected—all external elements that block the smooth running of the military machine—and most notably his argument that "In strategy, therefore, a course of action tends to become retroactive."[7]

The new US strategy covering the years 2020–40[8] reveals that the aim is to prolong the Syrian crisis and assess the options for regime change in order to ensure that the Russian, Iranian and Syrian governments do not triumph in this war. This strategy treats the fact that Syria would be completely wrecked by civil war as collateral damage. This is how civil wars have become the proxy wars of powerful and greedy capitalist nations. The terms of these wars are unambiguously dictated by the present unbalanced global political power systems in international relations, and thereby further paralyse peace arbitrating institutions like the United Nations (UN). Analysing these sovereign strategy documents, therefore, puts the answer on the right track.

The strategy demonstrates America's approach to foreign policy. It essentially attempts to justify America's drive towards controlling emerging world political systems by all means possible, including, but not limited to, the use of power, even unilaterally, whenever and wherever it serves American interests. The central emphasis of the project remains the drive for crucial energy resources that can add to its economic strength. Therefore, the strategy disregards all other nations' interests and announces the return of US forces back home. Whether or not the political objective was achieved is debatable. If the objective was achieved, the next question that emerges is: how would the US proceed to maintain its control over the Middle East region, and why? The answer one feels is "to use the partners and allies" in proxy wars and conflict.

Currently, the most aggressive and dangerous NSS[9] regarding national and international security is that of Trump's administration. It clearly exposes in my assessment "Trump's egoism". On the other hand, the Russian doctrine speaks volumes about its return to a bipolar world system.[10] These two major sites of power notwithstanding, it is also worth mentioning that China's rise and soft power approach are directly tied to the achievement of China's global aspirations.[11] The One Belt One Road initiative is aimed at ensuring that China regains its position as a leading world economy and becomes a strong military power to reckon with. It is too early to assess whether the Chinese political assertion will be converted into military assertion or not. The US and its Western counterparts feel threatened by China's rise and its closeness with Russia. This is what has made them obsessed with the rapid growth in both the countries. The growth and competition between the Western countries and the China–Russia flanks of the world has been further exacerbated by how each of them could go about achieving their goals and interests, namely, in gas and oil. The ultimate conclusion echoes in Churchill's famous words, "he who controls oil controls the nations". How that control and dominion is to be established can be interpreted as the power struggle for the Middle East conducted through proxy wars, under the mantra of a newly invented adversary—terrorism and political systems. The method places value on the nation-state rather than its stateness, implying an erosion of state sovereignty and good governance.

Thus, the reason that the Arab world, rich in natural resources, is the epicenter of conflict of the global powers is self-evident. This is particularly true in an age where natural resources are scarce and there is a competition between the giant companies ruling the world economy. The lust for oil and gas has shifted the sphere of dominance from Europe to America–Israel, which has now moved towards Russia and China. The unrest has been further exacerbated with the discovery of more oil and gas in the Mediterranean which is shared by Syria, Egypt, Lebanon, Palestine, Cyprus and Israel. Former regional players like Turkey and Iran have also increased their sphere of influence in the region. This new discovery has put the Gulf Cooperation Council (GCC) in direct competition with the above-mentioned countries, since their future (Qatar, the Arab pipeline and Nabucco pipeline) projects depend on the approval of the passage countries (Saudi Arabia and Syria) that have refused to give their permission This could be what triggered the war against the Middle East in general, and Syria and Iraq in particular.[12] While the Arab–Israeli conflict and the rise of national resistance should not be forgotten, it will also be helpful to keep in mind that the pricing of oil is determined by the American dollar since the collapse of the Bretton Woods system, and the rising dominant US concern is the future pricing of gas.

The Arab Levant, originally known as "natural Syria", currently comprises five independent states: Syria, Lebanon, Iraq, Jordan and occupied Palestine. The turmoil in the Middle East/West Asia has been on for a century. It started with the division of the Arab world into different states, under Sykes–Picot Agreement of 1916, a secret deal between France and Britain to split the Arab world under their different spheres of influence. Earlier, the successful Ottoman emperors had ensured that no Arab leader was allowed to hold an important position, and racism was practiced. The regime saw the killing of Arab scientists and the closing of all borders with the outside world, which eventually culminated in the surrender this part of the world to France and Britain. The culmination of First World War saw the drawing of haphazard boundaries of the said states without any social, economic or political considerations of the people's will, or their social constructs. Originally, they formed a nation-state of multicultural, multi-religious and multi-ethnic social constructs. Thus, the formation of incoherent ethno-religious, social-based political systems in the newly rising independent units sowed seeds of continuous conflicts in the region. This was part of the well-known British policy of "Divide and Rule".

The attempt here is not to undermine the plight of the Arab world and only put the blame squarely on Western powers. Instead, I want to point out that while there are internal conflicts and squabbles within the region, the fact remains that nations facing continuous threats to their security by outsiders cannot absolutely implement their constitutions and achieve their political ends. Their primary motive will always be survival. This fact could explain the types of volatile political systems that currently exist in the Arab world since the countries are primarily governed by shadow governments.

An overview of the support to radical movements shows that it started as early as the eighteenth century with Wahhabism in the Arab Peninsula, and the new doctrine of Islam, and a condition to be followed by Al-Saud tribe who conquered the peninsula. Ambassador Dore Gold's book, *Hatred's Kingdom: How Saudi Arabia Supports the New Global Terrorism*, explains to a large extent the link between the current global terrorism and jihadists strategy. Gold talks about Wahhabism as the foundation of the Saudi state. He says that "the struggle between Saudi pan-Islamism and Nasser's (secular Arab Nationalism) had other side effects that lasted for decades".[13] It was Saudi Arabia that revived Islamic fundamentalism in Egypt and the rest of the Arab countries, which was then used as a tool to topple secular leaders and thwart any Arab leader movement to unite the Arabs.

In the face of transnational political systems, the advent of globalisation, spread of ideas, knowledge, mass communication and the emergence of complex dependence and independence theories, multinational companies ruled the world. It appeared as if the liberals had won the race, and their doctrine dominated the world scene with the neo-realist school of thought as propagated by the complex interdependence theory offered by Robert Keohane and Joseph Nye.[14] This theory shifted the "closed-security area" to flexible "specific-areas" that were on top of the agenda of foreign policy. They thereby diversified the concept of security to include other matters, such as development, rational decision making, building the nation-state by empowering all the strata of the society to participate in decision making and the gradual erosion of the state's sovereignty and its monopoly of use of force.

I believe, the Anglo-Saxons recycled their old sinister plan to gain influence in the Arab world by creating "Projection Forces" and promoted the Arab Spring to make it look like a civil war through ethno-religious conflicts, inter-faith clashes and the revival of tribalism and primordial conflict. In his book, *Shadow Wars*, Christopher Davidson stated that "CIA regard ISIS–Al Qaeda a strategic but volatile assets to be wielded against their enemy."[15] *Thicker than Oil*,[16] by Rachel Bronson, speaks of:

> US allowing Saudi monarch, after signing an accord, to protect Al Saud tribe. US first considered Saudi an asset but it eventually became a liability after the fall of USSR as there was no more threat of communism but the growing menace of Islamization by rich gulf states that continued unabated.

However, when it comes to the dilemma, that is, the option between values and norms promoted by liberals or ensuring sovereign interests through stability by maintaining the status quo, the second option becomes the best, as Vijay Parshad, an American scholar of Indian origin, documented in his book, *Arab Spring: Libyan Winter*.[17] He quoted what Frank Wisner, the special US representative to Egypt, said after meeting with the Democrats and Republicans, "if achieving security and stability is more difficult, and if the short-term necessities will contradict with the long-term objectives, and if the long term objective is to achieve democracy, it is good to sacrifice it in favor of the short term necessity." [18]

This led to the support of authoritarian regimes in newly independent Arab states that did not allow any democratic institutions to be established. The social injustice, lack of distribution of wealth, low economic growth, anti-West policy feeling, rise of hatred and political unrest led to instability and rise of religious fundamentalism. This was compounded by the covert interference of the West in the internal affairs of these states, by toppling regimes, assassination or military intervention, as the case in Iraq, Libya, Syria and Yemen. All these events culminated in the Balfour Declaration and the creation of Israel in the heart of the Middle East. Given the preponderance of the Arab masses in the region, it gave the dispossessed, divided ethnic groups another slogan to fight with, fuelling religious discourse and suiting the emergence of more radical groups.

Osama bin Laden was recruited by the US in the fight against the Union of Soviet Socialist Republics (USSR). Mujahideens from all over the globe joined him. Mosques and imams were allowed to call for jihad against the Soviet Union. Extremist ideologies were nourished, and it was motivated by the end goal of toppling the regimes. A terrorist Takfiri bureau, an overseas network, was established in Afghanistan with the help of Saudi Arabia and Inter-Services Intelligence (ISI) (Pakistan)—and it effectively served as a Muslim brotherhood. It spread its roots all over the globe to recruit young people. The evidence is for all to see.

Global Terrorism

A purview of Islamist movements as political instrument to achieve political ends, versus secular political movements in the Middle East, reveals a clash between political Islamism and secularism. The former is confined to the "text" promoting Salafi and Wahhabi traditions and calling for an adherence to the text as interpreted by the clerics and imams. This apparently clashes with other movements, such as the "Damascene school of Islam", that call for the separation of religion from politics and thereby encourage secularism in building the nation-state as a guide for modernity. What adds insult to injury, in my opinion, is that the Zionist project according to me is based on manipulating religion for political ends. It is predicated on creating and establishing Israel in the region on the claim of it being the "national home for the Jews" in Palestine, which was the grassroots of political conflict based on religion. This Zionist project, according to me, has nurtured and paved the way for the rise of political Islam. Thus, one sees different political projects in the Middle East: the Zionist project supported by the West; and Islamist projects—Iran, Saudi Arabia, Turkey; and the nationalist project.

From the negative consequences of the October liberation war (1973), to the vested Western world interests, the region has seen a tremendous number of plans aimed at undermining and destroying the whole of Middle East. This is self-explanatory and can be proven by examining the Turkish invasion of Cyprus in

1974, which was followed by the breakout of civil war in Lebanon in 1975, the Morocco–Algeria War in 1975 and the Iraqi–Iranian War in 1980. The last one primarily paved the way for the rise of Iran as a regional power supporting the just Arab cause. That war diverted Arab attention away from the Arab–Israeli conflict to the Arab–Persian conflict, as well as to inter-faith conflict.

Turkey, a member of North Atlantic Treaty Organization (NATO) and an ally of the US and Israel, entered the scene through the political Islam doctrine, projecting itself as a representative of moderate Islam. It thereby managed to introduce "zero-sum" problems with its neighbours, which proved to be a ploy following the tenets of "game theory" used frequently in politics. This explains its behaviour towards the ongoing wars in the region and its direct involvement in supporting the terrorists. The region has thus played a major role in spreading political Islam and has been looked at as a model to be implemented in different Arab capitals. Paradoxically, it has been promoted as one by the US, Europe and some other Arab countries as well. However, this model has now developed problems with not only its people but also Europe and ostensibly, the US. There is a deep and strong belief that Muslim Brotherhood has to bring back Islamic glory, with a modern caliph, who can unite the Arab region under an Islamic umbrella, as it was under the Ottoman Empire.

Thus, as evident, the region was subjected to division, internal fighting and military intervention for a regime change. External folly led to the creation of ISIS and other such radical militant groups. This also led to increased fundamentalism through the promotion of political Islam and the sheltering of all Islamists and radicals in their own homeland. After providing initial shelter, these radicalised groups were later sent back to their respective native countries to further promote jihadist culture and radicalism. This led to the growth of international terrorism and its spread from being a regional nuisance to a global menace.

The world woke up to the menace of terrorism only when it started to backfire on them. Terrorist acts were carried out in many European capitals by their own citizens, who were returnees from Syria and Iraq.[19] It was then decided that an end to the menace and massacre in Syria would need to be facilitated.

What is the global implication of the diminishing of ISIS in the region? What are the lessons that Asia can learn to tackle this menace and outbreak of terrorism? Before we answer this, we must acknowledge the fact that not many nations are serious about fighting this menace and it is often used to create more battle zones. Some countries, which are sheltering such malicious actors, are also responsible for the spread of extremism ideology by providing safe havens to terrorist organisations. How else can the interventionist politics of American and European nations in the domestic politics of Middle Eastern countries be interpreted?

We must remain aware that the kind of terrorism we are facing is sponsored by certain countries. The US and the West, in my understanding, are responsible for the spread of terrorism and extremist ideology from Afghanistan to Maghreb Al-Arabi in Northern Africa. This menace will continue to spread to new regions. The developing world is actually fighting terrorism that has been imposed on them. This scourge has occurred because of countries that have aided the activities of certain militant groups, by allowing them to recruit and be trained, with the intent of using these terrorists as a tool. Countries falling on the Maritime Silk Route will be more vulnerable to internal strife and foreign "humanitarian intervention".

The world is witnessing turbulent times, new alliances, new battle zones and increased rivalry. There is an urgency to reshape the new international order but until then, many countries need to fasten their belt, come together and fix the issues that have been created thus far.

Conclusion

Taking all the above-mentioned complications into consideration, I can extrapolate what Marxist historian Eric Hobsbawm said about the Cold War and the US hegemony and question if America will learn this lesson, or will it be tempted to maintain an eroding global position by relying on politico-military force, and in doing so not promote global order but disorder, not global peace but conflict, not the advance of civilization but of barbarism?[20]

Since 11 September, the US foreign policy has been driven by the principles of megalomania. The Trump strategy does not seem to be easing up on those expansionist tendencies. The concept of security is increasingly linked to the question of control and domination, and the play of world politics in the modern age still furled by the shadow of oil.

NOTES

1 The seize by the US led coalition, was made by secret deal and as per the deal, hundreds of ISIS fighters and their families were allowed to escape. (Editor's Note: For more see "Quentin Sommerville and Riam Dalati," *Raqqa's Dirty Secret, BBC,* 13 November 2017, available at https://www.bbc.co.uk/news/resources/idt-sh/raqqas_dirty_secret, accessed on 22 July 2018.)

2 Assessment based on author's access to local sources.

3 Ibid.

4 See note 1.

5   For more see: "The National Security Strategy of the United States of America," September 2002, available at https://www.state.gov/documents/organization/63562.pdf, accessed on 22 July 2018.

6   For more see: "The National Security Strategy, February 2015," available at https://obamawhitehouse.archives.gov/sites/default/files/docs/2015_national_security_strategy_2.pdf, accessed on 22 July 2018.

7   E.N. Luttwak (1987), *Strategy: The Logic of War and Peace*, Cambridge: Belknap/Harvard University Press.

8   US Memo 2012, available at http://www.justicewatchfoundation.org/, accessed on 17 February 2018.

9   For more see "The National Security Strategy of the United States of America", December 2017, available at https://www.whitehouse.gov/wp-content/uploads/2017/12/NSS-Final-12-18-2017-0905.pdf, accessed on 22 July 2018.

10 For more see "Russia's national security strategy and military doctrine and their implications for the Eu" Directorate-General For External Policies Policy Department, January 2017, available at http://www.europarl.europa.eu/RegData/etudes/IDAN/2017/578016/EXPO_IDA%282017%29578016_EN.pdf, accessed on 21 February 2017.

11 For more see: Dennis J. Blasko "Peace Through Strength": Deterrence in Chinese military doctrine" 15 March 2017, available at www.warontherocks.com; https://warontherocks.com/2017/03/peace-through-strength-deterrence-in-chinese-military-doctrine/, accessed on 22 July 2018.

12 For more see: Bronson, Rachel, (2008), "Thicker Than Oil: America's Uneasy Partnership with Saudi Arabia," OUP Catalogue, Oxford University Press.

13 For more see : Gold, Dore (2003), "Hatred's kingdom: How Saudi Arabia Supports the New Global Terrorism." Washington, DC: Regnery Pub.

14 For more see: Keohane, Robert O., and Joseph S. Nye (1977), "Power and Interdependence: World Politics in Transition." Boston: Little, Brown.

15 For more see: Davidson, Christopher M. (2016), Shadow Wars: The Secret Struggle for the Middle East. London: Oneworld/Bloomsbury

16 For more see note 10, p. 41.

17 For more Prashad, Vijay. 2012. Arab spring, Libyan winter. Oakland, CA: AK Press Pub.

18 Ibid.

19 For more see note. 10.

20 For more see "Hobsbawm's history", *The Guardian*, October 2012, available at https://www.theguardian.com/books/2012/oct/01/eric-hobsbawm-history-book-extracts, accessed on 22 July 2018.

SECTION TWO

New Wave of Global Terror:
Ideas, Resources and Trends

Special Insight II
Hostage Taking as a Tool of Terrorism and Methodology of Negotiations

Baker Atyani

Statistics show that politically motivated kidnappings have risen dramatically over the last decade.[1] The reasons may appear inhumane but they arise from the need to prove a statement, hold leverage for demands and most importantly, spread fear and terror. Some of the easiest targets for these kidnappings are journalists; particularly those who take risks with their lives to try and understand and track political conflicts in the hope of shedding some light on the situation, or finding a solution. I have worked for 18 years in conflict zones and specialised in violent extremist groups. The aim behind going into conflict zones was to track and interview leaders and members of terrorist groups in Asia in order to try and understand the psychology behind their agendas. In June 2012, however, I became the subject of my study when I was kidnapped and held hostage for 18 months by the Philippines-based Abu Sayyaf Group (ASG).[2] During those 18 months, I was able to observe the social behaviours and patterns of the terrorist group first-hand and noted that they exhibit the same social patterns and behaviours as any group of people. The group had established its own set of accepted norms, identified their enemies—and like all other groups, they had their own insecurities, professional rivalries, competitions—and had also forged alliances against the common "threat". Kidnapping was therefore used as a weapon, to coerce states into cooperating. The reason for the same is because it is easy to accomplish compared to other methods. This is primarily why it is being used increasingly by Islamic terrorist groups, with the aim of ensuring financial benefits or achieving certain political and social gains.

At the outset, it needs to be stated that reliable statistics on hostage taking and ransom payments are not easily available. According to some estimates, between 12,000 and 30,000 kidnappings are carried out every year around the world.[3] Most of these abductions are carried out purely for criminal profit. The United States (US) government has recorded 1,283 cases of kidnapping motivated by Islamic terrorist group in 2012.[4] This makes the share of terrorist groups responsible for kidnappings around the world around 4.5–11 per cent every year. In 2017, the figure was at 8,900 for 920 terrorist attacks.[5] While traditional criminals do not want political gains and publicity, terrorist groups attempt to maximise their benefits in any hostage situation. The monetary gains help them maintain their future activities and enable them to recruit new members. Aside from the financial demands and gains, terrorist groups may also use kidnapping as a tool to coerce governments into changing their policies, or releasing their fellow members from government prisons. While "kidnapping" as a tool may not be considered as big a deal as violent extremism, its overall impact in the long term is as deadly and toxic as instant large-scale violence.

According to Strategic Forecasting (Stratfor), al-Qaeda made 89 million dollars in the last decade in the Islamic Maghreb.[6] Reports known to me reveal the ASG and its subgroups have made only 7.5 million dollars in 2016. This shows that counter-terrorism strategies that were put in place after 9/11 have dried out the financial sources backing terrorist groups around the world. Therefore, kidnapping is now seen as one of the main sources of income for many terrorist groups. Hostage takers usually gather intelligence about their potential hostages by using varying sources of information, such as surveillance, open-source information or intel from their supporters. Easy access to vulnerable but high-profile targets and a cost–benefit analysis are significant factors that determine how the perpetrators select their victims.

Living with my kidnappers, their life, their fear, for 18 months gave me first-hand look at how they operate, coordinate and kidnap. In Solo Island alone, there are eight to ten communities all called "Abu Sayyaf Group". Every community has a leader who is responsible for gathering food and ensuring protection for the community—sometimes even from other ASG communities. This leader is the one who is in touch with the main leader of the ASG, Radolan Sahiron, who belongs to one of the most influential families in Solo. It is normal to see every community hold a hostage or two for ensuring their own survival. In my case, Kasman Sawadjan, who leads a community of two families, planned my kidnapping. In order to successfully carry out the operation, he cooperated and coordinated with several elements as outlined:

1. Individuals who do not belong to the group but want to benefit from the exercise. The group usually adopts this approach of utilising external

resources when it lacks roots outside the jungle in cities. The resource is usually either a believer or a beneficiary.

2. Corrupt elements in law enforcement agencies, who act as negotiators, but actually serve the interests of the kidnappers for their own gain. They effectively serve as middlemen.

3. The community of civilians in the jungle that tips-off such groups, thereby providing cover and protection. These civilians are always aware of the hostages' whereabouts and the terrorist hideouts. They usually consist of either family members, supporters, beneficiaries or, at times, even people coerced into obeying the groups' traditions out of their own compulsions.

4. The smaller and poorer families who have joined the terrorist community of Sawadjan, offering logistic support in an attempt to get a piece of the pie.

5. While Rodolan Sahiron may not be a part of the initial kidnapping, he receives a 20 per cent share of the income generated in exchange for letting the groups use the ASG name.

Given the structural patterns and parameters mentioned here, the ASG is a perfect example of crimes like kidnapping evolving into militancy under the name of jihad. Other kidnapping cases in Iraq, Syria and Pakistan also demonstrate how criminals kidnap and sell their victims to the Islamic State of Iraq and Syria (ISIS), al-Qaeda and the Taliban. Terrorist groups with more links and connections with other groups—including but not limited to criminals and smugglers—tend to be more able to operate and kidnap. The question that remains, nonetheless, is whether or not political entities like states should negotiate with "terrorists". From an experiential and personal standpoint, it is a resounding yes! The most essentialist and fundamental reason for the same is that it saves lives. The nitty-gritties and complications of the hostage takers and their politics is not enough of an excuse to bargain with innocent lives. Despite the fact that governments say, "we do not negotiate or pay ransom", statistics show that ransom was paid in 64 per cent of kidnappings in the past decade.[7] While governments, individuals or groups should not blindly accept the demands made by hostage takers, they should nevertheless institute a serious process of negotiations with the intent of saving lives. Successful strategies aimed at opposing and countering terrorist kidnappings must begin by subjectively believing that every situation and every group calls for a customised strategy. There is a need to understand and study the goals of each group, who they target, what their networks are, where they operate and what the end strategy is. A broad-based solution will be ineffective. Traditional counter-terrorism tools cannot minimise the threat alone.

NOTES

1   James J.F. Forest, "Global trends in kidnapping by terrorist groups," *Global Change, Peace & Security*, Vol. 24, No. 3, pp. 311–330.

2   The ASG is one of the smallest and most violent jihadist groups in the southern Philippines. Its name means "bearer of the sword" and it is notorious for kidnapping for ransom, and for attacks on civilians and the army.

3   Assessment based on author's survey.

4   National Consortium for the Study of Terrorism and Responses to Terrorism, *Annex of Statistical Information: Country Reports on Terrorism 2012*, Baltimore, Maryland, 2013, p. 3. Office of the Coordinator For Counterterrorism.

5   Ibid., *Country Reports on Terrorism 2017*.

6   "Mali: Al Qaeda in the Islamic Maghreb's Ransom Revenue," STRATFOR, 15 October 2012, available at https://worldview.stratfor.com/article/mali-al-qaeda-islamic-maghrebs-ransom-revenue, accessed on 23 February 2017.

7   "Kidnapping for Ransom as a Source of Terrorism Funding," Report No 141, Center for Security Studies (CSS), ETH Zurich, 2013, accessed on http://www.css.ethz.ch/content/dam/ethz/special-interest/gess/cis/center-for-securities-studies/pdfs/CSS-Analysis-141-EN.pdf 23 February 2017.

6

Terror Finance in Kashmir

A Brief Overview

Atul Goel

Introduction and Outline

The chapter intends to provide a brief outline of the sources and transfer and distribution mechanisms of funds that are used for the financing of terrorism in Jammu and Kashmir (J&K). The scope of this chapter is limited to the funding of terrorism for violent activities, as opposed to the financing of the separatist political activity, even though the two are correlated. Also, the chapter is limited to the funds that are raised and transferred from Pakistan. The bulk of the finances for terrorism-related activities in J&K emanate from Pakistan and are raised, transferred and distributed through an intricate network of operators.

The three major terrorist organisations operating in J&K are: the Hafiz Saeed-headed Lashkar-e-Taiba (LeT); the Masood Azhar-headed Jaish-e-Mohammad (JeM); and the Syed Salahuddin-headed Hizbul Mujahideen (HM). These organisations (particularly the LeT and the JeM) maintain a substantial presence in Pakistan and its socio-religious space. The LeT, for instance, is organically linked to the Jamaat-ud-Dawa (JuD) and the Falah-i-Insaniyat Foundation (FIF), sharing the same leadership and resource base. Whereas the JuD is "officially" bandied as a socio-religious organisation involved in the spread and preaching of Islam, the FIF is primarily a charity and relief organisation. Similarly, the Al-Rahmat Trust projects itself as a charity and social service organisation, whereas in reality it is no more than a front. Organisations such as the JuD, the FIF and the Al-Rahmat Trust are used as major vehicles for the collection of funds for the Kashmiri "cause".

The chapter is divided into five sections, including this section. The second section discusses various methods through which funds are raised for the financing of terrorism in J&K. The third section highlights the ways in which funds raised in Pakistan are transferred to India for their use in J&K. The fourth section outlines the process through which these funds are distributed to their ultimate intended recipients—the self-styled terrorist "commanders" operating in J&K. The final section summarises the inferences that may be drawn from the funding patterns of terrorist organisations operating in J&K.

Before moving on to the main body of the chapter, a disclaimer is in order. This chapter does not claim completeness. While the prominent sources of funds and their transfer and distribution mechanisms have been identified and discussed, there may be others that are not mentioned here. There are two reasons for this. The first reason is because a substantial part of the financing activities is undertaken clandestinely. Therefore, finding and exposing clear trails is slightly more challenging. Second, methods, channels and mechanisms for funding are ever-evolving, in response to national and global legal and regulatory regimes as well as the new vulnerabilities and opportunities that present themselves to the networks of terrorist financiers. This factor makes it impossible to capture the entire gamut of the funding activities at any given point of time in totality.

Raising of Funds

As mentioned earlier, the bulk of the funds for financing terrorism are raised in Pakistan. There is no single channel through which these funds are raised and a wide variety of channels and organisations (such as the JuD, FIF and Al-Rahmat Trust) participate in the raising of such funds. Moreover, the funds collected by these organisations are transferable. Despite being raised for certain proclaimed purposes, they may find their ultimate use for the funding of the "jihad" movement in J&K. The various sources through which these funds are raised are discussed next.

1. *Collections for charitable and religious purposes*: Collections for ostensibly charitable and religious purposes is one of the most important ways in which funds are crowd-sourced for the Kashmir cause. These collections take multiple forms, including, inter alia, donation soliciting outside mosques and other public places, collections on the Eid festivals in the name of *fitrana* and *zakat* and collections made during natural disasters. Weak or non-existent auditing standards also incentivise the diversion of these funds even when they are collected for causes other than Kashmir.

2. *The sacrifice of animals and the collection of animal hides during "Eid-ul-Azha"*: This point has been separated from the previous one to highlight

its importance as a source of funds for the terrorist organisations operating in J&K. Despite the official ban on the practice of collecting hides of sacrificed animals on the occasion of 'Eid-ul-Azha', the practice has continued unabated. Though precise estimates of the volume of funds are not readily available, it has been estimated that the earnings for organisations such as LeT, JuD and FIF from the collection and sale of animal hides can go up to a million dollars or more.

3. *Income from profitable business enterprises*: The over-ground wings (in Pakistan) of the terrorist organisations operating in J&K are involved in operating profit-generating businesses. Profits from these enterprises contribute significantly towards supporting the infrastructure of terrorism in J&K. As mentioned earlier, several of these businesses are couched as religious and charitable enterprises and include educational institutions and hospitals. However, the user charges for availing the services of these institutions by most of their clients negate their claims of being service-oriented institutions. For example, the FIF runs a network of schools known as the Taqwa Model School. From the fee structure posted on the website of the school, it is apparent that the target clientele of the school is middle-class families since the fees would not be affordable for poor families in Pakistan.

4. *The supply of fake Indian currency notes*: The role of the Inter-Services Intelligence (ISI) in supplying[1] fake Indian currency notes is well-known. Furthermore, aside from the adverse impact wreaked on the monetary and financial system of India, the supply of fake Indian currency is also a profitable business for the ISI. There have been instances where fake Indian currency notes have been seized from terrorists infiltrating Indian territory. In a related but slightly different context, the LeT operative, David Coleman Headley, was also provided fake Indian currency during his stay in India to aid his operation of carrying out reconnaissance about possible targets for the Mumbai terror attacks of 26 November 2008.

5. *Bankrolling of terrorist organisations by the ISI*: A large part of the terrorism-related infrastructure and logistics are funded directly by the ISI. These include training camps for terrorists, mostly located in Pakistan-occupied Kashmir (PoK). The weapons, as well as the communications and navigation equipment provided to individual terrorists, are also believed to be financed out of the funds made available to the terrorist organisations by the ISI[2].

Transfer of Funds

Funds that are raised and collected in Pakistan are transferred to India using a variety of channels. The importance of the particular transfer channels tends to vary depending on the evolving legal and regulatory regimes, as well as the new exploitable opportunities that present themselves. For instance, the volume of funds transferred through formal banking channels seem to have declined due to the importance given to the regimes and protocols developed by institutions such as the Financial Action Task Force (FATF) in recent years. On the other hand, the opening up of the cross-Line of Control (LoC) trade in 2008 may have provided a new avenue for the transfer of funds aimed at fuelling terrorism in J&K. The following points provide a brief description of some of the channels used to transfer the funds raised in Pakistan for financing terrorism in J&K.

1. *Cash carried by infiltrating terrorists*: Infiltrating terrorists are invariably provided cash at the terror launching pads (colloquially referred to as "Dets"). This cash (often less than Rs 50,000 per infiltrating terrorist) is handed over to the field commanders once they meet. This is a ready source of funds for the terrorists operating in J&K. However, the amount of aggregate funds that can be transferred through this channel is constrained by infiltration activity. Successful counter-infiltration operations by the security forces can inflict severe losses to terrorist organisations.

2. *Transfer through hawala operations*: Hawala is the preferred medium for movement of funds by terrorist organisations. These transactions are difficult to detect and prosecute. Consequently, this low-risk, low-cost option is used extensively by Pakistan-based terrorist organisations to transfer funds to J&K.

3. *Cross-LoC trade*: Cross-LoC trade was initiated in 2008 as a confidence-building measure between India and Pakistan. There are allegations that this route is being increasingly used by Pakistan-based terrorist organisations to finance terrorism and separatism in J&K.

4. *Transactions between persons living on different sides of the LoC*: Transactions, such as sale and purchase of assets in J&K, between persons living on different sides of the LoC require transfer of funds and these opportunities are actively sought out by the terrorist organisations. Such opportunities arise particularly in cases such as the sale of properties of families whose members live on both the sides of the LoC. This is, therefore, a low-cost, low-risk option exercised by the terrorist organisations to fund their activities in J&K.

Distribution of Funds

The last link in the chain of the financing of terrorism in J&K is the distribution network of funds that are collected and then transferred to India. The distribution network—as in the case of transfers—is improvised in a manner aimed at minimising losses for the terrorist groups by way of detection and seizure of funds. Essentially, the distribution network working on behalf of the terrorist organisations consists of over-ground workers (OGWs). In the cases where funds are carried as cash by infiltrating terrorists, the distribution network is redundant because the cash is handed over directly to the field commanders. It is when the funds are transferred through the remaining channels that the distribution network comes into play.

Essentially, the distribution network consists of teams of OGWs who work for a particular commander. These teams, which may be two to three in number, work independent of each other. They are deployed on rotational basis to collect cash from the source, which could be a hawala operator, an LoC trader or someone who needs to send money to a relative across the LoC on account of a recently concluded sale of jointly owned family land. Once the OGW team collects the money, it is transferred to the field commander through a long chain of intermediaries. The rotational deployment of teams ensures that the detection of any one person does not hamper the working of the others. The flow of funds can, therefore, be maintained without major disruptions. The use of a long chain of intermediaries ensures that it becomes nearly impossible to track the assets from the source to the commander. Care is taken to break down the volume of transactions into smaller amounts, such as a maximum of approximately Rs 2 lakhs, so as to avoid major losses in case of detection.

Conclusion

Based on the given discussion, we can make some generalisations about the financing of terrorism in J&K by Pakistan-based terrorist organisations. The varied mechanisms through which these terrorist organisations raise, transfer and distribute their resources have evolved over the course of time and have been improvised so as to minimise the risk of detection, while also maintaining a continuous flow of funds for the purposes of fuelling terrorism. The funding of terrorist organisations in J&K is directly related to cross-LoC or cross-border exploitable opportunities. The opportunities mentioned in this chapter are then used to the terrorists' advantage to proliferate instability and anarchy within the region.

There is also a distinct dichotomy between how funds are raised on the one hand, and how they are transferred and distributed on the other. The former activity is carried out almost wholly in Pakistan where the operating environment for terrorist groups is permissive. This accounts for the relatively open nature of the activities related to fundraising for the Kashmir cause. On the other hand, the transfer of funds to India and their distribution involve risks of detection for terrorist organisations, hence special care is taken to keep these mechanisms clandestine. All in all, the terror finance networks are necessarily labyrinthine and complex, but nonetheless there are several issues that are known and documented already. While further research on the subject is still necessary, steps also need to be taken to control the environment as it exists. It is important to establish an efficient system of checks and balances that can control these points of vulnerability, thereby preventing the illegitimate influx and exit of questionable sources of finance.

NOTES

1   Assessment by the author is based on his experience as a serving officer of the Indian Police Service in various assignments in Kashmir.

2   Ibid.

7

Women and Support for Terrorism in Pakistan[1]
An Empirical Study

C. Christine Fair and Ali Hamza

Introduction

Pakistan attracts the attention of policymakers and scholars for numerous reasons. With over 196 million Muslims, Pakistan's population is larger than the populations of Iran (80.8 million), Egypt (86.9 million) and Saudi Arabia (27.3 million) combined.[2] Its location has long been of strategic importance to the international community, as it sits astride the Middle East, Central Asia and South Asia. Most recently, Pakistan has been an important—albeit problematic—United States (US) partner in the conduct of the US and North Atlantic Treaty Organization (NATO)-led military and stabilisation operations in Afghanistan. Pakistan's *madaris* (plural of madrasa, religious schools) and institutions of higher Islamic studies attract scholars from all over the world and therefore, Pakistan is an important leader in Islamic thought and scholarship across the Muslim world.

Pakistan is also a nuclear-armed state with the fastest-growing arsenal in the world, inclusive of battlefield nuclear weapons.[3] As the revisionist state, in the security competition with India, Pakistan has long sought to alter maps in Kashmir. In order to do so, Pakistan has started several wars with India, in 1947–48, 1965 and 1999, in an effort to seize territory in the portion of Kashmir controlled by India. More worryingly, the Pakistani state has employed Islamist militants as tools to achieve the state's goals in India as well as Afghanistan since 1947, essentially since the time when the state became independent from the erstwhile Raj.[4] With both India and Pakistan possessing nuclear weapons, analysts fear that such Pakistani provocations may incite the next war in South Asia with potential escalation to nuclear use.

While Pakistan suffers a vast array of political violence with sanguinary consequences, in this chapter we focus specifically on Islamist militant groups.[5] While there have been many scholarly inquiries about the sources of support for terrorism among the Pakistanis, but, to date, no scholar has sought to empirically demonstrate whether or not gender has predictive salience for support for Islamist militancy. Instead, most scholars and officials assume that "men of military age" are the most important segment of interest. Gender, if examined at all, is usually treated as a "control variable" rather than a "study variable", reflecting the paucity of interest in this subject.

In this chapter, we seek to address this scholarly lacuna. To do so, we use a large dataset collected by Fair *et al.* (2013), which is drawn from a large national survey of Pakistanis. We use these data to empirically investigate the differences in support for Islamist militancy between male and female respondents. The study finds significant gender effects. Specifically, we find that males are significantly less likely to support the sectarian group Sipah-e-Sahaba Pakistan (SSP), but more likely than women to support the Afghan Taliban. While these gender effects are statistically significant at the $p < 0.01$ level, the magnitude of these gender effects is smaller than several of the control variables.

The remainder of this chapter is organised as follows. In the next section, we briefly review the extant literature on support for Islamist violence in Pakistan and elsewhere. In the following section, we discuss the data and methods used herein and in the penultimate section, we discuss our findings. We conclude with a discussion of the implications of this study, specifically that gender should be an explicit focus of such efforts to exposit the determinants of support for Islamist militancy in Pakistan.

Explaining Support for Islamist Violent Actors

In this section, we briefly review the prominent arguments and empirical frameworks that scholars have used to explain support for Islamist violence and its purveyors generally, and in Pakistan particularly.

Economic Arguments for Respondent Support for Islamist Violence

While the body of literature examining support for violent groups has traditionally focused on grievances,[6] ethnic conflicts[7] and state repression,[8] the decision to support political violence is deeply personal and must be understood at the individual level.[9] One sort of personal motivation derives from poverty or perceived poverty. Scholars have studied these two dimensions of the interaction between poverty and support for violent politics and come to varying conclusions.

One cluster of studies examines actual poverty and support for violent politics. Several scholars have argued that low-income individuals are more likely to support militant organisations due to feelings of powerlessness and general dissatisfaction with the current political system.[10] These ideas rest on the underlying logic that if the existing governance paradigm is not meeting the needs of those in poverty, then they will turn to violent groups who offer the prospect of changing the status quo.

Another proposed mechanism for the relationship between poverty and support for violence focuses on opportunity costs. Individuals living in poverty have lower opportunity costs associated with supporting political violence than their wealthier counterparts, making them more likely to do so ceteris parabis.[11] However, the empirical evidence on the relationship between poverty and support for political violence is mixed.[12] Less well-studied is the interaction between perceived poverty and support for militant violence. One empirical study of perceived poverty and support for Islamist militant groups in Pakistan finds that "feelings of relative poverty decreased support for militant political organizations". Not only was the direction of the relationship the opposite of what is commonly assumed, but the critical variable was relative, not actual, poverty.[13]

Do Piety and Islamism Explain Support for Islamist Violence?

Another framework that some scholars have used is the "clash of civilizations" thesis outlined by Huntington,[14] which asserts that there is a fundamental conflict between the Christian West and the so-called Islamic world. As a result of this dynamic, several scholars posit that support for terrorism and/or militancy may derive from adherence to Islam itself.[15] Some anecdotal evidence supports the narrative that there is a link between Islamic piety and political violence.[16] While one analysis of a 2003–04 survey of Palestinian Muslims found a link between attendance at religious services and support for suicide attacks,[17] the majority of analytic studies find little association between simply believing in Islam and supporting violent politics.[18] When a correlation between embracing Islam and violence does exist, the linkage is limited to a specific and narrow understanding of Islam: for example, beliefs about the efficacy or compulsory nature of individual militarised jihad.[19]

Perhaps the most discussed contributing factor in determining support for militancy in the Muslim world is support for political Islam or Islamism, terms which are often used interchangeably. Scholars exploring this angle posit that support for political violence may derive from an affinity with political positions self-identified as Islamist. Analysts typically understand such positions as those which privilege the role of Islamic law (sharia) in political life or in the functioning of the state. Islamist politics have been extremely important in Pakistan (and elsewhere) because major Islamist parties have frequently and publicly backed violent action.[20] For example, the political group Jamaat-e-Islami (JI) supports militant groups such as Hizbul Mujahideen and al-Badr.[21] Another Islamist political party, the Jamiat ul Ulema (JUI), has long supported Deobandi groups such as the Afghan and Pakistani Taliban organisations and sectarian militant groups, as well as Deobandi organisations operating in India.[22] Support for these political parties is commonly used as a proxy for measuring support for militancy, the rationale behind this being that if an individual supports a group that supports militancy, they themselves must support militancy as well. While transitive logic may suggest that support for Islamist parties (especially those that espouse and even organise violence) should co-vary with support for Islamist violence, data do not consistently bear this out.[23]

Understanding the link between Islamist politics and militancy is further clouded by a tendency of scholars to measure support for political Islam only partially, largely because scholars generally rely upon extant datasets and the less-than-ideal questions they include on support for political Islam and related concepts. For example, scholars often operationalise support for "Islamism" as support for the implementation of sharia.[24] This has yielded contradictory results in the literature. Fair et al. contend that these conflicted results likely stem from the fact that there is no universally held understanding of what the application of sharia looks like.[25] Some individuals may conceptualise an Islamic government as a transparent regime that provides services, while others may understand sharia in the context of *hudood* punishments and restrictions on female participation in public life.[26] In other words, the imperfect questions that analysts use to instrument support for "political Islam" drive the results in their quantitative studies, in part because the questions were never intended to comprehensively assess support for "political Islam" in the first instance. Using the same data employed in this study, Fair *et al.* found that liberal understandings of sharia, such as a government that provides security and public services, are correlated with opposition to jihadi organisations.[27] Conversely, they also found that conceptualising sharia as hudood punishments and restricting women's roles was correlated with positive support for jihadi organisations. Therefore, it is important to note that there is no generalisation to be made about the interaction of support for Islamist politics and support for political violence, as the definition of Islamist politics is context dependent.

Support Democratic Politics and Support Islamist Violence?

Another area of academic inquiry probes the relationship between support for democratic values on the one hand, and support for militant politics on the other. Presumably, support for democratic values such as free speech, civilian control of the military and rule by elected representatives leads to the opposition of violent forms of political expression. There is considerable scholarly literature that outlines the ostensible relationships between supporting ideas associated with liberal democracy and resistance to autocracy,[28] more durable democratic institutions,[29] effective governance[30] and economic expansion.[31] Belief in the ability of democracy to reduce support for political violence, especially terrorism, remains a key tenet of the US foreign policy and the underlying logic behind international democracy promotion.[32]

A more nuanced examination of the topic provides varied examples of political movements that have advocated violence in hopes of achieving democratic outcomes. Especially in the Muslim world, there exist multitudes of violent political groups that claim to fight for freedom and political representation against oppressive governments. In Pakistan in particular, Islamist militant groups often espouse the concept of *azadi*, an Urdu word that means freedom and self-determination, as their casus belli. In fact, Fair, Malhotra and Shapiro, using a provincially representative 6,000-person survey of Pakistanis, find that support for a set of core democratic values is correlated with increased support for militant organisations.[33]

Sectarian Orientation

Sectarianism may promote political violence by entrenching ethnic and religious identities presented as inherently opposed to one another. Within Pakistan, four interpretative traditions of Sunni Islam exist. These *masalik* (plural of *maslak*) are Ahl-e-Hadith, Deobandi, Barelvi and JI. All of the Pakistani masalik are part of the Hanafi school of Islamic jurisprudence (fiqh), with the exception of Ahl-e-Hadith adherents, who do not follow any fiqh. A fifth maslak encompasses Shia Islam. All masalik, madaris and religious scholars affiliated with an interpretive tradition espouse the supremacy of their particular orientation. Although only a small percentage of children in Pakistan are enrolled in a madrasa full time, many attend religious schools in addition to other educational institutions.[34] As a result, many young people in Pakistan are exposed to potentially divisive rhetoric. Additionally, madaris train ulema (plural of *alim*, scholar) and other religious figures who preach and deliver sermons, further spreading the ideas of each maslak. Due to their influence on Pakistani society, these madaris are often accused of promoting sectarianism by fostering the belief in the primacy of particular maslak.[35] However, madaris are not the only pathway by which sectarian identities can be spread. Existing literature points to the role of family and social networks,[36] public schools,[37] Islamist-influenced civil society groups[38] and religious television, radio, Internet and print content[39] in this process as well. These pathways, especially madaris, are resistant to change pushed by outside actors, making it difficult to envision a scenario in which their role in spreading sectarianism changes in the near future.

Fair finds that "a person's *maslak* is a far more stable predictor of support for various aspects of sharia or evidenced piety…even those who simply identify as 'Sunni'—in contrast to 'Deobandi' or 'Ahl-e-Hadith'—are more inclined to support sectarian militancy."[40] The significant and positive relationship between self-identification with a maslak and support for militancy is persistent across districts. Notably, effects were consistent when controlling for all relevant variables (marital status, education, income and age), with the exception that those 50 years of age and older were found to be significantly less likely to support sectarian violence. Therefore, maslak affiliation as spread via Pakistani institutions, such as madaris, generates support for militant groups among parts of the population that embrace the primacy of specific sectarian identities.

Does Respondent Ethnicity Explain Support for Islamist Violence?

Less studied is the role of ethnicity in explaining support for militancy. Kaltenthaler *et al.*, using data derived from a nationally represented survey of 7,656 respondents fielded in late 2013, explored the connections between respondent ethnicity and support for the Pakistani Taliban, which is a network of Pashtun and Punjabi militant groups operating in Pakistan against the Pakistani state.[41] Citing the historically important role that ethnic identity has played in intra-state conflict in the country, they hypothesised that ethnicity should have greatest importance in low-information environments like Pakistan, because persons may have little else on which to base their political support.[42] They found evidence that ethnicity is indeed an important predictor for popular support of the Pakistani Taliban.

Knowledge of Islam and Support for Islamist Violence: Putting Forth an Alternative Explanation

There is limited work suggesting that those who are more knowledgeable about Islam may be less resistant to the appeals of militant groups. Their work draws upon Wiktorowicz's[43] insights from his work on al-Muhajiroun in the United Kingdom (UK): the "vast majority of Muslims are not trained in the complexities" of Islamic jurisprudence and are thus ill-equipped to evaluate the claims offered by recruiters and/or ideologues and the evidence they employ to buttress their arguments in defence of non-state actors perpetrating violence in the name of Islam.[44] He observed that religious seekers drawn to organisations such as al-Muhajiroun generally "are not in a position to objectively evaluate whether al-Muhajiroun represents an accurate understanding of Islam."[45] Implicit in this argument is the possibility that persons who are more knowledgeable about Islam will be less reliant upon these heuristics in assessing the credibility of the leader and their arguments about foundational questions, such as: who can wage jihad and under what circumstances and for whom is jihad obligatory and what kind of obligation is it? Fair *et al.* test this hypothesis using survey data for Pakistan and find important evidence for this hypothesis.[46]

Gender: What, if Any, Salience in Predicting Support for Islamist Violence?

Finally, turning to gender, there is no empirical literature from which we can draw hypotheses. However, we do know that many of Pakistan's militant groups explicitly target women to cultivate their support for their so-called jihadi missions.[47] Lashkar-e-Taiba (LeT) places a premium upon mothers offering their blessing to their sons before they are deployed on a mission.[48] We also know that the LeT has a vast infrastructure to specifically recruit women. They hold annual women's congregations and have an extensive publications line which explicitly targets women.[49] The LeT also has a famed female propagandist named Umm-e-Hammad, who has authored several books intended to recruit women to LeT's cause with the aim of encouraging them to dispatch their sons to Kashmir. While the LeT has the most developed effort to cultivate women, Pakistan's other militant groups cultivate mothers as well.[50] However, the particular survey employed here did not query respondents about support for LeT. Rather, it queried support for the SSP which is a vicious sectarian group targeting Pakistan's Barelvis, Shias, Ahmedis, Christians and Hindus. The SSP not only commits sectarian attacks, it is also involved in communal violence, and it is an important collaborator in violence perpetrated by the Pakistani Taliban and even the al-Qaeda. In recent years, its cadres have also left to fight abroad, such as in Syria and Iraq, and have shown support to the Islamic State of Iraq and Syria (ISIS) domestically as well. There is no evidence that SSP specifically attempts to recruit women. For this reason, we pose the null hypothesis that:

H0: Support for Islamist militancy should not vary by gender.

Data and Analytical Methods

To assess whether or not gender is salient for predicting support for Islamist militancy, we employ a dataset collected in 2011 and 2012.[51] This survey effort featured the first large-scale, agency-representative survey, with extended interviews on the topics of support for militancy and knowledge of Islam in the Federally Administered Tribal Areas (FATA), as well as within the four normal provinces of Pakistan (Punjab, Balochistan, Sindh and Khyber Pakhtunkhwa). The FATA is afflicted by multiple active militant groups, providing an especially relevant region to study individuals' views of violent political groups. In conjunction with SEDCO, a major survey firm in Pakistan, the research team administered a face-to-face survey with a sample of 16,279 individuals. Pakistanis from the four main provinces accounted for 13,282 of the interviews, while 2,997 interviews were conducted in six of the seven agencies in the FATA (Bajaur, Khyber, Kurram, Mohmand, Orakzai and South Waziristan). Fieldwork in the four main provinces was done in January and February 2012; and in the FATA, in April 2012.

The data drawn from Punjab, Sindh, Balochistan and Khyber Pakhtunkhwa include district-representative samples of between 155 and 675 households in 61 districts. The SEDCO sampled the two largest districts within each province and then proceeded to select a random sample of additional districts. In the FATA, the data consists of agency-representative samples of 270–675 people in each of the six agencies where the survey could be administered. The total response rate for the survey was 71 per cent. Of the households that were not interviewed, 14.5 per cent refused to take the survey and 14.5 per cent had no one home when contacted. Here we employ data for Muslim respondents only, yielding a final sample size of 14,508.

This study enumerates support for two militant groups, the first being SSP, which is also known as Lashkar-e-Jhangvi (LeJ) and, more recently, as Ahle Sunnat Wal Jamaat (ASWJ). The SSP is rooted in Pakistan's Deobandi interpretive tradition. While it is most known for its attacks against Ahmedis and Shias, it has also launched a sanguinary war against Pakistan's Barelvis and has long attacked Hindus, Christians and other non-Muslims in the country. It is tightly allied with other Deobandi militant groups operating against India as well as the Afghan Taliban and even al-Qaeda.[52] The second group for which we estimate support is the Afghan Taliban. The Afghan Taliban also draws from Pakistan's Deobandi tradition. Formed in the early 1990s, the Afghan Taliban uses its base in Pakistan to engage in insurgency against the Afghan government and international backers.[53] Both the SSP and the Afghan Taliban have ties to the Pakistani Taliban through overlapping networks and a shared infrastructure of Deobandi institutions and religious scholars.[54]

We, therefore, derive two dependent variables which measure respondent support for both organisations taken from answers to two survey items. One asked respondents: "How much do you support SSP and their actions?", while the other queried: "How much do you support the Afghan Taliban and their actions?" Respondents answered both questions on a five-point scale ("not at all", "a little", "a moderate amount", "a lot" or a "great deal"), with higher numeric values indicating higher support for these groups.

Our principal study variable is gender. In addition, we have included several control variables building upon previously published work.[55] These control variables include the respondent's maslak, ethnicity, marital status, level of education, age group and income. We have also included an additive knowledge index that measures the respondents' basic knowledge of Islam, as per Fair *et al.*, using five questions for which there are no ambiguous responses.[56] This index is scaled from zero to one, with higher values indicating greater knowledge.[57] The descriptive statistics for the dependent, independent and control variables are provided in Table 7.1.[58]

Table 7.1. Summary Statistics of Dependent and Independent Variables (Muslim only)

	Categories	Frequency	Percentage (%)
Dependent Variable			
How much do you support SSP and their actions?	Not at all	5,621	38.74
	A little	2,105	14.51
	A moderate amount	2,338	16.12
	A lot	1,146	7.9
	A great deal	1,062	7.32
	No answer	2,236	15.41
Total		14,508	100
(q1012) How much do you support Afghan Taliban and their actions?	Not at all	7,129	49.1
	A little	1,840	12.7
	A moderate amount	2,024	14
	A lot	934	6.4
	A great deal	897	6.2
	No answer	1,684	11.6
Total		14,508	100

(Contd.)

	Categories	*Frequency*	*Percentage (%)*
Independent Variables			
Gender	Female*	5,994	41.32
	Male	8,514	58.68
Total		14,508	100
Control Variables			
Knowledge Index (0.00–1.00)	0.00	312	2.15
	0.04	55	0.38
	0.08	220	1.52
	0.12	298	2.05
	0.16	152	1.05
	0.2	737	5.08
	0.24	98	0.68
	0.28	296	2.04
	0.32	717	4.94
	0.36	525	3.62
	0.4	1,342	9.26
	0.44	93	0.64
	0.48	211	1.45
	0.52	588	4.05
	0.56	580	4.0
	0.6	2,089	14.4
	0.64	66	0.45
	0.68	134	0.92
	0.72	470	3.24
	0.76	500	3.45
	0.8	3,404	23.46
	0.84	17	0.12
	0.88	31	0.21
	0.92	80	0.55
	0.96	154	1.06
	1.00	1,338	9.22
Total		14,508	100
Maslak: Type of Madrasa	Shia*	601	4.14
	Sunni	7,394	50.96
	Deobandi	5,928	40.86
	Ahl-e-Hadith	585	4.03
Total		14,508	100
Ethnicity	Other*	662	4.56
	Punjabi	4,767	32.86
	Muhajiir	1,024	7.06

	Categories	Frequency	Percentage (%)
	Pashtun	5,051	34.82
	Sindhi	1,401	9.66
	Baloch	1,519	10.47
	No response/don't know	84	0.58
Total		14,508	100
Marital Status	Married	11,301	77.89
	Divorced	30	0.21
	Widowed	337	2.32
	Single/never married*	2,806	19.34
	Don't know/no answer	34	0.23
Total		14,508	100
Level of Education	Less than primary*	5,612	38.68
	Primary	1,734	11.95
	Middle	1,935	13.34
	Matriculate	2,607	17.97
	Higher education	2,493	17.18
	Don't know/no response	127	0.88
Total		14,508	100
Age Group	18–29*	5,199	35.84
	30–49	7,212	49.71
	50+	2,076	14.31
	Don't know/no response	21	0.14
Total		14,508	100
Income Quartiles	First quartile*	5,185	35.74
	Second quartile	3,940	27.16
	Third quartile	1,804	12.43
	Fourth quartile	2,766	19.07
	Don't know/no response	813	5.6
Total		14,508	100

Source: Survey conducted by authors
Note: * denotes regression reference group.

To conduct the analysis, we ran ordinary least squares regression using the above-mentioned dependent, independent and control variables. To run the regression, we converted categorical variables (for example, ethnicity and maslak) into dummy variables. We denote the reference group for each categorical variable by "*" in Table 7.1. We clustered standard errors at the primary sampling unit (PSU) as the survey sample was drawn at the PSU level. To capture district-level characteristics, we ran regressions for both militant groups with district fixed effects.

Regression Results

As the regression results in Table 7.2 demonstrate, we find significant gender effects. Curiously, gender operates differently in both of our models. While males are less likely than females to support the SSP, they are more likely to support the Afghan Taliban. These findings are significant at the $p < 0.01$ level. While these results are statistically robust, the magnitude of the gender coefficients is somewhat smaller than that observed for some of the other control variables. The most important variables in terms of magnitude are variables for maslak. However, the gender variable is on the same order of magnitude as the ethnicity variable and notably larger than the estimates for statistically significant knowledge, age and income variables.

Table 7.2. Regression Results

	How much do you support SSP and their actions?	*How much do you support Afghan Taliban and their actions?*
Independent Variables		
Male	-0.4403 (-8.07)***	0.1736 (3.43)***
Control Variables		
Knowledge Index	-0.0496 (-0.69)	-0.08873 (-1.35)
madrasa_sunni	0.5145 (4.25)***	0.4828 (3.49)***
madrasa_deobandi	0.7455 (5.76)***	0.7267 (5.01)***
madrasa_ahl_e_hadis	0.6471 (3.97)***	0.6138 (3.48)***
maritalstatus_married	0.0391 (0.98)	0.0409 (1.08)
maritalstatus_divorced	0.0316 (0.10)	-0.0987 (-0.40)
maritalstatus_widowed	0.0176 (0.17)	0.0457 (0.48)
ethnicity_punjabi	-0.312 (2.37)**	-0.3450 (-3.39)***
ethnicity_muhajir	-0.1763 (-1.04)	-0.1338 (-1.37)
ethnicity_pashtun	-0.1448 (-0.96)	-0.1441 (-1.37)
ethnicity_sindhi	-0.4700 (-3.05)***	-0.3625 (-2.83)***
ethnicity_baloch	-0.3375 (-2.07)**	-0.1987 (-1.44)
educ_primary	0.0268 (0.63)	0.0577 (1.41)
educ_middle	0.0782 (1.80)*	0.0373 (0.87)
educ_matric	0.0987 (2.12)**	0.0049 (0.12)
educ_higher	0.0467 (0.93)	0.0172 (0.37)
age_30to49	0.0030 (0.09)	-0.0057 (-0.19)
age_50plus	-0.0758 (-1.69)*	-0.0617 (-1.45)
quartile_second	0.0600 (1.82)*	0.0627 (2.02)**
quartile_third	0.0320 (0.68)	0.0060 (0.14)
quartile_fourth	0.0528 (1.10)	0.0223 (0.47)
_cons	1.044 (5.64)***	0.7215 (4.18)***
R^2	0.2178	0.2355
N	11,601	12,057

Source: Survey by authors
Notes: 1. t-value in parenthesis.
     2. *** $p < 0.01$; ** $p < 0.05$; * $p < 0.10$.

At this juncture, we have no theoretically derived explanation for why gender seems to function differently in both of these models. In another empirical work of this nature, Fair, Hamza and Hellman examined determinants of support for suicide bombing using data for Bangladesh from the Pew Foundation's "World's Muslims Data Set". These data are derived from a nationally representative survey of 1,918 adult respondents, conducted between November 2011 and February 2012 in Bangladesh's national language, Bangla (Bengali). In that study, they found males were more likely than females to support suicide bombing.[59] These two similar studies into gender effects suggest that this is an area that requires urgent inquiry and exposition.

Implications and Conclusions

Our findings that gender is an important predictor of support for Islamist violence is new. Given that there is no previous such study to examine gender, the mechanisms by which support for militant groups would vary by gender is an urgent empirical question. As noted earlier in this chapter, we know that some of Pakistan's militant groups specifically cultivate women. Thus, if this were a chapter that focused upon public support for LeT and we found that women were more supportive of that group, we would have a plausible explanation. The extant scholarship on both SSP and the Afghan Taliban provides no clues about the ways in which they reach out to men and women. On the one hand, it is not surprising that Pakistani women would be less enthusiastic about the Taliban. Pakistani women know more than the global public about the Taliban's horrific treatment of women. The Taliban, like Pakistani Pashtuns, are associated with the cumbersome "shuttlecock" burqa and significant constraints placed upon women's movement. Moreover, given the association of the Afghan Taliban with Pashtun ethnic group and the prevalent derogatory stereotypes that many Pakistanis embrace about Pashtuns and how they treat "their women", this finding is not so terribly puzzling.

On the other hand, what *is* puzzling is why women are more supportive of the SSP. The SSP, unlike LeT, does not provide social services. In fact, the only "public good" SSP provides is a "public bad": murdering Pakistanis because of their faith. Given that the SSP is an enormous contributor to insecurity in Pakistan, both due to terrorist acts it commits and also because it contributes commanders and foot soldiers to the Pakistani Taliban as well as the ISIS, understanding the sources of female support is incredibly important and merits much more research than currently exists.

Suggested avenues for further research should focus upon this gender difference in support for the SSP. It may be useful for Pakistani scholars to collect and analyse SSP literature and look for potential clues to solve this empirical riddle.

NOTES

1   This chapter is derived from a reformulation of C. Christine Fair, Jacob S. Goldstein and Ali Hamza, "Research Note: Can Knowledge of Islam Explain Lack of Support for Terrorism? Evidence from Pakistan", *Studies in Conflict and Terrorism*, Vol. 40, No. 4, 2017.

2   Central Intelligence Agency (CIA), "The World Factbook: Egypt", 7 June 2016, available at https://www.cia.gov/library/publications/the-world-factbook/geos/eg.html; CIA, "The World Factbook: Iran", 7 June 2016, available at https://www.cia.gov/library/publications/the-world-factbook/geos/ir.html; CIA, "The World Factbook: Saudi Arabia", 7 June 2016, available at https://www.cia.gov/library/publications/the-world-factbook/geos/sa.html on 21 February 2017.

3   Gregory D. Koblentz, "Strategic Stability in the Second Nuclear Age", Council on Foreign Relations, 19 November 2014, available at http://www.cfr.org/nonproliferation-arms-control-and-disarmament/strategic-stability-second-nuclear-age/p33809#, accessed on 31 August 2015; Jaganath Sankaran, "Pakistan's Battlefield Nuclear Policy: A Risky Solution to an Exaggerated Threat", *International Security*, Vol. 39, No. 3, 2015, pp. 118–51.

4   Praveen Swami, *India, Pakistan and the Secret Jihad: The Covert War in Kashmir, 1947–2004*, London: Routledge, 2007; Shuja Nawaz, "The First Kashmir War Revisited", *India Review*, Vol. 7, No. 2, 2008, pp. 115–54.

5   Isaac Kfir, "Sectarian Violence and Social Group Identity in Pakistan", *Studies in Conflict and Terrorism*, Vol. 37, No. 6, 2014, pp. 457–72.

6   Ted R. Gurr, *Why Men Rebel*, Princeton, NJ: Princeton University Press, 1970.

7   Donald L. Horowitz, *Ethnic Groups in Conflict*, Berkeley: University of California Press, 1985.

8   James C. Scott, *Moral Economy of the Peasant: Rebellion and Subsistence in South East Asia*, New Haven: Yale University Press, 1976.

9   C. Christine Fair, Rebecca Littman, Neil Malhotra and Jacob N. Shapiro, "Relative Poverty, Perceived Violence, and Support for Militant Politics", *Political Science Research and Methods*, 16 February 2016 (published online), doi:10.1017/psrm.2016.6.

10 See discussions in Alberto Abadie, "Poverty, Political Freedom, and the Roots of Terrorism", *American Economic Review*, Vol. 96, No. 2, 2006, pp. 50–56; John L. Esposito and John O. Voll, *Islam and Democracy*, New York: Oxford University Press, 1996; James A. Piazza, "Draining the Swamp: Democracy Promotion, State Failure, and Terrorism in 19 Middle Eastern Countries", *Studies in Conflict and Terrorism*, Vol. 30, No. 6, 2007, pp. 521–39; Mark Tessler and Michael D.H. Robbins, "What Leads Some Ordinary Men and Women to Approve of Terrorist Attacks against the United States?", *Journal of Conflict Resolution*, Vol. 51, No. 2, 2007, pp. 305–28.

11 Scott Gates, "Recruitment and Allegiance: The Microfoundations of Rebellion", *Journal of Conflict Resolution*, Vol. 46, No. 1, 2002, pp. 111–30; Ernesto Dal Bó and Pedro Dal Bó, "Workers, Warriors, and Criminals: Social Conflict in General Equilibrium", *Journal of the European Economic Association*, Vol. 9, No. 4, 2011, pp. 646–77.

12 Michael Mousseau, "Urban Poverty and Support for Islamist Terror: Survey Results of Muslims in Fourteen Countries", *Journal of Peace Research*, Vol. 48, No. 1, 2011, pp. 35–47; Brian Burgoon, "On Welfare and Terror", *Journal of Conflict Resolution*, Vol. 50, No. 2, 2006, pp. 176–203; Tessler and Robbins, "What Leads Some Ordinary Men and Women to Approve of Terrorist Attacks against the United States?", n. 10; Alan B. Krueger and Jitka Malekova,

"Education, Poverty and Terrorism: Is there a Causal Connection?", *Journal of Economic Perspectives*, Vol. 17, No. 4, 2003, pp. 119–44; Claude Berrebi, "Evidence about the Link between Education, Poverty, and Terrorism among Palestinians", *Peace Economics, Peace Science, and Public Policy*, Vol. 13, No. 1, 2007; Graeme Blair, C. Christine Fair, Neil Malhotra and Jacob N. Shapiro, "Poverty and Support for Militant Politics: Evidence from Pakistan", *American Journal of Political Science*, 2012, pp. 1–19.

13 Fair, Littman, Malhotra and Shapiro, n. 9.

14 Samuel Huntington, "The Clash of Civilizations?", *Foreign Affairs*, Vol. 72, No. 3, 1993, pp. 22–49; Samuel Huntington, *The Clash of Civilizations and the Remaking of the World Order*, New York: Simon & Schuster, 1996.

15 Walter Laqueur, *The New Terrorism: Fanaticism and the Arms of Mass Destruction*, New York: Oxford University Press, 1999; John Calvert, "The Islamist Syndrome of Cultural Confrontation", *Orbis*, Vol. 46, No. 2, 2002, pp. 333–49; Jessica Stern, *Terror in the Name of God: Why Religious Militants Kill*, New York: HarperCollins, 2003; Barak Mendelsohn, "Sovereignty under Attack: The International Society Meets the Al Qaeda Network", *Review of International Studies*, Vol. 31, No. 1, 2005, pp. 45–68.

16 Leonard Weinberg, Ami Pedahzur and Daphna Canetti-Nisim, "The Social and Religious Characteristics of Suicide Bombers and their Victims", *Terrorism and Political Violence*, Vol. 15, No. 3, 2003, pp. 139–53.

17 Ginges, Hansen, and Norenzayan, "Religion and Support for Suicide Attacks", *Psychological Science*, Vol. 20, No. 2, pp. 224–230.

18 Inter alia, Tessler and Robbins, "What Leads Some Ordinary Men and Women to Approve of Terrorist Attacks against the United States?", n. 10; John L. Esposito, *Unholy War: Terror in the Name of Islam*, New York: Oxford University Press, 2002; Mark Tessler and Jodi Nachtwey, "Islam and Attitudes toward International Conflict: Evidence from Survey Research in the Arab World", *Journal of Conflict Resolution*, Vol. 42, No. 5, 1998, pp. 619–36.

19 C. Christine Fair, Neil Malhotra and Jacob N. Shapiro, "Faith or Doctrine? Religion and Support for Political Violence in Pakistan", *Public Opinion Quarterly*, 2012, pp. 1–33.

20 International Crisis Group, "Pakistan: The Mullahs and the Military", 2003, available at http://www.crisisgroup.org/~/media/Files/asia/south-asia/pakistan/pakistan%20the%20Mullahs%20and%20the%20Military.pdf, accessed in April 2016; International Crisis Group, "Unfulfilled Promises: Pakistan's Failure to Tackle Eextremism", 2004, available at http://www.crisisgroup.org/~/media/Files/asia/south-asia/pakistan/073%20 Unfulfilled%20promises%20pakistans%20Failure%20to%20tackle%20extremism.pdf, accessed in April 2016; Zulfiqar Ali, "More the Better: MPA Wants End to Birth Control to Spurt 'Jihad'", *Dawn*, 29 June 2010, available at http://criticalppp.com/archives/17097, accessed in April 2016.

21 Husain Haqqani, "The Ideologies of South Asian Jihadi Groups", *Current Trends in Islamist Ideology*, Vol. 1, 2005, pp. 12–26; Husain Haqqani, *Pakistan: Between Mosque and Military*, Washington, DC: Carnegie Endowment for International Peace, 2005; C. Christine Fair, "The Militant Challenge in Pakistan", *Asia Policy*, Vol. 11, January 2011, pp. 105–37.

22 Ibid.

23 Tessler and Nachtwey, "Islam and Attitudes toward International Conflict", n. 18; Peter A. Furia and Russell E. Lucas, "Arab Muslim Attitudes toward the West: Cultural, Social, and Political Explanations", *International Interactions*, Vol. 34, No. 2, 2008, pp. 186–207; C. Christine Fair, Clay Ramsay and Steve Kull, "Pakistani Public Opinion on Democracy, Islamist Militancy, and Relations with the United States", Working Paper, US Institute of Peace, 2008.

24 C. Christine Fair, Rebecca Littman, and Elizabeth Nugent, "Conceptions of Shari`a and Support for Militancy and Democratic Values: Evidence from Pakistan", *Political Science Research and*

Methods, 31 January 2017 (published online), doi.org/10.1017/psrm.2016.55.

25   Ibid.

26   Ibid.

27   Ibid.

28   ·Mathew Kirwin and Wonbin Cho, "Weak States and Political Violence in Sub-Saharan Africa", Afrobarometer Working Paper No. 111, 2009.

29   Russell J. Dalton, "Communists and Democrats: Democratic Attitudes in the Two Germanies", *British Journal of Political Science*, Vol. 24, No. 4, 1994, pp. 469–93; Torsten Persson and Guido Tabellini, "Democratic Capital: The Nexus of Political and Economic Change", *American Economic Journal: Macroeconomics*, Vol. 1, No. 2, 2009, pp. 88–126.

30   Gabriel A. Almond and Sidney Verba, *The Civic Culture: Political Attitudes and Democracy in Five Nations*, Princeton, NJ: Princeton University Press, 1963.

31   Samuel Huntington, "Will More Countries Become Democratic?", *Political Science Quarterly*, Vol. 99, No. 2, 1984, pp. 193–218.

32   US National Security Council, *National Strategy for Combating Terrorism*, Washington, DC: US National Security Council, 2011, available at https://www.whitehouse.gov/sites/default/ files/counterterrorism_strategy.pdf, accessed in April 2016; Shadi Hamid and Steven Brooke, "Promoting Democracy to Stop Terror, Revisited", *Policy Review*, Vol. 159, No. 159, 2010, pp. 45–57.

33   Contrary to what some observers may believe, Pakistanis tend to remain committed to the concept of democracy even when they are unhappy with their country's democratic institutions. Fair, Littman, Malhotra, and Shapiro, n. 9.

34   C. Christine Fair, "Explaining Support for Sectarian Terrorism in Pakistan: Piety, Maslak and Sharia", *Religions*, Vol. 6, No. 4, 2015, pp. 1137–64.

35   C. Christine Fair, *The Madrassah Challenge: Militancy and Religious Education in Pakistan*, Washington, DC: US Institute of Peace, 2008; Fair, Littman, Malhotra, and Shapiro, n. 9.

36   Victor C. Asal, C. Christine Fair and Stephen Shellman, "Consenting to a Child's Decision to Join a Jihad: Insights from a Survey of Militant Families in Pakistan", *Studies in Conflict and Terrorism*, Vol. 31, No. 11, 2008, pp. 973–94.

37   Azhar Hussain, Ahmad Salim and Arif Naveed, *Connecting the Dots: Education and Religious Discrimination in Pakistan—A Study of Public Schools and Madrassas*, Washington, DC: US Commission on International Religious Freedom, 2011, available at http://www.uscirf.gov/ sites/default/files/resources/Pakistan-ConnectingTheDots-Email(3).pdf, accessed in April 2016.

38   Mohammad Qadeer, *Pakistan: Social and Cultural Transformations in a Muslim Nation*, New York: Routledge, 2006.

39   Zafrulla Khan, "Cyberia: A New Warzone for Pakistan's Islamists", in Moeed Yusuf (ed.), *Pakistan's Counterterrorism Challenge*, Washington, DC: Georgetown University Press, 2014, pp. 69–186.

40   Fair, "Explaining Support for Sectarian Terrorism in Pakistan", n. 34, p. 1158.

41   Karl Kaltenthaler, William Miller and C. Christine Fair, "Ethnicity, Islam, and Pakistani Public Opinion toward the Pakistani Taliban", *Studies in Conflict and Terrorism*, Vol. 38, No. 11, 2015, pp. 938–57.

42   Ibid. Wiktorowicz, Quintan. 2005. *Radical Islam rising: Muslim extremism in the West.* Lanham, Md: Rowman & Littlefield

43   Ibid.

44   Ibid.

45   Fair et al., "Research Note: Can Knowledge of Islam Explain Lack of Support for Terrorism?", n. 1.

46 Muhammad Amir Rana, *The A to Z of Jehadi Organizations in Pakistan*, translated by Saba Ansari, Lahore: Mashal, 2004; Farhat Haq, "Militarism and Motherhood: The Women of the Lashkar-i-Tayyabia in Pakistan", *Signs*, Vol. 32, No. 4, 2007, pp. 1023–46.

47 Mariam Abou Zahab, "I Shall be Waiting at the Door of Paradise: The Pakistani Martyrs of the Lashkar-e-Taiba (Army of the Pure)", in Aparna Rao, Michael Bollig and Monika Böck (eds), *The Practice of War: Production, Reproduction, and Communication of Armed Violence*, New York: Berghahn Books, 2007, pp. 133–58.

48 Ibid. See also Haq, "Militarism and Motherhood", n. 47; C. Christine Fair, "Insights from a Database of Lashkar-e-Taiba and Hizb-ul-Mujahideen Militants", *Journal of Strategic Studies*, Vol. 37, No. 2, 2014, pp. 259–90.

49 Haq, "Militarism and Motherhood", n. 47.

50 Fair, Littman, Malhotra and Shapiro, n. 9.

51 Fair, "Explaining Support for Sectarian Terrorism in Pakistan", n. 34.

52 Antonio Giustozzi, *Koran, Kalashnikov, and Laptop: The Neo-Taliban Insurgency in Afghanistan*, New York: Columbia University Press, 2008; Naematollah Nojumi, "The Rise and Fall of the Taliban", in Robert D. Crews and Amin Tarzi (eds), *The Taliban and the Crisis of Afghanistan*, Cambridge: Harvard University Press, 2008, pp. 90–117.

53 Shehzad H. Qazi, "Rebels of the Frontier: Origins, Organization, and Recruitment of the Pakistani Taliban", *Small Wars and Insurgencies*, Vol. 22, No. 4, 2011, pp. 574–602.

54 Fair et al., "Research Note: Can Knowledge of Islam Explain Lack of Support for Terrorism?", n. 1; Najeeb Shafiq and Abdulkader H. Sinno, "Education, Income and Support for Suicide Bombings: Evidence from Six Muslim Countries", *Journal of Conflict Resolution*, Vol. 54, No. 1, 2010, pp. 146–78.

55 Fair et al., "Research Note: Can Knowledge of Islam Explain Lack of Support for Terrorism?", n. 1.

56 The first survey item used to create this index asked respondents to "Name as many of the five pillars of Islam as you can", with score ranging from zero to one, if the respondent could name all five. The second item we used asked respondents whether or not the way in which Muslims should pray namaz (salat or salah) is described in the Qu'ran. If they answered no (the correct answer), they received one point. Third, we used a question which asked respondents: "What is the percentage amount required to be given as Zakat?" They received one point if they answered 2.5 per cent, which was the correct answer. Fourth, we used a question that asked: "How many months do you have to hold wealth for Zakat to be due on it?" If they answered "12 months", the correct answer, they received one point. The fifth and final question we used asked respondents: "What is the first revealed verse in the Qu'ran?" If they indicated "al-Alaq", the correct answer, they received one point. If the respondent provided an incorrect answer or refused to answer a particular item, they received zero points on the item in question. To calculate the final index score for respondents, we summed the respondents' total score and divided it by five to produce an individual knowledge index that ranged from zero to one, with higher index value indicating greater knowledge of Islam.

57 It should be noted that respondents were indirectly asked about their maslak due to respondent social desirability bias. The following open-ended question was used to determine the maslak: "If a child in your house were to study hifz-e-Quran or nazira, what kind of madrassah or school would you like them to attend?" (responses were "Sunni", "Shia", "Deobandi", "Ahl-e-Hadith", "Non-Muslim" and "don't know").

58 This work is under review and not published as of March 2017.

8

Women and Da'esh[1]

Lamya Haji Bashar

The recent years have witnessed the rise and proliferation of extremist ideologies and terrorist outfits across the world. The mushrooming of such groups in a globalised world order has had consequences across the interconnected geopolitical spectrum. Terrorism as an act, and as a tool, attempts to ideologically control target demographics through physical manifestations of power. The act of power projection necessitates the subversion of an inferior/other who can effectively be made an example of. The roots of the extremist act and the concomitant need to project power can be traced to historical, socio-political and socio-economic inequalities, all of which contribute towards the irrational anger driving the oppressor's actions. While anger, dispossession and hatred are all elemental drivers of the human desire for violence, stating that every single terrorist outfit follows the same principles, in the exact same order, would be a grave misconception. Extremism and terrorism both differ according to the ideological type and political motivations driving the outfits. Varying groups would require varying levels of complicity from those that they control and contain. Fear balance and power projection aside, what remains common across most instances of these aberrant "States" is the suspension of certain fundamental human rights. Torture, pain, fear and death, all serve as tools on the axis of power projection and become ideological means of control in socio-political vacuums. When terrorist groups come to power, the act usually originates from/replicates itself through the domination of weaker sections of society. This is one of the key reasons that conflict zones suffer so rampantly from issues of conflict-related sexual violence (CRSV). While the United Nations (UN) has come up with several resolutions— most notably, Resolution 1888—to end CRSV, it has not been enough to prevent terrorist outfits from using brutality as a means of socio-political control. The Islamic State of Iraq and Syria (ISIS), in particular, has used various arguments to justify its genocidal attacks on Yazidi people and its proselytising tool, *Dabiq*, provides the ideological justifications that the group uses to defend such dehumanisation.

There are varying motivations driving such terrorist actions—from economic gains to political power—and on occasion, there may even be target demographics/ powers whose attention they are trying to gain. Nonetheless, the fact remains that the only way they can spread their message, gain recruits as well as instil fear about the brand is by targeting the "average global citizen". While terrorism may manifest locally given the rising interconnectivity of the age, it is certainly not limited to being a local threat and affects people across the world. The spectre affects people across class, race and gender. While recruited young men are celebrated as fighters and ideologically indoctrinated into the system to further the cause, being captured by these groups is a torturous and barbaric experience. Affected groups include women, children, the elderly and the infirm, all of whom are used by the group purely from a utilitarian standpoint. While some women are used to create support systems for the group and are effectively used as slave labour, others are exploited physically for labour and violated sexually for pleasure. The extent of the torture may vary from group to group; but aside from serving as political leverage, captives also become the means through which terrorists reinforce their structural hierarchies and assert power and domination within the group themselves. For groups like ISIS or Daesh, people—particularly women— that don't follow what is considered "the right religion" are effectively heathens and animals and can be treated as such. There are no ethical or moral constraints on the brutality inflicted on captives of war. Daesh ravages and raids villages with the intent of gaining fighters as well as submissive slave labour.

Once captured, escapees are rare and few and far between. Furthermore, even those who escape often suffer from severe cases of trauma, have a tremendous amount of difficulty readjusting to society and are often plagued by flashbacks and nightmares of their traumatic pasts. Survivors are often unwilling to speak about their experiences because the relived trauma itself becomes a triggering experience. There are, nevertheless, some survivors who escaped the terrorist camps, who attempt to not only spread a counter-message against the seeming harmony the groups intend to provide but are also willing to do all it takes to build a network that can get other such victims out and provide them with the care and rehabilitation they need. Lamya Aji Bashar is one such survivor who currently works to not only build awareness regarding the brutality of Daesh as a group but also exhorts international powers to rescue other such victims who might still be suffering within the confines of Daesh camps. Lamya was captured by Daesh and suffered excessively at their hands, but ever since she escaped she has been actively campaigning for the Yazidi community to build awareness and develop a response aimed at countering the large-scale crimes Daesh is committing.

Lamya recounts her story in an attempt to build outreach, provide insight into the functioning of the group as well as develop an effective response mechanism to prevent such incidents from occurring in the future. Lamya states that in 2016, a subsection of the ISIS invaded her village of Kocho in northern Iraq. Lamya, her father, her two brothers and three sisters were all captured and taken captive as prisoners along with the rest of her village. The men—including her father and brothers—were murdered, while the women were split up. The married women and younger children were taken to Tel Afar, while the unmarried women and teenagers were taken to Mosul. The older women, considered useless from the terrorist standpoint, were shot dead the next day. The younger women were gathered together and sold as sex slaves. Rebellion or refusal were not options for the captives as they were forced to submit to the dehumanising demands of their captors, or else they were brutalised for insubordination. Lamya was held captive for a period of 20 months during the course of which she was taken to various places in Syria and Iraq, tortured and abused, until she escaped in April 2016.

While detailing the experience and recounting the levels of dehumanisation, Lamya iterates that she was sold five times, if not more, and also draws attention to the fact that human flesh was bartered as a mere convenience within the camps. Further speaking about her captivity, she states that "They treated women not as human beings, they treated us like animals." As evinced by her testament, a large part of the ideological control manifested by Daesh can directly be attributed to their refusal to engage with any other religious system. The extreme nature of the violence unleashed on captors and victims was based on a system of othering, where women, infidels and animals all fall under the same category. The establishment of a caliphate has been the sole priority of the Daesh and this core belief manifested at every stage, from the attempted eradication of all other religious structures to the rampant brutalisation of women from other communities. Furthermore, the narratives of organisations like ISIS are based on extreme interpretations of religious scriptures and the usage of alternate schools of thought as defences allowing for such brutality. Lamya recounts that the Daesh fighters repeatedly beat and raped them by using the argument that the Qu'ran allowed for such behaviour against women.

Another major aspect of the brutalisation and dehumanisation committed by the ISIS is that they target communities that are very easily "othered" on religious and ethnic grounds. The Yazidis are a majority Kurdish-speaking religious group living mostly in northern Iraq. They number less than one million worldwide and throughout their history, the Yazidis have been persecuted as infidels by Muslim rulers and considered apostates by fundamentalists. Daesh has singled out the Yazidi religious and ethnic minority as a particular enemy to be destroyed, and this often manifests most notably through the brutalisation of Yazidi women and children. Lamya states that thus far, more than 3,500 women and children are still held in captivity by Daesh. Furthermore, these networks are not static and there are several roots and organised systems through which the buying and selling of female slaves can be undertaken. This brutalisation of Yazidi women and the Yazidi people by Daesh, as mentioned earlier, is based on an othering founded on historical and social religious persecution. This alienation is reinforced through the messages that the group sends out in their magazine, *Dabiq*. *Dabiq* is one of the many tools used by the ISIS to control and proliferate their narrative and their agenda. It is a constant site of hate speeches, misogyny and violent proselytisation. The fourth issue of the magazine mentions that the Yazidis were never an Islamic group but "became Islamized by the surrounding Muslim population, language, and culture, although they never accepted Islam nor claimed to have adopted it."[2]

It further talks about how the Yazidis should be dealt with and the ways in which the Yazidi women could be captured and enslaved unlike other female apostates. The enslaved Yazidi families are to be then sold by the ISIS soldiers and a fifth of the captured sales sent to Daesh leadership as *khum*s (a tax on war spoils) and those remaining are to be divided among Daesh fighters in accordance with sharia. In order to defend these actions, they cite religious authorities and discuss various commentaries which indicate that "actual slavery was a likely interpretation".[3] The group bases its arguments on the fact that slavery was mostly abandoned since the rise of the *taghut* law and the desertion of jihad.

> Before Shaytan (devil) reveals his doubts to the weak-minded and weak hearted, one should remember that enslaving the families of the kuffar and taking their women as concubines is a firmly established aspect of the Shari'ah that if one were to deny or mock, he would be denying or mocking the verses of the Qur'an and the narrations of the Prophet, and thereby apostatizing from Islam.[4]

The ISIS has also stated[5] that the desertion of slavery had led to a rise in adultery, fornication, etc., because the sharia alternative to marriage is not available, so a man who cannot afford marriage to a free woman is surrounded by temptation towards sin.

In December 2014, the Research and Fatwa Department of ISIS released a list of rules in a Q&A format for having sex with captured and enslaved women and girls who are not Muslim. It was apparently written by Daesh's scholars to regulate the "violations" by fighters. It is a manual carrying rather disturbing details of how and when a fighter should have sex with prisoners and the rules of their ownership. Through this document, they not only justify slavery of "unbelieving" women but also permit sex and bondage labour. The document says that it is permissible to sell a female captive for they are "merely property which can be disposed of as long as they don't cause [the Muslim ummah] any harm or damage." The document also mentions that a female slave can be owned in "partnership" (by more than one man) and outlines the rules of ownership of the female captive. It states: "If two or more individuals are involved in purchasing a female captive, none of them are permitted to have intercourse with her because she is part of a joint ownership."[6] It also explains that fighters should not have sex with women while they are pregnant, and that they cannot resell them if the fighter impregnates the female captive. The fatwa was recovered by the United States (US) Special Forces, and released by Reuters, after a raid on the home of Abu Sayyaf, ISIS's chief financial officer in Syria.

On 7 April 2016, the Global Justice Center published a paper tilted, "Daesh's Gender-based Crimes against Yazidi Women and Girls include Genocide",[7] highlighting the treatment meted out to ethnic minorities, in particular the Yazidi community. It mentioned how the Yazidi women, once captured, are separated into three groups:

1. married women with children;
2. married women without children; and
3. young women and girls.

Women who are too old to be sold as sex slaves or used for physical labour are killed and buried in mass graves. The Yazidi women and girls are inspected by the Daesh fighters, evaluated according to their beauty and made to undergo various examinations in order to determine whether they are virgins. While in captivity, they are subjected to sexual violence and are forcefully impregnated by Daesh fighters. According to them, a child cannot be Yazidi without two Yazidi parents and therefore, by forcefully impregnating the Yazidi girls and women, Daesh fighters prevent another generation of Yazidi's from being born.

Lamya's story provides a first-person account about the brutal manner in which the ISIS treats its captives. She, through her outreach,[8] is working towards the improvement of the state of Yazidi community worldwide, while also bringing awareness regarding the work that needs to be done to rescue the victims captured.[9]

Her story is proof that the current global efforts at rescue and rehabilitation are limited if not insufficient, and as she repeatedly warns, "Nobody from international community did anything for our victims. But if there is no response, Daesh ideology will reach every single one of you."[10] The reality of terrorism impacts the global community as a whole and therefore the response to it must also emerge from all state parties equally. In her account, Lamya mentions that contrary to popular belief, the Daesh fighters were not only Iraqi or Syrian but also Afghani, Pakistani and from European countries as well.[11] The ISIS proliferates its agenda wherever it finds a willing audience. Hence, there is a need for the counter-measures to be equally expansive, especially towards eradication of such inhuman practices. Lamya ends by saying that "she won't wish such a fate to her worst enemy."

NOTES

1 Editor's Note: This chapter is drawn from Lamya Haji Bashar's inspiring speech at the ASC 2017 and conversation with her after the conference on the terrifying experience of women enslaved in Daesh camps. Lamya was captured by Daesh and suffered excessively at their hands, but ever since she escaped she has been actively campaigning for the Yazidi community to build awareness and develop a response aimed at countering the large-scale crimes Daesh is committing

2 For more see: Clarion Project, "Islamic State's (ISIS, ISIL) Horrific Magazine, Clarion Project," 2017, available at https://clarionproject.org/islamic-state-isis-isil-propaganda-magazine-dabiq-50/, accessed on 28 September 2017.

3 (ISIS, 2014) Ibid.

4 (ISIS, 2014), Ibid.

5 For more see Human Rights Watch, "Slavery: The ISIS Rules," 2017, available at https://www.hrw.org/news/2015/09/05/slavery-isis-rules, accessed on 28 September 2017.

6 See Note 2

7 For more see Olszewski, S., "Daesh's Gender-Based Crimes against Yazidi Women and Girls Include Genocide - Global Justice Center," *Globaljusticecenter.net*, 2017, available at http://globaljusticecenter.net/publications/advocacy-resources/284-daesh-s-gender-based-crimes-against-yazidi-women-and-girls-include-genocide, accessed on 28 September 2017.

8 For more see "Former IS sex slaves get EU prize." *BBC News* 2017, available at http://www.bbc.com/news/world-europe-37787061, accessed on 28 September 2017.

9 For more see Barnett, D., "Yazidi women are not just Isis sex slaves. It is genocide, *The Independent*, 2017, available at: http://www.independent.co.uk/news/world/middle-east/isis-sex-slaves-lamiya-aji-bashar-nadia-murad-sinjar-yazidi-genocide-sexual-violence-rape-sakharov-a7445151.html, accessed on 28 Sep. 2017.

10 For more see "Kidnapped teenager escaped after five attempts and told her story of captivity," *The Online Citizen*, 2017, available at https://www.theonlinecitizen.com/2017/01/11/kidnapped-teenager-escaped-after-five-attempts-and-told-her-story-of-captivity/, accessed on 28 September 2017.

SECTION THREE

The Age of Instant Terror: Technology, the Game Changer

9

Breaking the ISIS Brand

Trajectories into and out of Terrorism and the Social Media Recruitment of the ISIS

Anne Speckhard and Ardian Shajkovci

Introduction

Despite the fact that the Islamic State of Iraq and Syria (ISIS) is rapidly being defeated on the Syrian and Iraqi battlefield, their online presence has not died down as they continue to use the Internet to radicalise and recruit followers to the extent possible. Till date, they have an unprecedented success rate among the various terrorist groups. Using various mediums, the ISIS has successfully recruited over 30,000 foreign fighters and inspired dozens of home-grown terror attacks with their polished and prolific online campaign.[1] They are adept at attracting the curious and confused denizens of the Internet and then "swarming" them with information that is coded with their ideological messaging and indoctrinating them into the group. Thus, while the military battlefield is looking to be a success, there is still a need to win against ISIS in the digital space.[2] All the current evidence available points towards the ISIS continuing its Internet recruiting success in the West, which is an issue because even if their physical presence is eradicated, the persistence of their online existence could serve as a point of proselytisation in the future. We have seen that the longer the ISIS goes unchallenged, the more dangerous they become. It has also been recently discovered that many supposedly "lone wolf" attacks were actually directed by the ISIS, from a virtual command centre. As the ISIS continues to lose physical territory, it is increasingly attempting to regain virtual ground and instructing new recruits to turn to home-grown terrorism, instead of travelling to Syria and Iraq. Most of their target base is particularly aimed at Western countries. The fight against the ISIS is not only on the battlefield, but has increasingly moved towards digital space where it is currently winning.

The West must understand that the ISIS is not just a terrorist organisation. It is a brand that sells its vision of a utopian Islamic "caliphate". The core ideology being peddled is a path to justice for those who feel marginalised, discriminated against, fearful of their governments, or who feel as though they are under attack by the West. The narrative that they are using to proliferate their message is increasingly gaining ground and unless the West takes the fight to the online battlefield, more victims will continue to buy what the ISIS is selling. The ISIS operates with impunity and unless countered effectively, we will continue to see attacks in the places we routinely frequent: airports, restaurants, nightclubs, concerts, parks, trains and sporting events, just to name a few. And ISIS, like all terrorist organisations, continues to learn from its mistakes and intensify the lethality and horrifying power of their attacks. Of late, they have begun using explosive-laden aerial drones to attack targets in Iraq. Also, signs point to them teaching their Western cadres to do the same, perhaps to swarm in on crowded areas or add a new element of horror to attacks involving guns and suicide vests, as was the case in the Paris 2016 attacks.[3] This chapter attempts to examine what goes into the making of a terrorist, how online proselytisation has increased extremist outreach and what counter-measures can be taken to put a stop to it.

The Lethal Cocktail of Terrorism

After interviewing 500 militant jihadi terrorists, their family members, close associates and even their hostages, from places ranging from Palestine, Lebanon, Iraq, Jordan, Syria, Russia, Kosovo, Krygyzstan, Chechnya, Israel, Canada to Western Europe, it has been possible to identify the necessary factors for the lethal cocktail of making a terrorist. These factors point out the individual vulnerabilities/motivations that also play a role—depending on the context and the individuals involved in motivating the decision to embrace extremism.[4] The factors that usually play a role in the making of a terrorist include:

1. *A group*: Ted Kaczynski (the Unabomber) and Chris Dorner (the former Los Angeles policeman and shooter) each formed their own manifestos and attacked on their own, but these types of true lone wolves are rare. There is usually a group purporting to represent some faction of society and offering terrorism as an answer.

2. *An ideology*: The group offers an ideology or a narrative that its believers can rally around. The ideology usually attempts to justify terrorism and the attacking of innocent civilians for a "greater" cause.

3. *Social support*: There is usually some level of social support that can vary widely by context. A young person thinking about joining a terrorist group in Gaza, for instance, is likely to have many friends who are also part of Hamas or Fatah. The youth may then choose his group the way the youths in other countries choose a football team. Whereas a youth growing up in Boston, as Tamerlan Tsarnaev did, will have to dig deeper in his community to find other like-minded individuals. What might have been an inhibiting factor earlier has completely broken down under the connectivity provided by the Internet. These days, one can quickly and easily tap into social networks that support and recruit for terrorist groups.

   The ISIS currently maintains a 24/7 presence on the Internet; and produces thousands of videos, posters and memes for individuals to interact with on all their social media sites. When someone shows interest in their activities through social media, they use feedback mechanisms, identify the person and quickly swarm in, providing them with one-on-one attention and care that is often lacking in their own lives. This initial provision of support serves to convert the victim to their cause and to recruit them further into the group. This psychological process mirrors cult recruitment processes as well.

4. *Individual vulnerability*: Another key factor that goes into this proselytisation is that there is a certain amount of individual vulnerability that resonates with the first three factors and serves as the clinching cog in the machine. The group, its ideology and the social support provided by the group all serve to allay individual vulnerability.

Speckhard has identified, in a paper, 50 such factors that have to do with individual motivations and vulnerability.[5] Those are broken into two cases: by whether the person lives inside or outside a conflict zone.

Those who reside in conflict zones are most often primarily motivated by trauma and revenge as well as frustrated aspirations. More often than not, they have family members who have been killed, raped, tortured, imprisoned or otherwise unfairly treated. They may have lost their home, territory, jobs and resources and may be living under occupation. Often, there are checkpoints and conflicts that keep them from engaging in their studies or block them from steady employment. They are angry, hurt and easily resonate to a group that offers to equip them with the tools that would help them strike back. They often want their enemies to feel the same pain they do, even if they know their terrorist act may be futile in every other way. Their feelings of persecution reach levels where they may be willing to even engage in suicide attacks in order to express their outrage. They become blinded by the idea of making their enemies suffer similarly, without paying attention to the costs entailed. Furthermore, sometimes these actions are not driven by rage but by despair and a desire to end their own pain. If they are highly traumatised, a suicide mission may offer them psychological first aid of a short-term nature—they can honourably exit a life overtaken by psychological trauma, painful arousal states, flashbacks, horror, anger, powerlessness, survival guilt and traumatic bereavement. If the group is good at selling suicide, they may even believe that they immediately go to paradise, and also earn paradise for their family members. These soft belief systems serve to create networks of unquestioning soldiers who buy into the idea that they will reunite with lost loved ones by taking their own lives in a suicide attack.

In contrast, those living in non-conflict zones are usually motivated by feelings of disenfranchisement, marginalisation and a resentment of the success of the people they see around them. Their lives may be off-track mentally, emotionally or economically and as a result, they become more susceptible to the ideology being sold and resonate more easily to a dream in which purpose, dignity, success, prosperity, adventure, romance or utopian living is offered to them.

Breaking the ISIS Brand: Way Forward

Research interviews conducted with actual terrorists have thus demonstrated that the lethal cocktail of terrorism is contextual and stems from the interaction of the four aforementioned factors: a terrorist group, its ideology, the social support it enjoys and the resonance of the terrorist group's ideology with the individual's own motivations and vulnerabilities. We see then that the drivers of violent extremism derive on a personal level from a desire for personal significance, adventure, justice and dignity to frustrated aspirations and anger at social inequalities, in addition to many other potential factors. Loosely grouped, individual vulnerabilities and motivators can be categorised as contextual, grievance-based, socio-cultural, social–psychological and ideological. Some of these, such as unemployment, discrimination, marginalisation and nepotism, are difficult to quickly and efficiently address, while others are less difficult.

For instance, delegitimising terrorist ideologies and groups and reducing their social support is less difficult if one can manage to raise the defectors' voices. The ISIS defectors, who have been inside the group, are likely the most powerful voices to raise to delegitimise the current terrorist groups operating globally and discredit their ideology (particularly the dream of a just and prosperous "caliphate" run by terrorists). This process of invalidating their narrative would serve to convince victims susceptible to recruitment and thereby diminish social support for violent extremism.

By using the voices of ISIS defectors and their experiences inside the ISIS to create a counter-narrative that is turned back against the group, it is possible to make it less desirable for individuals to seek or find any type of solution/salvation in terrorist groups presently operating in the victims' area. Individual needs and vulnerabilities may still exist, but the terrorist group's ability to make vulnerable individuals believe that the group or its ideology offers any type of viable solution will be diminished. Social support for the groups and their ideologies will be discredited and delegitimised.

Breaking the ISIS Brand—The ISIS Defectors Interviews Project

The International Center for the Study of Violent Extremism (ICSVE) team spent a year-and-a-half capturing ISIS defectors' stories on video in the "Breaking the ISIS Brand—The ISIS Defectors Interviews Project". Under the project, the ICSVE staff collected 43 stories of defectors inclusive of various geographies, genders and professions: Syrian, European, Central Asians and Balkan former ISIS fighters; and men, women, teens, fighters, guards, wives, morality police, etc., all of whom shared personal horror stories of ISIS brutality and hypocrisy. These former ISIS cadres witnessed Muslim children as young as 6 year old being manipulated into committing suicide bombings, as also the systemic rape of Muslim women as sex slaves. They witnessed the massacres of Muslim dissenters and the complete perversion of their faith. In addition to the defectors, 12 parents of the ISIS fighters and two ideologues were also interviewed for the project.

The sample was collected between the time frame of November 2015 to February 2016 from returnees of Western European and Balkans countries as well as Central Asian actors, and from Syrians fleeing the ISIS by escaping into Turkey. Interviews were conducted in a semi-structured manner, allowing the defectors to tell their stories of being recruited into the group, serving and then defecting. These stories were followed by in-depth questioning involving a series of 25 questions that examined, in great detail, topics they had personal experience with inside the group. The defectors were not asked to give their names and were judged to be genuine on the basis of four things: referral from prison authorities and prosecution records; referral from defectors who knew them from inside the group; insightful knowledge about experiences inside the group; and intense post-traumatic responses during the interview evincing they had been present and taken part in events they were describing. The subjects were contacted via smugglers, other defectors, personal introductions and prison authorities, thus the sample remained entirely non-random. The defectors did not give their real names (except for those in prison or those who were already prosecuted) and were told not to incriminate themselves during the interviews.

From the 13-year-old child soldier who watched other young boys behead prisoners as a part of their induction as ISIS fighters (and he likely did the same), who left because children were being tricked into dying in suicide bombings, to a European bride of ISIS who, widowed while pregnant, was rescued by her father when the ISIS demanded that she give up her baby to the "caliphate" before leaving, they all described the horrific realities of life inside the ISIS.

Four short video clips[6] were produced from the longer videotaped interviews. The process was to edit the interview down to its most damaging elements and to the content denouncing the organisation and deriding the structureless belief. The cropped content added to the speaker's presentation of emotionally evocative video footage and the pictures taken from actual ISIS content were coupled with these tools to graphically illustrate what the speakers were saying. The finished video clips were named with pro-ISIS names and started with an opening screen that mirrored ISIS materials so that an individual looking for and viewing ISIS recruiting videos might accidently watch an ICSVE video and be surprised to encounter an ISIS defector denouncing the group. The video clips were also subtitled in the 21 languages that the ISIS uses for recruitment, such as French, Dutch, German, Uzbek and Malay. Once produced, the videos were then uploaded to the Internet with the hope of catching the same audiences that ISIS engages with on a 24/7 basis. Recently, ICSVE staff have also begun experimenting with targeted placement of the videos, which they are trying to get pinned onto the social media accounts of those endorsing and promoting violent extremism.

The ICSVE aims to break the ISIS brand by creating and flooding the Internet with powerful counter-narratives to their claims of creating a utopian "caliphate". Providing disenfranchised victims with an alternative narrative to rally around might reduce the Internet seduction of vulnerable sectors of society. Given the prolific use of the media by terrorist organisations such as ISIS to spur their global reach and propaganda, fighting ISIS and similar groups in the digital and information realm has become a major pillar of research activities. These field-based primary research and evidence-based educational video materials are being carefully crafted to counter the efforts of extremist and terrorist organisations to publicise their propaganda to garner support for violence.

Prior Counter-narrative Attempts

Counter-narrative materials produced up until recently have suffered from a lack of emotional impact. For instance, during the last 15 years, the United Kingdom

(UK) Home Office has commissioned a plethora of websites and groups to argue against al-Qaeda's use of "martyrdom". These counter-narratives were meant to oppose the calls to militant jihad using Islamic scriptures and logical arguments, thereby presenting more moderate views of Islam. These measured responses, however, were not effective. They fell flat particularly in the face of al-Qaeda's use of emotionally evocative pictures, videos and graphic images arguing that Islam, Islamic people and Islamic lands are under attack by the West and that jihad is an obligatory duty of all Muslims and "martyrdom" missions are called for in Islam.[7] Likewise, the ISIS's creative and emotionally evocative use of videos, alongside their leverage of social media feedback mechanisms, made counter-narratives that are based on logical arguments pale in comparison to emotionally evocative proselytisation calls.

The ISIS defector videos, in contrast, were created by seasoned professional storytellers with experience in Hollywood and documentary film production, with an eye for capturing emotions. To produce them, the researchers first worked through the time transcript of the entire article and picked out emotionally compelling material that would serve to denounce the ISIS. Likewise, the defectors had been asked at the end of their interviews to give advice to anyone thinking of joining the ISIS—a time when they strongly and emotionally denounced the group and warned others of the dangers and disappointments of joining. Further, emotionally evocative ISIS video and images were also used to illustrate what the defectors were narrating—to make their stories come alive and also to turn the ISIS back on itself.

Another effort has been to use former extremists to undertake CVE work, including undercover infiltration into terrorist groups, such as the case of Mubin Shaikh and Morten Storm. Google created a formers network and a recent Jigsaw-sponsored study by Frenett and Dow (2015) used formers to try to dissuade jihadist endorsing Facebook holders away from their views. This has not always worked out well in the past however, with some cases leading to reversions from forward motion on the terrorist trajectory and in the cases of using them as undercovers, prosecutions and drone kills.

Problems in working with formers include issues of trust and reliability. Some formers find it stressful to speak about their experiences and others simply refuse. Still others are not trusted enough by law enforcement to be used in that capacity as they vacillate in their opinions about the terrorist groups that they formerly endorsed or belonged to. Not surprisingly, many are not psychologically healthy as they were seduced into the group because of their needs/vulnerabilities. As a result, the groups became their last resort as they hoped the group would meet their expectations. When the organisation failed to provide the human support they required, they suffered a tremendous amount of post-traumatic stress after serving in conflict zones inside a horrifically brutal organisation.

In contrast, the ISIS defector videos do not suffer from these complications as there is no danger of face-to-face interaction with vulnerable audiences. Furthermore, unlike the case with the formers, the videos are pre-vetted, set and almost constructed with the intent of opposing extremism and violence, so the support ensures that the counter-narrative being created does not get lost in the confusion. Also, even if the defector later changed his mind and reverted back to the group, the viewer is not made aware/negatively influenced, so the danger of relapse that stems from using "formers" is removed. The videos become an effective means of instilling disgust, fear and disillusionment in the viewer who may have been gravitating towards the ISIS and other such organisations.

Tools to Counter Violent Extremism and Violent Extremist Propaganda

Cogent cognitive arguments should certainly be made against extremist ideologies. However, cognitive arguments are not enough, as is clearly evinced by the UK's previous efforts that failed to counter al-Qaeda and the ISIS' use of graphic images and emotions to seduce youth and propel them along the terrorist trajectory. Emotion-based and graphic multimedia tools to counter violent extremist groups need to be developed better in order to fight these groups.

In addition, by introducing real defector voices, we strive to bring some sort of credibility with the target group, specifically introducing the voices of those who have experienced real and harsh realities of being a victim or belonging to a terrorist group. Equally important, our video products are disseminated in multiple languages to ensure that we reach out to a broad and geographically diverse audience.

One of the primary goals of these educational videos is to showcase the stories of individuals profoundly impacted by violent extremism, whether they be victims of terrorism, family members or actual members of extremist or terrorist groups. During the course of interviewing extremists worldwide for over two decades, ICSVE has found that in order to identify the personal needs of those prone to radicalisation and extremism (for example, vulnerabilities, grievances and capabilities), there is a need for personalised engagement and conversation. The ICSVE firmly believes that such conversations, including the process of identifying personal grievances, can start by engaging the emotions and one way to do so is by showing videos that depict the actual real-life stories of defectors and provide the inside story of living in terrorist groups. Such counter-narratives can pave the way to more personalised engagements and productive discussions in which needs, grievances and vulnerabilities are made apparent and can begin to be addressed. In this regard, our educational videos are designed to:

1. Tell actual stories of individuals affected by extremist and terrorist groups such as the ISIS and Al-Nusra, in their own words, in order to delegitimise both the group and its ideology.

2. Depict the harsh realities of belonging or being a victim of terrorist groups such as ISIS or Al-Nusra.

3. Use the emotional appeal of real-life stories told on videos to reach out to vulnerable populations. Reaching their hearts first and powerfully engaging emotions and relatability with the speakers who regret choices and portraying vulnerability is the best way to do it.

4. Employ a powerful narrative and visual that appeals to human emotions and depicts a mistaken path taken by individuals. The admission of human fallibility makes the viewers identify with individuals who share their grievances, vulnerabilities and motivations that led to them to make the wrong choice. Using logical arguments and evidence alone can often be challenged or countered, as seen in previous failed counter-messaging campaigns. Such materials also fail to engage the emotions and personal motivations involved in joining terrorist groups.

5. Start conversations on extremism and terrorism-related topics and create a safe environment in which young and other vulnerable demographics can openly discuss contentious issues related to extremism and terrorism.

6. Create a platform for discussions that can help serve as a diagnostic to cater to the needs, grievances and vulnerabilities that become apparent and can begin to be addressed.

7. Generate additional educational materials and activities to engage with, especially to encourage the young to think critically about emotional and controversial issues as well as simulate real-life scenarios on what it means to belong to extremist or terrorist groups, specifically in terms of consequences and effects of extremist violence. The discussions could also spark constructive discussion on the root causes of radicalisation and violent extremism.

8. Serve as a resource and platform to channel potential doubt, frustration and anger into positive change and participation.

9. Serve as a platform to challenge extremist ideas that exploit the idealism

of young people, including vulnerable populations, as well as challenge extremist narratives that offer facile and easy solutions to real-life problems.

10. Serve as a platform to ignite the passions of the youth into positive and meaningful paths and divert them away from violent extremism.

11. Offer a compelling counter-narrative to extremist and terrorist stories that are rooted in the expert understanding of counter-narrative tactics, the religion of Islam and community concerns.

12. Ensure that ICSVE's positive message reaches vulnerable populations before extremist messages do or, when later, powerfully counters theirs.

13. Not only keep vulnerable populations out of harm's way but also empower them to think critically and independently and equip them with real-life stories that help them speak out against violent extremism.

14. Offer necessary tools to practitioners in the field (for example, law enforcement, teachers, civil society employees, healthcare practitioners, imams, psychologists and social workers) to deal with confidence and knowledge when it comes to addressing contentious issues related to extremism and terrorism in their respective communities.

15. Offer tools to practitioners in the field to further construct and develop alternatives to extremist messages.

16. Increase digital literacy, knowledge and critical thinking about online propaganda, especially among the young.

In the four elements making up the lethal cocktail of terrorism—the group, its ideology, social support for terrorism and individual vulnerabilities and motivations—only the first three are addressed by the ISIS defector videos. The defectors denounce and delegitimise both the group and its ideology and thereby reduce social support for both, but they do nothing to address the underlying individual needs and vulnerabilities that first led to the terrorist group and its ideology resonating with the individual in the first place. This is a drawback of most counter-narrative messaging in fact, and points to the need to have follow-ups or links taking the disillusioned viewer to help for addressing those needs and desires.

The defector testimonies deal with disillusionment in the Islamic nature of the ISIS and its so-called utopian "caliphate", referring to corruption, brutality, inescapability and the criminal nature and terrifying practices of its members, thereby creating disgust and turning away from the group. However, the videos are likely limited in these ways:

1. They may not necessarily turn away those already committed to extremist and terrorist movements and organisations, although they can be used to

facilitate discussions with committed extremists as the emotional and personal nature of the true-life stories engages them to speak as well— even if to argue that the videos are untrue, contrived or the speaker has failed in his Islamic path.

2. They may not prevent radicalisation solely on their own. Video messages, online propaganda and the Internet, in general, are not considered the sole instruments of radicalisation. Counter-narratives would also necessarily have to be multilayered as a result. Equally important is the fact that when terrorist groups are powerfully meeting the needs of their recruits, messaging can delegitimise the groups but may not delegitimise their actual support.

3. While the primary purpose of defector videos remains prevention and counter-radicalisation, they may not necessarily be solely effective in the realm of deradicalisation or disengagement. Nevertheless, as an intervention tool they are likely to start a lively discussion that may lead to openings for treatment. They can also serve to deconstruct and give meaning to extremist messages in the case of individuals already at risk.

4. The videos do not serve as a substitute for other forms of personalised engagement, such as helplines, expert insight or peer-to-peer discussions, but are designed to be tools that facilitate all of the aforementioned.

Focus Testing the Tools

The ICSVE research fellows are currently focus testing the first video materials for prevention and intervention purposes, specifically with ISIS endorsers on Facebook, YouTube and in Telegram chat rooms. The primary goal of the project is to identify individuals online (for example, Facebook, YouTube and Telegram) who are at risk or already expressing sympathies for the terrorist groups. Once identified, such individuals are then sent one of the defector videos. The assumption is that the voices of defectors are the most credible voices that could reach the target group and start a discussion on extremist groups and narratives. The reactions are also monitored by professionals with experience in such interventions in an offline environment. While the research is still in progress, the goal is to focus-group the effectiveness of our videos as well as elicit discussion and cast doubts on extremist groups and narratives to the target individual and their online connections. The ultimate goal is to link those vulnerable and willing to appropriate intervention providers based on their specific needs and preference (for example, ideological inclination, age and gender) and to break them free of ISIS's online influence and terrorist recruitment.

The question of how to measure the effectiveness of the video products, or any other video product with a focus on counter-messaging for that matter, is complex. That said, the ICSVE is constantly striving to refine its videos and measure their effectiveness. It has focus tested its videos in various settings, such as in Jordan, Central Asia, Europe, the Balkans and the United States, and constantly strives to adjust the videos accordingly, in order to find the most effective messages to reach to our target audience and to learn how the videos spark conversations and can lead to helpful interventions.

We will continue to assess both short and long-term impact of our videos on user behaviour (for example, supporting extremist ideas by liking, tweeting, etc., and monitor user behaviour over sustained period of time to determine changes due to measures implemented) while also continuing to understand better the relationship between our online interventions and offline behaviour.

NOTES

1   A. Speckhard, A. Shajkovci and A.S. Yayla, "Defeating ISIS on the Battle Ground as well as in the Online Battle Space: Considerations of the 'New Normal' and Available Online Weapons in the Struggle Ahead', *Journal of Strategic Security*, Vol. 9, No. 4, 2016, pp. 1–10.

2   A.S. Yayla and A. Speckhard, "The Potential Threats Posed by ISIS's Use of Weaponized Air Drones and How to Fight Back", ICSVE Brief Report, 28 February 2017, available at http://www.icsve.org/brief-reports/the-potential-threats-posed-by-isiss-use-of-weaponized-air-drones-and-how-to-fight-back/. Accessed on 28 February 2017

3   Ibid.

4   A. Speckhard, "The Lethal Cocktail of Terrorism: The 4 Necessary Ingredients that Go into Making a Terrorist & 50 Individual Vulnerabilities/Motivations that May Play a Role", ICSVE Brief Report, 26 February 2016, available at http://www.icsve.org/the-lethal-cocktail-of-terrorism—the-fournecessary-ingredients.html, accessed on 28 February 2017.

5   Ibid.

6   For more on this, the ICSVE channel can be accessed on https://www.youtube.com/channel/UCumpEsozixbl-PyKw12hmnw/playlists.

10

Technology and Intelligence in Countering Terrorism
An Intuitive Approach

Saikat Datta

Finding Extremism Online

In 2004, an internal audit carried out by the Federal Bureau of Investigation (FBI) revealed the organisation's thousands of hours of untranslated intercepts, hampering its counter-terrorism efforts.[1] Unable to keep up with the growing backlog, the report made 18 recommendations to address the problem. An audit carried out the following year showed that the backlog had increased and the recommendations had failed to achieve the desired output.

Post 9/11 also saw a proliferation of private entities monitoring the growing online violent extremism. In May 2004, the al-Qaeda posted the video of a beheading of a 26-year-old American, Nicholas Berg, by the Jordanian-born Abu Musab al-Zaraqawi on a Malaysian website. Traffic to the site spiked, leading to a realisation that the Internet was helping extremist groups to exploit the medium to expand their reach. As a counter to this phenomenon, private groups came up, evolving a business model that generated revenues by monitoring extremist behaviour using algorithms to understand, analyse and interpret information into actionable intelligence.

Rita Katz[2] emerged as a leading private entity in the business of monitoring online violent extremism. She founded the Search for International Terrorist Entities (SITE) intelligence group[3] to monitor groups online and sell its analysis to interested parties for a price. The SITE worked primarily in tracking posts "on Arabic message boards" and discovered networks, some leading to future terror attacks. Most of the material discovered by Katz and SITE turned out to be propaganda material and others training videos. Some turned out to be messages that led to planned terror attacks. Soon, she was generating adequate information to be taken seriously by government agencies, and the media reported on her extensively and even pointed out her controversial methodology that involved some of her staffers posing as extremists and joining chat rooms to track down potential terrorists.[4]

According to research published in 2005, the use of the Internet for terror and extremist activities had specific outcomes.[5] It established the broad uses of the Internet by terrorists:

1. psychological warfare;
2. publicity and propaganda;
3. data mining;
4. fundraising;
5. networking;
6. sharing information; and
7. planning and coordination.

Weimann's research[6] also established the different kinds of audiences that were targeted by extremist groups he studied for his paper. Primarily three kinds of audiences were targeted by extremist groups using the Internet on a regular basis:

1. Current and potential supporters—to keep the faithful happy and build new networks.
2. International public opinion—address a global audience to legitimise terror attacks.
3. Public in inimical nations—target the population of the country deemed by the extremist organisation as the "enemy".

While Weimann's research captured the growing phenomenon of extremists using the Internet, a later study by the United Nations Office on Drugs and Crime (UNODC) confirmed the earlier trends:

> ...the benefits of internet technology are numerous, starting with its unique suitability for sharing ideas and information, which is recognised as a fundamental human right. It must also be recognised, however, that the same technology that facilitates such communication can also be used for terrorist purposes. The use of the internet for terrorist purposes creates both challenges and opportunities.[7]

This forms a useful framework to build credible counter-mechanisms that can be embedded into an overall counter-terrorism strategy. The strategy has to be built intuitively, keeping in mind the sensitivities of the target audience, and shape the counter-narrative accordingly.

Anonymity and Security

A key aspect to the use of the Internet and it related technologies for terrorism is the anonymity that it can grant to extremist groups. The lack of attribution makes it difficult for security agencies to track perpetrators. In some ways, the rise of non-state threats is synonymous with the use of Internet technologies from a doctrinal perspective.

The rise of non-state actors rewrote the fundamental rules of modern conflict, moving away from a conventional, mutual deterrence models to a loose global federation. These non-state actors did not hold territory, thus rendering them rootless and therefore harder to deter. Unlike the past, when conventional adversaries would threaten to invade territories or achieve deterrence through mutual destruction of assets and/or economies, the new enemy had neither land nor assets to hold on to. Therefore, the formulation of a counter-terrorism strategy needed a fundamental doctrinal shift.

The key to this loose, ideological federation of extremist ideologies centred around the ability to communicate securely and with speed across vast distances. For example, the al-Qaeda, a loose federation, served as the ideological "base" that allowed a federated structure, where the name was the only connection between disparate groups of individuals. This was facilitated by the emergence of Internet-based technologies, allowing groups to use secured chat rooms or messaging boards to share information, tactics and ideologies. India too witnessed cases of communication between extremists, where emails were used to transmit messages, surprising the security agencies. Mails would be saved in draft folders, while the password would be shared offline, allowing people across disparate distances to communicate with each other without actually transmitting the mail.[8] This, in theory and in practice for a while, allowed people to communicate securely with minimum threat of detection.

Technology and Terrorism: Cases from India

Three cases from India are illustrative of how quickly extremists can adapt to emerging technologies in their bid to evade the state's surveillance mechanisms.

The interrogation report[9] of Mohammed Ahmed Sidibapa Mohammed Zarar, better known as "Yasin Bhatkal", an extremist who is alleged to have been behind several terror attacks across India, is indicative of how secure communication technologies can be used by extremist groups.[10]

The 26/11 terror attacks on Mumbai by a group of 10 men trained by the Pakistan-based Lashkar-e-Taiba (LeT) proved to be a paradigm shift, serving as a precursor to several other attacks that took place across the globe. What surprised Indian investigators during and after the attack was the use of Voice over Internet Protocol (VoIP) communications between the attackers and their Karachi-based handlers.[11] A protracted investigation revealed that online accounts had been created by members of the LeT using fake identities to avoid detection. The terrorists had also been trained in the use of hand-held Global Positioning System (GPS), using it to navigate from the sea to specific landing points in Mumbai and head towards their targets.

As investigations would reveal subsequently, the GPS coordinates had been fed in by a Pakistani-American, David Coleman Headley (aka Daood Gilani), who gathered extensive details during visits to India. The fact that the GPS systems had also been fed data to return to Karachi via the sea indicated that the terrorists had planned to return to Karachi after carrying out their attacks. The Snowden documents show that the British technical intelligence agency, General Communications Headquarters (GCHQ), was monitoring the computer of LeT's Zarar Shah, but did not inform its Indian intelligence counterparts during the months preceding the attack on Mumbai.[12]

The final case from India that illustrates the ability of extremists to adapt to new technologies in the Indian context is the series of bombings that were carried out by the group known as the Indian Mujahideen (IM). The attacks stared in 2007 and the group continued to be active until 2013, carrying out attacks across India, from Delhi to Rajasthan, Gujarat, Maharashtra and Bihar. Believed to have been created by individuals associated with the banned Students Islamic Movement of India (SIMI), the IM began to use hacked Wi-Fi networks to send across messages claiming credit for the attacks. However, what surprised the investigators was the plethora of literature that was made available to the extremists online, to pick up skills in bomb making and other offensive capabilities. Employing these skills, the extremists used material that was available in the open market to create explosives, detonators and timing mechanisms to build improvised explosive devices (IEDs), sometimes using pressure cookers and nails to act as shrapnel to maximise explosives with limited explosive materials.

But the IM was also using secure communications that slowly unravelled as investigations proceeded.[13] The IM was found to be using emails that would disappear if they weren't accessed every 24 hours, secure messaging chat applications and proxy servers that hopped across continents.

While the use of the Internet by members of the IM might be considered rudimentary when compared to the use of technology by international terror groups to evade traditional surveillance mechanisms, it is indicative of the gap between the capabilities of the Indian law enforcement agencies and terrorists, as the latter proved to be far more imaginative and capable than the former.

Emerging Technologies and Jurisdictional Issues

In 2008, an assault on the Baku–Tbilisi–Ceyhan pipeline in eastern Turkey was initially presumed to be a traditional physical terror attack. Subsequent investigations established it as an act of "cyberwar".[14] Although information about the attack in the open domain is still sketchy, it is believed that vulnerabilities in the software running the Internet Protocol (IP)-based security cameras were exploited by hackers who "super-pressurised the crude oil in the line" to cause a series of devastating explosions.[15] The claims of it being purely a cyberattack have been disputed in some quarters, but experts have not ruled out the possibility of such an attack in theory.

Analysts and intelligence officials also see the emergence of the militant outfit from the Syrian civil war, the Islamic State of Iraq and Syria (ISIS) (aka Daesh), and its use of social media as a fascinating case study of a "next generation security threat",[16] which although traditional at one level, has grown in complexity, reach and ability on the arrival of next-generation networks (NGNs).[17]

Since the first ISIS recruits surfaced from India in 2014, it has emerged as the only terror group with a global footprint to be able to attract recruits from India, a phenomenon that had never been seen before.[18] The recruits were part of the ISIS plan to create remote-controlled attacks by contacting them online and as investigators discovered, "In the most basic enabled attacks, Islamic State handlers acted as confidants and coaches, coaxing recruits to embrace violence."[19]

Their ability to recruit people from different economic, regional classes as well as gender has perplexed security agencies across the globe. This can be partly evidenced by the discovery of some social media influencers who would actively use social media networks to propagate and if necessary recruit people to the cause. The discovery of the Bangalore-based Mehdi Masroor Biswas, with Twitter handle @ShamiWitness, as one of the most influential social media proponents of the ISIS has reinforced this belief.[20] The terror attacks in Gulshan, Dhaka, Bangladesh, by a disparate group of college-going youth in 2016, once again reinforce the ISIS' ability to carry out remote-controlled attacks from afar.

Countering Tech Terror: Back to the Basics

To understand how terror aided by technology and the emergence of NGNs can be countered, it would be helpful to frame the problem as a series of queries.

Query 1: Why do Terror Groups Innovate while Security Agencies Lag behind?

This is obvious. Groups that are threatened will always innovate, while those tasked with responding to emerging threats will always lag behind. Therefore, the answer, though it seems obvious, does not lie in merely innovating technology. It lies in creating mechanisms that can adapt intuitively. This is similar to the way emerging technologies are leveraging machine learning and artificial intelligence to build threat intelligence programmes. A good example of this approach can be understood from General Stanley McChrystal's account of his time as the commander of the Joint Special Operations Command (JSOC) in Iraq. McChrystal's tenure has been documented by him in his part-autobiographical, part-management treatise, *Team of Teams*, where he examines the problems of losing a counter-insurgency war *despite* the availability of technology.[21]

A key discovery that McChrystal made once he arrived in Iraq was that even though the United States (US) Special Forces and the teams from the National Security Agency (NSA) were situated just a few hundred metres apart, they were not working together. The disjointed operations were leading to failed operations, giving the Iraqi insurgents a major edge. He found the Iraqi groups far more organic and intuitive than the standard operating procedure (SoP)-driven US military and intelligence units. His views on the availability of big data and analytics are illuminating:

> Big Data will not save us because the technological advances that brought us these mountains of information and the digital resources for analysing them have at the same time created volatile communication webs and media platforms, taking aspects of society that once resembled comets and turning them into cold fronts. We have moved from data-poor but fairly predictable settings to data-rich, uncertain ones.[22]

He admits that the JSOC task force understood very little of this and instead, using the classic management approach of trying to build SoPs, began to respond to a "complex" challenge by creating a "complicated" response. In simpler terms, military and intelligence bureaucracies had created a response mechanism that ticked all the right boxes, but had little to show for all its efforts. Instead, he decided to take a more intuitive approach at simplifying processes so that he could produce effective results.

McChrystal's experiences in Iraq established that basic, intuitive and simple-to-understand protocols were the best ways to beat the technological challenges that the Iraqi insurgents threw up. If the Iraqis depended on secure communications to disrupt the US operations, the NSA's cyber experts would break into the code to not only spread disinformation but also set up false meetings that would be passed on the special forces units in real time. This led to a series of successful raids that broke the back of the Iraqi insurgency, producing major successes such as the raid on a key insurgent command centre at Sinjar,[23] through a special forces' operation codenamed "Operation Massey", that would yield nearly 5 terabytes of intelligence.

McChrystal advocated a radical change in the way the military functions. As illustrated in Figure 10.1, the conventional military and intelligence was hierarchical in structure and worked in neat silos of command and control. However, the Iraqi militants worked as teams, some in complex and nebulous relationships, allowing them far greater adaptability as well as capability. To counter them, McChrystal came up with the concept of an interconnected team (Figure 10.2) that could also function as a team of teams. This, in actual practice, meant putting people from different groups and silos to work together as complex units, complementing each other's strengths as well as being sensitive to their operational requirements. So cyber hackers would sit and plan with special forces teams, working jointly to take on the Iraqi insurgency.

Figure 10.1

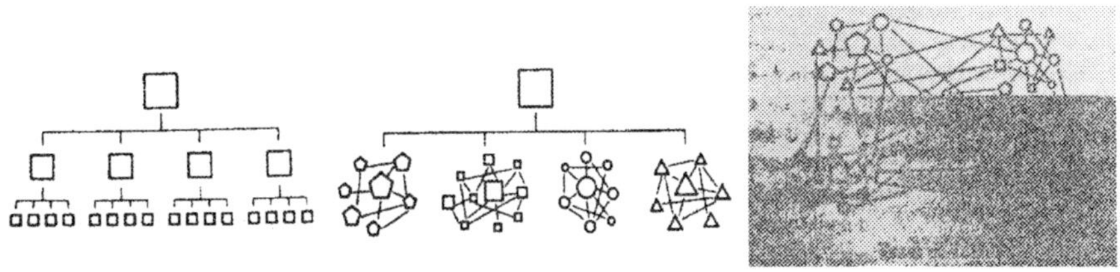

Command   Command of Teams

Figure 10.2

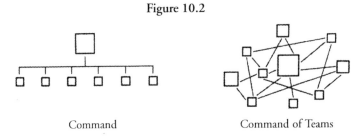

Command   Command of Teams

Source: McChrystal, Stanley A., Tantum Collins, David Silverman, and Chris Fussell. 2015. Team of teams: new rules of engagement for a complex world, New York: Penguin.

Query 2: How do We Prioritise Technology as a Counter-terrorism Response

The plethora of technological solutions available to counter-terrorism professionals today can be mind boggling. This creates a legitimate query: how do they prioritise the development and adoption of a technology that will deliver results? The answers are not simple, but intuitive.

For instance, today while most cell phones offer apps that can provide end-to-end encryption, some of them have code scripts that are stored on the device. These scripts can be used to decrypt some kinds of encrypted messages using the keys stored on the device. But that will need expertise from digital forensics, and has to be extracted in manner that also makes it available as evidence under the relevant provisions of the Indian Evidence Act. However, it is also a fact that the lack of capacity at central forensic institute(s) can cause delays up to 6–12 months, rendering the investigation meaningless. Unless such capacity shortcomings, both in terms of processes and technology, are not filled, it will never be possible to deploy the rights kinds of technology in the right manner to yield meaningful results.

This also underscores the need to build privacy frameworks that ensure that data of citizens is not violated unless an established set of norms have been met. Unless these provisions are met, it will allow shortcuts to counter-terrorism professionals, that can inevitably lead to wrong decisions driving counter-terrorism efforts with less-than-desirable results.

Therefore, the key to adapting technology to modern-day counter-terrorism efforts must start at the weakest links in the chain.

1. Is the beat constable, who is embedded in the local community, equipped adequately to deal with anomalies when they show up?
2. Are security agencies networked adequately to share data in real time,

ensuring that they are able to analyse information and arrive at actionable intelligence?

3. Are counter-terrorism professionals building credible counter-narratives to counter online violent extremism, which can be deployed in optimum ways to reach the target audience? This is important because people who deal with social media networks often forget the *social* aspects of media and get overwhelmed with the technological aspects of the medium rather than its *sociological* underpinnings.

4. Are counter-terrorism professionals taking a multidisciplinary approach to their challenges, or are they entirely driven by singular aspects? Unless this is addressed in a networked manner, allowing all stakeholders to interface and build "Team of Teams", it is likely that most counter-terrorism efforts will use disproportionate resources to deliver meagre results.

NOTES

1   See FBI audit report, *Translation of Counterterrorism and Counterintelligence Foreign Language Material*. US Department of Justice, Office of the Inspector General, 2004, available at https://oig.justice.gov/reports/FBI/a0425/final.pdf, accessed on 3 March 2017.

2   See siteintelgroup.com/blog/index.php/blogger/634-rkatz for an official biography.

3   Available at http://siteintelgroup.com/.

4   For more see, Benjamin Wallace-Wells, "Private Jihad :How Rita Katz got into the spying business", 29 May 2006, available at http://www.newyorker.com/magazine/2006/05/29/private-jihad, accessed on 3 March 2017.

5   See, for example, James Carafano, "The Future of Anti-Terrorism Technologies", www.Heritage.org, 6 June 2005, available on http://www.heritage.org/homeland-security/report/the-future-anti-terrorism-technologies and Gabriel Weimann "www.terror.net How Modern Terrorism Uses the Internet", Special report 16, United States Institute for Peace, March 2004, available at https://www.usip.org/sites/default/files/sr116.pdf. Both accessed on 3 March 2017.

6   See Note 5.

7   "The use of the Internet for terrorist purposes," Report by UN Office on Drugs and Crime In collaboration with the United Nations Counter-Terrorism Implementation Task Force, 2012, available at https://www.unodc.org/documents/frontpage/Use_of_Internet_for_Terrorist_Purposes.pdf, accessed on 3 March 2017.

8   Views of author based on his experiences as a reporter covering the issue and research as a cyber security expert.

9   An interrogation report is an investigation document based on the questioning of an accused in the presence of a police officer. This report is an inadmissible document in a court under most Indian laws. It is mostly used to extract intelligence from the accused and should be viewed as such. This is a document which is restricted and not for public consumption.

10 The *Interrogation Report of Yasin Bhatkal*. See pp. 77–79 for details on the use of secure chats, fake emails and proxy addresses by the 'Bhatkal Group' to communicate with each other and transfer funds.

11　"VoIP Used by 26/11 Planners, 150 Test Calls Made before Attack", *India Today*, 18 August 2009, available at http://indiatoday.intoday.in/story/VOIP+used+by+26-11+planners,+150+test+calls+made+before+attack/1/57314.html, accessed on 3 March 2017.

12　James Glanz, Sebastian Rotella and David E. Sanger, "In 2008 Mumbai Attacks, Piles of Spy Data, but an Uncompleted Puzzle", *The New York Times*, 21 December 2014, available at http://www.nytimes.com/2014/12/22/ world/asia/in-2008-mumbai-attacks-piles-of-spy-data-but-an-uncompleted-puzzle.html?_r=0., accessed on 3 March 2017.

13　Muzamil Jaleel, "NIA Probe Shows IM Men Tech-savvy; Used Proxy Servers, Complex Code to Chat", *The Indian Express*, 4 July 2014, available at http://indianexpress.com/article/india/india-others/nia-probe-shows-im-men-tech-savvy-used-proxy-servers-complex-code-to-chat/, accessed on 3 March 2017.

14　Jordan Robertson and Michael Riley, "Mysterious '08 Turkey Pipeline Blast Opened New Cyberwar", Bloomberg, 10 December 2014, available at http://www.bloomberg.com/news/articles/2014-12-10/mysterious-08-turkey- pipeline-blast-opened-new-cyberwar accessed on 3 March 2017.

15　Ibid.

16　Marc Goodman, *Future Crimes*, London: Transworld Books, Bantam Press, 2015, pp. 317–48.

17　J.M. Berger, "How ISIS Games Twitter", *The Atlantic*, 16 June 2014, available at http://www.theatlantic.com/international/archive/2014/06/isis-iraq-twitter-social-media-strategy/372856/ accessed on 3 March 2017.

18　Saikat Datta, "Why do More Indians Seem to be Joining Global Jihadi Outfits?", www.Scroll.in, 4 January 2016, available at https://scroll.in/article/801335/why-do-more-indians-seem-to-be-joining-global-jihadi-outfits, accessed on 3 March 2017.

19　See Rukmini Callimachi, "Not 'Lone Wolves' After All: How ISIS Guides World's Terror Plots from Afar", *The New York Times*, 4 February 2017, available at https://www.nytimes.com/2017/02/04/world/asia/isis-messaging-app-terror- plot.html. Callimachi's work in *The New York Times* on the ISIS has been the most expansive so far based on interviews of recruits arrested by security agencies, interrogation reports and online chat boards and official releases by its news agency *Amaq*.

20　See Saikat Datta, "Hunt on for Bengaluru Man Who Ran Influential IS Twitter Handle", *Hindustan Times*, 13 December 2014, available at http://www.hindustantimes.com/india/hunt-on-for-bengaluru-man-who-ran-is-twitter-handle/story-QHv3CzEbXHXOTlhlZBhyqO.html., accessed on 3 March 2017

21　For more see: McChrystal, Stanley A., Tantum Collins, David Silverman, and Chris Fussell. 2015. *Team of teams: New rules of engagement for a complex world*, New York: Penguin.

22　Ibid., p. 73.

23　For a more detailed account of the Sinjar raid, see Michael R. Gordon, Wesley S. Morgan, "The General's Gambit", 1 October 2012, Foreign Policy, available at https://foreignpolicy.com/2012/10/01/the-generals-gambit/, accessed on 3 March 2017.

11

Online Radicalisation and India

Sanjeev Singh

Terrorist groups in India have been using modern equipment and technology as force multipliers for sustaining their disruptive and violent activities. Depending on the specific requirement, state-of-the-art technology has been innovatively adapted and used by the terrorist groups in activities that range from capacity building to post-attack operations. This chapter attempts to examine and deal with different aspects of technology that have been used by the Islamist jihadi groups in India, as well as the threats posed by such groups that have been enabled with "network technologies". The chapter draws heavily from the Rand Corporation study report of 2007 on the use of network technology by terrorists.[1] The report helps provide some basic definitions and lists nine basic terrorist functions that depend significantly on the use of technology. The statements/ disclosures made during the personal interviews of arrested terrorists in India and case documents have also been used for outlining trends regarding the use of modern technology by terrorist groups.[2] This chapter will briefly analyse the salient features of a few terror attacks planned and executed by terrorist groups, such as Jaish-e-Mohammad (JeM), Lashkar-e-Taiba (LeT), Indian Mujahideen (IM), Jamaat-ul-Mujahideen Bangladesh (JMB), elements of Students Islamic Movement of India (SIMI) and the Islamic State of Iraq and Syria (ISIS), in order to see the extent of use of technology in planning and executing attacks.

From 2008 Mumbai Terror Attacks to 2016 Pathankot Airbase Attacks: The Technology Leap

In my opinion, the 2008 Mumbai terror attack presents an example where network technology and the latest equipment was used alongside military expertise in order to plan, prepare and execute the attack. In late 2005, senior leaders of the

LeT and elements of Pakistani intelligence agency took a decision to organise a simultaneous multi-target mass casualty attack in Mumbai on strategic locations by launching specially trained suicide attackers using the sea route. Two individuals were selected for establishing a base in Mumbai and engaging in tactical surveillance. One was an immigration agent of Canada (Tahavvur Hussain Rana) located in Chicago and the other was a United States (US) citizen of Pakistani origin (Dawood Gilani). In February 2006, Dawood Gilani changed his name to David Coleman Headley in the US and got a fresh US passport in order to hide his Pakistani origin and Islamic faith. Dawood, now David Headley, obtained a business visa to India by providing false information that he was required to be in Mumbai for running the business of Rana. After reaching Mumbai in September 2006, he used stolen identities for: hiring houses, staying in the hotels which were attacked, acquiring cell phone connections and using the services of an Internet cafe. Selection of specific targets was done by military tactical experts after a careful study and analysis of the surveillance videos and related information collected by David Headley during the course of his nine visits to India over a period of two years. Financial, tactical and communications support was provided by using online transfer of funds to buy services on fake or stolen identities. The services of a New Jersey-based Voice over Internet Protocol (VoIP) calling platform, Callphonex, were used for passing on instructions to the attackers during the attack process. Direct inward dialing numbers with Austrian code were used. Virtual numbers carrying the US country code were set up and the account was activated through an online transfer of money. Services of Western Union Money transfer were also used (for conspirators, planners, fund providers, persons who did reconnaissance, persons who trained, equipped, launched, monitored, guided and directed the attack , since they were all located at faraway places, few even in different continents). An attack of such magnitude could be organised because of the effective use of network technology with modern recording, communication and navigation devices.

The most striking feature of this attack was the tactical use of live television (TV) footage, with running commentary being shown on news channels, for guiding and directing the terrorists on the ground about what to do and what not to do. Experts manning the Mumbai attack control centre in Karachi had set up multiple TV sets and computers to watch the ongoing attack and guide the attackers based on their analysis of the combined inputs being seen on TV screens and live media coverage. This was done for the first time in the history of terrorism.

Eight years after the Mumbai attack, when the people of India were waiting for the first sunrise of 2016, terrorists of JeM launched a suicide attack inside the

Pathankot airbase. The terrorists were tactically guided during the entire attack process from a control centre in Pakistan. While the attack was still in progress, a 20-minute statement claiming responsibility for the attack was uploaded to a website owned by the Pakistan-based terrorist organisation, JeM. The statement put forth an emotionally compelling narrative aimed at sending the message that while pursuing jihad, even a small group could take on a mighty army. This idea tied in with the Islamist rationalisation of jihad which was defended with the understanding that since the attackers were on their way to defend their faith (shahada), they were receiving supernatural help in their endeavours. This logic was also extended to the afterlife and the belief that attackers would receive special rewards post death. The statement and associated coverage was widely circulated amongst the target population and it resonated with sympathisers over social media, increasing their recruitment numbers and aiding them in resource acquisition. Knowing that they would become heroes in Pakistan, the attackers indulged in wanton violence till death. While waiting to launch an attack, one of the attackers called his mother and repeatedly told her to record his speech saying that he had achieved something great for which he would be remembered as a hero.

According to the police reports of investigated suspects, at the stage of planning, the attack images of the campus of Pathankot airbase available on Google were minutely studied to identify the strengths and weaknesses of the perimeter security. Google map was used for finalising the route from international border to Pathankot airbase. The route map was fed into a Global Positioning System (GPS) device for navigation. Mobile phone was used for real-time communication.

The analysis of trends in the use of communication and navigational devices indicates a growing sophistication. In almost all the cases where terrorists were/ are launched from Pakistan, very high frequency (VHF) wireless sets were/are modified by trained electronic engineers for patching mobile phones with VHF sets. Wireless sets (ICOM IC-V82, made in Japan) were/are modified to enable and ensure mobile communications in places without mobile connectivity. The complementary applications were/are downloaded and installed on a smartphone. As a result, the phone established/establishes a connection with the modified wireless sets enabling smartphones to send and receive short message service (SMS) messages where there was/is no mobile phone coverage.

Indian Mujahideen: Using Technology to Enforce Organisational Structure

A group of terrorists, who later assumed the name "Indian Mujahideen" (IM), was responsible for carrying out at least 13 blasts and causing nearly 400 deaths and injuries to over 1,400 persons.[3] As per police investigations, this group was raised by Pakistani agencies to show that Indian nationals were involved in bomb blasts. Majority of the members of IM were taken to Pakistan by Pakistani agencies for training in the various skills required for terrorism, particularly bomb making and the use of weapons. All the senior leaders of IM, like Riaz, Iqbal, Afeef, Dr Shahnawaz, Bada Sajid, Sultan Armar, Mohsin Chowdhry and several others, were and are located in the safe houses of Pakistani agencies in Pakistan. Several others were taken to Pakistan after the Indian Police found evidence of their involvement in mass casualty attacks. Police investigation has found evidence of IM leaders, located in Pakistan, organising terror attacks in India.[4]

Disclosures made by the arrested members of the IM have shown the group's sophistication in the use of Web-based services in ensuring the maintenance of a hierarchical structure with a canonical command system. The senior leaders, located in the safe houses at Karachi, assigned multiple email IDs with dynamically coded passwords to each member for receiving/sending commands and feedback. These processes were also used for auxiliary operations, such as sending funds, and for planning and executing attacks. Furthermore, each of the members also had multiple email IDs that they would use alongside chat platforms and Web-based encryptions to send and receive messages. Riaz Bhatkal would regularly direct other members regarding which Web-based services were to be used and what procedures were to be followed. The members would strictly follow the communication protocol as recommended by the senior leaders. Leaving offline messages was also a mode used to ensure that message leaks/decryption risks were minimised.

It is interesting to see how the group adapted available technology when it came to propaganda. They sent emails, from a cybercafe, to news channels on 23 September 2007, claiming responsibility for blasts in the court premises of Varanasi, Lucknow and Faizabad. In July 2008, the group improved and stole the services of a private Wi-Fi account to send mails to groups of 30 recipients after the Ahmedabad serial blasts on 26 July 2008. Furthermore, two months after the above incident and just before the serial blasts of Delhi, emails were also sent out with video clippings of earlier blasts. Subsequent mails were sent in Portable Document Format (PDF) with attached video clips of the Delhi blasts. In September 2010, an Internet-enabled Tata Docomo mobile phone was used to send mails after the Jama Masjid attack using opera.com (a Norwegian browser) for claiming responsibility. In one of the mails, the terrorists wrote, "this is their third consecutive e-mail" and police experts have failed to "find out their technique of sending the Message of Death".

A careful study of the emails sent by IM claiming responsibility for bomb blasts show a high degree of expertise in various skills needed to develop text of the mails. This was made possible by integration of expertise of various individuals located at different places in downloading, patching and developing a final draft of mail. One can see a Pakistani design of linking the objectives of jihadist ideology with emotive issues specific to India.

Jamaat-ul-Mujahideen Bangladesh (JMB) Technological Innovation and Capacity

In October 2014, the JMB was involved in an accidental blast that took place on the second floor of a house in the Khagragarh locality of Burdhman, West Bengal. Locals tried to provide help to the victims, but the two young mothers, whose husbands were dead/injured as a result of the blast, would not let anyone enter. They locked the channel gate and kept threatening the people who were trying to help—even the police—stating that if anyone tried to enter, they would blow up the entire house. They were members of the JMB and were making grenades when the accidental blast took place. The JMB had established its training and bomb-making facilities in three districts of West Bengal which shared border with Bangladesh. It was an eye-opener for the police to see the sophisticated use of digital media, digital communication and computers in organising training programmes for the semi-literate Bengali-speaking individuals. All the members had a clear vision about their ultimate goal of jihad and understood the tasks that needed to be performed by them. Female terrorists were arrested in India for the first time, and they said that they were given inputs on suicide mission as well. The training video produced by JMB used a DSL camera and was edited using sophisticated software. They further innovated and transferred the audio video materials on pen drives and on the memory chips of mobile phones in order to increase the ease of distribution and use. Members of this group also procured cans of picric acid (which comes under the category of high explosive) by placing orders using the Internet.

After the Bodh Gaya serial blasts of 2013,[5] the public relations office of the Bihar government in Patna received an eight-page photocopy of a handwritten letter claiming responsibility for the attack. The issues raised in the letter repeated the narrative of a global jihad in the strain of the ISIS ideology and it was clear that the person who wrote the letter had a deep understanding of the jihadi Salafist Islamist ideology. A few months after these attacks, serial blasts took place at different places in Patna, especially targeting the Bharatiya Janata Party's (BJP) election rally. Hyder Ali was the leader of the group which carried out both the serial blasts. He was raised in a secular environment and had received a good education. He was pursuing his graduate studies in a college in Ranchi. He was exposed to jihadi ideology as a result of his personal contact with individuals associated with SIMI and subsequently, by seeing/reading materials available on the Internet. He decided to fight for the cause of jihad and planned the bombings at Bodh Gaya and Patna. He collected a few boys and turned them into jihadis by showing them online material. He also mastered the art of preparing improvised explosive devices (IEDs) by accessing *Inspire* magazine for directions and practising repeatedly. He and his associates would routinely watch videos preaching global jihad and the idea of attacking Buddhists came through online material. References to organising attacks in Bodh Gaya have been found in Web chats between masterminds Riaz Bhatkal and Yasin Bhatkal well before the Bodh Gaya attacks happened. The group had also planned to attack Shia Muslim shrines. This attack was the first of its kind in India, in which, from the stage of radicalisation to the stage of planning, the attackers used online materials.

The ISIS: Branding Global Jihad Online

The ISIS and its affiliates have mastered the art of using the combined power of social media, Internet-based services, twitter, modern recording devices and editing software for terrorist activities. The ISIS has been successful in running a very effective propaganda targeting vulnerable sections of population for recruitment and subsequent travel to Syria and Iraq. Indians have also been exposed to their ideology and a few Indians have travelled to the so-called caliphate after they were radicalised and recruited online. They were assisted by online entities in their travel plan. Analysis of use of Internet by them shows a growing sophistication. For example, in 2014, four individuals who travelled to Syria from Mumbai did not use any proxies or anonymisers for Internet access; they did not use secure operating systems for traffic or data forensics; they did not use additional encryption over and above what was provided by the service providers; and they used Google Play Store to download the applications used for operations. But two years later, in 2016, another set of ISIS recruiters used proxy/anonymisers, after working around the system. For instant messaging, they used ChatSecure, Telegram and Signal as private messaging platforms. The use of these services makes it extremely difficult for service providers to retrieve/provide plaintext email/attachment data. Additionally, because of the usage of such services, identifying service providers with Internet Protocol Detail Record (IPDR) data becomes almost impossible and login details provide misleading information.

The Threat Online: Challenges for India

It is clear from above-mentioned narration that terrorists have been proactive in adapting to emerging technologies for sustaining their activities. It will be useful to revisit those specific functions of terrorist attack cycle which have been greatly benefited by emerging technology and list the threats of use of technology by terrorists in India.

1. *Communication*: Major characteristic of new terrorism is its ultra-flexible networked and less hierarchical organisational structure, enabled by state-of-the-art technologies. Terrorist groups within these networks become very autonomous but are still connected through advanced communication and common objectives. In this manner, terrorist organisations can adjust more easily to various situations. Although members may communicate with their leaders, groups can operate independently.[6] Communication is central to the functioning of terrorist groups and therefore, emerging technologies in this field have been used by them. Terrorist groups have traditionally tried their level best to acquire and use such modes and devices of communication that are difficult to track/monitor, and also provide uninterruptible communication between individuals, location notwithstanding. Smartphones now have all the capabilities of a computer. They are used for emails, text messaging, VoIP, etc., by accessing Wi-Fi networks, Code Division Multiple Access (CDMA) cell phone networks and wired Internet. Police investigations have shown that Internet-enabled smartphones form the backbone of terrorist communication system. For example, terrorists of IM located in Pakistan were communicating regularly with their associates in India by using Web-based chat services. The easy availability of encryption software in hand-held devices greatly enhances the security of terrorist communication and thus poses a difficult challenge.

2. *Recruiting*: Recruiting is defined as the process and tools that an organization uses to *attract* and *indoctrinate* new members. In Pakistan, the terrorist groups have been openly using public channels, along with videos, pamphlets, Websites, sermons, friendly news media, religious schools and congregations, to attract and indoctrinate youngsters into carrying out attacks in India. This process will continue and more terrorists will be recruited in Pakistan for conducting terror attacks in India. However, the process of recruitment of Indians into terrorist ranks in India, so far, has been clandestine. The trend is using Web-based services for radicalisation/indoctrination after establishing personal contact. For

example, Yasin Bhatkal recruited several members for IM. He would look for intelligent young boys seeking answers to questions relating to jihad and get in touch with them. He would convince them to follow the Ahl-e-Hadith way of life by showing online sermons and videos. Once the boys were indoctrinated into the Ahl-e-Hadith way of living, it was not difficult for Yasin to bring a person into the fold of jihadi rank. Several arrested members of the IM stated that they were encouraged to watch material posted by Salafi groups on Internet-enabled mobile phones advocating extreme forms of Islamist ideology.

With the proliferation of smartphones, accessing jihadi websites has become easier. A significant number of vulnerable youths have been exposed to online material espousing the Islamist jihadi ideology through their phones, which has resulted in the increase in the amount of radicalisation. An example is worth quoting. On 7 March 2017, a bomb blast took place in a passenger train compartment near Ujjain in Madhya Pradesh. National Investigation Agency report says that the group involved in the bombing was self-radicalised by watching online videos and reading online jihadi material. Members of this group sent their oath of allegiance to the chief of the ISIS by using Internet and they decided to follow the ideology of leaderless jihad advocated by al-Suri. They read *Dabiq* and *Inspire* magazines by downloading them on Internet-enabled phones to learn to make bombs. One member of this group, Saifullah, was so motivated that he did not surrender and kept firing on police till he died. Efforts of the local police to use the father and brother of Saifullah to convince him to surrender did not work.

As per the study by the Rand Corporation, the potential use of virtual settings in the indoctrination process, by using massively multiplayer online games (MMOGs), offers another tool in the hands of terrorist groups to scout, identify and indoctrinate vulnerable individuals. There is also the threat of use of data on individuals collected and warehoused in electronic form for remote recruiting—a method often adopted by the ISIS and its affiliates. The Internet as a platform provides recruiters with a fairly large number of individuals who could be targeted by the appropriate use of network technology.

3. *Acquisition of Resources*: Acquiring resources (both weapons and funds) for conducting a terrorist attack in India has not been a difficult task for terrorists, given the support they receive from across the border. We have seen open appeals through websites and posters, with announcements for public contributions at different places in Pakistan exhorting people

to support terrorist activities in India. Terrorist groups in India have been getting funds from Pakistan through most modern methods of fund transfers. Over and above currently used methods, terror groups may also use modern advertising techniques (used in legitimate business) for sending tailored appeals directly to individuals who are likely to respond favourably. In terms of receiving funding for operations, online transactions and digitised fund transfers are also used.

4. *Training*: The massive and dynamic online library of audio-video training materials covering bomb making, handling of weapons, undercover operations, identity forging and ways to withstand police interrogation have all been used to train and control the emergent crop of extremists. There is threat of use of computer simulations and associated graphics for repeated practice/rehearsals as opposed to conducting practice missions in actual settings for planning terror attacks. These tools have the potential to greatly enhance the attacker's familiarisation with the selected targets of attack. Combined use of simulation and computer gaming can also be used for teaching a range of skills needed for making combat decisions (who to engage and who not to engage) and for improving leadership skills of the terrorists.

5. *Creating false identities, forgery and other deceptions*: The easy availability of hardware, such as highly capable scanners, computers and printers, and photo editing software has enhanced the capacity of terrorist groups to create authentic-looking forged documents and photo identity cards that can pass the cursory inspection performed by undertrained or hurried clerks/police officers. The Rand Corporation study has predicted that terrorists may develop the capacity to "determine the exact parameters of critical public or private identity documents (or devices as in the case of Radio Frequency Identification Documents (RFID) chips and smart cards)."[7]

6. *Attack operations*: As more functionalities are integrated into personal electronic devices, obviously clusters of technologies are most likely to play an increasingly important role in enabling terrorist operations. Cell phone sets also work as GPS devices, digital video recorders, digital cameras and personal memory devices. They can therefore be used in various stages of the operation to facilitate and ensure efficiency. The RFID tags and similar technology can also be easily used as trigger mechanism tags. Wireless devices that uniquely identify an individual (for example, Bluetooth-aware phones or Wi-Fi personal digital assistants [PDAs]) could also be used as triggering mechanisms to initiate attacks on specific people.

India, till date, has not seen many cases of suicide bombers. However, there may be an increase in the number of suicide bombing attacks in the future as emerging technologies, which can be adapted in remote detonation devices, can be used to turn an individual into a suicide bomber without his/her knowledge.

7. *Propaganda and persuasion*: Modern technology has tremendously increased the capacity of terrorist groups in this function of the terrorist attack cycle. Terrorists in India have used all available aspects of mass media for propaganda and persuasion, and are likely to continue with this trend. With the increasing reach of social media, there appears to be a clear shift towards decreasing dependence on news channels. The reason for this shift is because the terrorists have no control over what will be shown and what will not be shown.

[T]errorist groups are no longer dependent on few media outlets:

The Internet, in particular, allows terrorist groups or their supporters to have dedicated Web sites...and to post messages, videos...for direct consumption by the public, without any need to employ media organizations, which might mistranslate or misstate the message.[8]

The Digital Scenario in India: Trends and Forecasts

As per Department of Telecommunications, Government of India's report, there are 121.12 million wireless phone connections in India. Public sector share in terms of the number of total telephones is merely 10.32 per cent. The number of Internet subscribers is over 500 million. The number of subscribers accessing the Internet through wireless phones is 409.55 million (end of June 2017).[9] Industry figures put the number of smartphone users in India anywhere between 35–36 crores. As per Cisco's Visual Networking Index Complete Forecast, Internet users in India will be 829 million in 2021 and there will be two billion networked devices in India in 2021, up from 1.2 billion in 2016.[10] According to the chief executive officer of the company: "Mobile networks, devices and connections in India are not only getting smarter in their computing capabilities but are also evolving from lower-generation network connectivity (2G) to higher-generation network connectivity (3G, 3.5G, and 4G or LTE)". The forecast also says that "India will reach 84 billion internet video per minutes per month by 2021, which is 160,000 years of video per month, or about 32,000 video minutes every second." Digital transformation of this scale poses serious challenges to law enforcement authorities as this will multiply the capacity of the terrorists in all of their functions. Of particular interest is the fact that almost all smartphone users are individually part of online groups where they share pictures, videos and other materials. An individual becomes member of multiple groups and satisfies his need to remain connected. These groups espouse a shared narrative and reinforce the belief in that narrative, thus providing opportunity for online radicalisation, and guidance to become a Jihadi.

India has seen so many examples of use of online videos in propaganda, radicalisation, recruitment and bomb making. This situation poses bigger challenge in the prevailing scenario where Internet service providers are based outside India and act as limiting factor on the capacity of the agencies to interdict, monitor and investigate.

Based on the trends in the use of technology by terrorist groups in India, it can be said that following emerging technologies may be used by the terrorist group in varying degrees depending on their appropriateness:

1. virtual gaming technology for recruitment,
2. cyberpayment systems that can be used anonymously by any bearer for fund transfer,
3. massively multiplayer games for training and populace influence,
4. ubiquitous replication of high-quality forged documents,
5. impersonation of key persons in electronically mediated individual communication,
6. worldwide, secure, multimode mobile data and voice communication,
7. falsified video and audio avatars of leadership figures for public propaganda, and
8. electronic highjacking of news and media outlets.

With these technologies, the terrorist may gain a useful set of tools, previously available only to larger and more established organizations. These tools could allow terrorist organizations to work faster and control activities vis-à-vis recruitment, training and even planning without moving peole out of the country.

Conclusion

Admittedly, the above threats may appear futuristic, and terrorist groups attacking India may not use them anytime in the near future. But they still need to be examined and prepared against given the fact that trained technicians and engineers have also joined the jihadist ranks. Counter-terror agencies need to be well prepared to deal with such threats. There are a large number of reported cases where the circulation of doctored videos and the distortion of the statements of public figures have caused widespread public order disturbances. If the terrorists hijack a media channel and broadcast falsified videos of important authorities saying that a simultaneous chemical weapon attack has taken place, the implications would be very damaging.

Despite tremendous improvements in technology and their possible use by terrorists, trends suggest that operational trade crafts mastered by the terrorist groups will determine the extent of their use of available technology in attack operations. This is also because terrorists work under severe limitations and they cannot afford a failure. Additionally, it is also not easy to adapt emerging technologies to develop a disruptive device to perfection. Unfortunately, Pakistan-supported groups do not suffer from the above limitations and India will continue to face the threat of terror attacks by them.

Dynamites were one of the first advancements that aided and abetted terrorist activities by providing them violent means to fulfil their agendas. Similarly, digital communications, network technologies and a multitude of fusing devices have given additional capacity to the terrorist groups to sustain their activities despite being located at faraway places. Easy availability of highly potent drones poses a threat of remotely controlled attacks on individuals and facilities which are guarded. All these threats considered, what needs to be reiterated is that technology—particularly technology related to communication—is a double-edged weapon. On the one hand, it is a great enabler and force multiplier, but on the other, it also provides substantial scope/opportunity for security agencies to exploit the vulnerabilities of these terrorist groups. Therefore, the latter would have to use discretion in choosing appropriate technology and training their members in associated skill sets. Police agencies, meanwhile, must rally together to capitalise on loopholes while they exist, in order to put an end to the scourge of global terrorism.

NOTES

1   Bruce W. Don, David R. Frelinger, Scott Gerwehr, Eric Landree, Brian A. Jackson, "Network Technologies for Networked Terrorists Assessing the Value of Information and Communication Technologies to Modern Terrorist Organizations," Rand Corporation, 2007, available at https://www.rand.org/content/dam/rand/pubs/technical_reports/2007/RAND_TR454.pdf, accessed on 21 June 2018.

2   Editor's note: This paper draws heavily from the author's personal experience of dealing with the issue as a senior officer in the Indian Police Service. The officer has also served with the National Investigative agency, the nodal agency established to combat terror in India

3   For more see South Asia Terrorism Portal, available at https://www.satp.org/terrorist-profile/india-islamistotherconflicts/students-islamic-movement-of-india-or-indian-mujahideen, accessed on 23 June 2017.

4   See Note 2.

5   For more see "Bodh Gaya Blasts: NIA Says explosives set off to show solidarity with Rohingya", *NDTV*, October 2018, available at https://www.ndtv.com/india-news/bodh-gaya-blast-nia-says-explosive-set-off-in-bodh-gaya-to-show-solidarity-with-rohingya-1925100, accessed on 27 October 2018.

6   Rohan Gunaratna, Matusitz, Jonathan Andre (2013), "Terrorism and Communication: A Critical Introduction," Thousand Oaks: SAGE.

7   Rand Corporation, "Network Technologies for Networked Terrorists", n. 2.

8   The SITE (Search for International Terrorist Entities) Institute, quoted in ibid., p. 42.

9   For more see *Annual Report 2017-2018, Department of Telecommunication*, GoI, accessed on http://dot.gov.in/sites/default/files/Telecommunications%20Annual%20Report%202018 % 20 ENGLISH_0.pdf, accessed on 6 October 2018.

10 Cisco VNI Global Fixed and Mobile Internet Traffic Forecasts (2016–2022), available at https://www.cisco.com/c/en_in/solutions/service-provider/visual-networking-index-vni/index.html accessed on 6 October 2018.

12

Tackling Malicious Profiling Online
The Indian Experience

Manjula Sridhar

Introduction[1]

Sybil attacks are named after a fictional character with dissociative identity disorder. Sybil attacks are attacks against the reputation of online social networks through the proliferation of fake profiles using false identities. Fake profiles have become a persistent and growing menace in online social networks. As businesses and individuals embrace social networks, the line between the physical and online world is getting blurred. Hence, it is critical to detect, prevent and contain fake accounts in online communities. This chapter looks at the specific dangers caused by fake profiles and solutions that can be used to detect and prevent them.

Fake Accounts and the Problems Arising from Them

The root cause of fake accounts is the popularity of open systems such as Facebook, Twitter and LinkedIn. Identities have become porous, instant and temporary, leading to easy creation of fake profiles. There are a few types of fake accounts:

1. accounts created using fake identities;
2. accounts created using stolen identities; and
3. compromised accounts.

These can cause serious issues and break the trustworthiness of online communities by:

1. manipulating the reputations of businesses, individuals, entities, using paid fake accounts and fake voting, reviews;
2. adversely affecting the news and trends by spreading false information and spam; and

3. acting as an anonymous front for harassment and extortion.

Fake accounts are not limited to online social networks (OSNs) alone; they also affect all forms of online open identities, such as cryptocurrency wallets, email accounts and phone numbers.

Solution Spectrum

There are two ways to look at the problem:

1. Preventive approach that relies on making the signup process closed, linked to a robust real-life identity (Closed Systems).
2. Detection of fake profiles after the signup (Open Systems).

The first one is harder to implement as many business models depend on more and more people signing up. Ease of signup is therefore their number one priority. There is also the aspect of privacy that takes precedence over the detection of fake accounts. So, many open systems, such as Facebook, Twitter and LinkedIn, completely do away with any form of verification of identification.

The more pragmatic solution is to figure out methods of detecting and blocking fake accounts after the signup. Some networks rely on the wisdom of a crowd or the action of an aggrieved party aimed at flagging down the fake or problematic account. While this has had some success in cases of standalone fake accounts, it is less effective against clusters of fake accounts and automated Sybil attacks.

Another approach would be the use of a set of behavioural thumb rules that would determine who to let in and keep. Accounts can be monitored for: type and frequency of posts; nature of interactions; devices and Internet Protocol (IP) addresses used to login; time of activity; and other such parameters. For instance, a person who is a friend of a trusted person is also considered trustworthy. But as social spheres grow online and users begin adding people who are not part of their physical circles, this method becomes harder to manage and rely upon. Moreover, these solutions do not address the problems of constructed, stolen and compromised identities that are the root causes in the first place.

More evolved solutions that aim to solve the problem rely on the use of artificial intelligence (AI) to recognise fake account patterns. The standard procedure for an AI (machine learning)-based solution is as follows:

1. Collection of data with manually (or otherwise) tagged known fake accounts.

2. Training models used to learn the complex patterns and rules.
3. Automation to enforce the rules (see Figure 12.1).

Figure 12.1: Process of AI Application

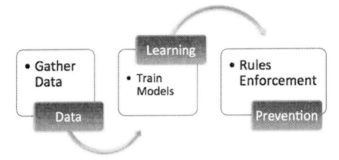

Source: Manjula Sridhar.

Machine Learning Classifiers

Training the machine to learn is one of the most critical points of any AI-based system. It requires a thorough understanding of the domain, the datasets and the interrelation of the datasets. Based on this, the right type of classifier is chosen and implemented. Some of the most commonly used classifiers in the context of fake profile detection are:

1. Naive Bayes classification;
2. Decision Tree classification;
3. Support Vector Machine; and
4. Logistic Regression.

These classifiers are mere starting points and in order to improve accuracy, it is better to try different classifiers, vary the parameters and compare the emergent matrices against known data.

So, in order to ensure maximum learning, an availability of known diverse data is essential for designing a detection and prevention system. In order to increase the accuracy, it is better to get the data in the context of targeted geography and demographics.

Indian Scenario and the Need for Collaboration

The virtual Indian scenario, much like its physical counterpart, is complex. Digital India has given unprecedented power to many people and the Internet is available in many remote areas, including sensitive areas. This makes it important for law enforcement to use the latest technologies to manage crime and terrorism. A cursory look at the Indian open data yielded the following.

Figure 12.2: Cybercrime Numbers in Each State

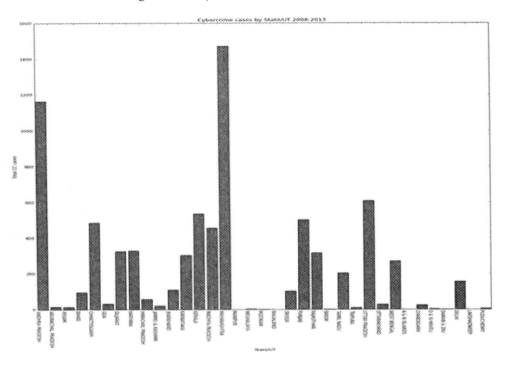

Source: Manjula Sridhar.

Figure 12.2 represents the number of reported cybercrime incidents in India plotted against each state. This provides some information, but there is nothing one can make out of it. In other words, there is no intelligence in this data.

However, if we map the data against the number of computer devices in each state (Figure 12.3), very important information emerges. In many states, the number of computers correlates with number of reported cybercrime incidents. However, few states, like Chhattisgarh, have disproportionate cybercrime numbers compared to the computing devices available. Does this mean those states have more cybercriminals? Perhaps. The next logical step would be to plot cybercrimes against the regular crimes and see if there is a correlation. However, it is clear that the number of parameters necessary to crunch to get real facts is quite high.

Figure 12.3: Plot of Cybercrime Incidences versus Computing Devices

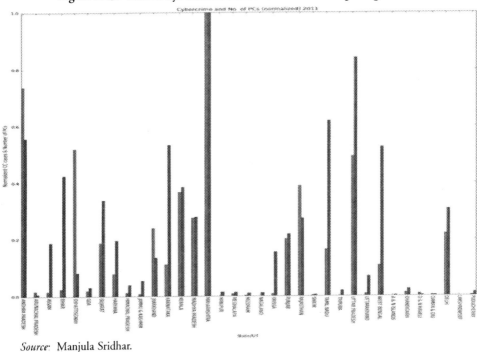

Source: Manjula Sridhar.

This is where advances in AI add immense value. They can process large amounts of data in relatively short spans of time to depict patterns that might escape the human eye due to limited processing capacities. However, in order for this to work out, it is essential to first gain access to relevant data. It is important that law enforcement officials in every country share this data with each other in order to build better monitoring and evaluative systems that can ensure a safer digital tomorrow.

NOTES

1   Editor's Note: Since Manjula is a practitioner in a field which is niche, she has recommended the following references for further information on the subject.

     1. "Detecting Clusters of Fake Accounts," available at http://theory.stanford.edu/~dfreeman/papers/clustering.pdf, accessed on 3 March 2017.

     2. "Detecting Anomalous social Behaviour," available at https://people.mpi-sws.org/~gummadi/papers/anomalous-socialbehavior.pdf, accessed on 3 March 2017.

     3. "Detecting Compromised Accounts on Social Networks," available at http://www.cs.ucsb.edu/~vigna/publications/2013_NDSS_compa.pdf, accessed on 3 March 2017.

     4. "Uncovering Large Group of Malicious Accounts," available at https://users.cs.duke.edu/~qiangcao/publications/synchrotrap.pdf, accessed on 3 March 2017.

     5. "Advagato Trust Metric," available at http://www.advogato.org/trust-metric.html, accessed on 3 March 2017.

SECTION FOUR

Regional Perspectives:
The West Asia Conundrum—
Unravelling Geopolitics and Global Response

Special Insight III
Countering Terrorism in the Maghreb
Implications for Global Security

Mustafa El Sagezli

This chapter is about Maghreb (Al-Arabi), or North Africa and the western part of the Arab world. The primary focus remains the issue of terrorism, radicalisation and violent extremism in the region. As a Libyan, the issue is personal and political for me as my country is a part of al-Maghreb, and therefore affected by the changes taking place in the region. This chapter will attempt to trace a brief history of the region in order to contextualise the conflict, and then proceed to examine the ways in which it has developed and can be countered. Maghreb is composed of Morocco, Mauritania, Algeria, Tunisia and Libya. It is in the north of Africa, close to Europe, Mediterranean and the Middle East. Arabic is spoken in most if not all the countries. There are some minorities that speak other languages as well, but on the whole Maghreb is in many ways homogeneous. Most of the people in the region are Sunni Muslims of Arab origin.

Homogenous in Culture, Diverse in Political Institutions

While the culture across the area is similar in many ways, the political institutions are extremely different. There are republics as well as constitutional kingdoms in the region. Morocco is an example of the latter. This situation has changed once again with the political turmoil that has occurred over the last few years. Libya and Tunisia were affected directly by the Arab Spring, while Algeria went through its bloody decade in the 1990s as it suffered from terrorism and struggled with counter-terrorism measures. So, there is some amount of diversity when it comes to the politics within the region. There is a certain level of diversity from an economic standpoint as well. While countries like Libya and Algeria rely on oil and gas for sustenance, others like Tunisia and Morocco depend more on tourism. As just mentioned, from a religious standpoint, the vast majority are Sunni

Muslims. This is the broad spread of the land as it exists currently. There are complicated opinions and varying viewpoints emerging, all of which need to be taken into account while debating the future of the region, particularly the voices emerging from the region who have a stake in how the future plays out. While military strategy and efficiency may dictate certain actions, on the whole my responses and principles differ on the whole while talking about terrorism as I approach this issue as a revolutionary who participated in the Libyan Revolution seeking freedom, seeking liberty, seeking democracy. Having lived the suffering of my people and empathised with the struggles of the youth in the last decade, my perspective is not about containment or an endgame solution, but more from a lived experience point of view. In order to do so, I would like to begin by concentrating on the root causes of terrorism, radicalisation and violent extremism.

Political Exclusion and Socio-economic Grievances

One of the root causes for radicalisation in Maghreb is political exclusion and injustice: political exclusion in terms of preventing people from participating in political decisions that affect their life, their future and the future of their kids. Most terrorist groups or terrorist organisations recruit their youth based on political grievances and the rhetoric of being oppressed. Extremist outfits reach out to their victims by informing them that they are oppressed and offering to provide socio-political power in exchange. Political exclusion and injustice is, therefore, a very crucial factor inciting violent extremism.

Another key issue is the problem of socio-economic grievances harboured by the residents. These usually manifest in the form of living inequalities. An example that can be seen is Libya, which is a very rich country when it comes to oil resources, gas resources and its location on the Mediterranean. But there have been times in the 1990s when doctors' salaries were less than 300 Libyan dinars, with an inflation rate of 3.8 dinars per dollar at the time. The wealth was distributed incredibly unequally across the populace and so, while the salary of a Libyan doctor was less than 100 dinar, the billions invested in Africa were controlled by a small part of the regime. Thus, socio-economic grievances and factors play a key role in fuelling radicalisation and extremism. The same problem exists in Algeria where not only is the wealth distributed unequally but there are also extremely high unemployment rates. The same situation holds true for Tunisia, Morocco and the rest of the region.

Ideology and Terrorism in the Maghreb

Certain key factors aiding the spread of extremism have been just been mentioned. However, there are some ideological issues as well that need to be examined in greater detail. These can be attributed to varying religious, ethnic and cultural backgrounds. There is a preponderance of Muslims in the region who follow the traditional Maliki school of thinking. It was traditionally a moderate school but the dispossessed and disenfranchised youth reinterpreted the Qu'ran to allow for and engender extremist activities within the region. This pattern spread across several countries in the region. Countries without universities and education systems were the ones that were affected more adversely in the bargain. A case for comparison can be Libya and Morocco. Morocco had traditional Islamic schools and universities and therefore, it was less affected by this extremist school of thought. Since young people had religious scholars whom they could refer to, they could clarify their queries and doubts without necessarily resorting to violent means. On the other hand, countries like Libya that lacked social welfare schemes, accessible public education institutions and scholars well versed in theosophical matters suffered from the spread of violent extremism. The only university in Libya was built in the time of King Idris and closed in the time of Gaddafi. There was no source of a fatwa. Even the position of the mufti was cancelled. Thus, there was no place for young people to take fatwa from, except from tapes and books that were coming from other countries and harboured/proliferated extremist views.

History plays an extremely important role in our thinking and the thinking of the youth today. It provides a means for people to orient themselves and their existence. Colonial history—that witnessed some of the most brutal acts of inhumanity—holds a particular space in the minds of the people today. Western Europe colonised the Maghreb region with France laying its claim over Morocco, Algeria and Tunisia, and Italy doing so in Libya. When colonised by France, Algeria became the country of one million martyrs. Similarly, 25 per cent of the Libyan population was killed by the Italians. These grievances are not too far back in history and are relatively fresh wounds on socio-political memory. The opposers of the regime were jihadis who were turned by a colonised society into martyrs and heroes. These role models thereby affected and influenced the youth and their understanding of what the purpose of a "successful life" is. History, and specifically a violent history, also has a key role to play in shaping the way events in the region occurred. Al-Mukhtar, for example, is a hero in Libya. Many of these heroes are jihadis or young people who turn into extremists and further propagate violent extremism. In order to deal with it, it is important to address the issue of colonial history and its remnant grievances in a way that helps to develop the country instead of breeding extremist groups.

Furthermore, the rising radicalism has also sparked a climate of fear within the region with legal enforcement authorities placing suspects under detention and internment. Such acts reinforce ideas of powerlessness and dispossession in their minds, thrusting them further into the arms of extremist retaliation. When young people aged 20 and below are arbitrarily placed in jails and holding cells for years at a time, their resentment grows and they further incite other people to revolt with them. The personal and political injustices coalesce and narratives are formed. This anger drives them to seek revenge against society as a whole, disregarding consequences and costs.

There are several groups spreading their message through the region, including Salafi-e-Jihadi-e (Salafi jihadism)—that mixes the Salafi thinking with the jihadi school of thought—the al-Qaeda, Daesh, etc. While Daesh has mostly been active over the last two years, it has since been beaten and almost eliminated from Surt, its stronghold in Libya. Aside from these key players, there are also certain domestically emergent terrorist groups that consist of tribal grievances, separatist agendas and criminals who engage in drug trafficking, weapons smuggling and so on.

Countering the Spread of Violent Extremism or Terrorism in al-Maghreb

The question that emerges, after laying the history and the context, is: what are the implications of the spread of violent extremism or terrorism in al-Maghreb? Given the increased globalisation and the rise of interconnected economies, such activities will impact not just the Maghreb region but the world. Al-Maghreb is no longer distinctly distanced from Europe, or the rest of the world. The travel from Libya to Italy is barely a few hours; people can go across on a boat. This increased connectivity poses several critical vulnerabilities as well. Malicious actors such as Boko Haram and other such groups could infiltrate the region as well. That is mostly how the network spreads and this includes the movement of groups across countries. Furthermore, recruitment and breeding are further issues that need to be considered as networks proliferate and replicate themselves. Some of the Daesh members that were found in Libya came from Europe. They were of North African origin, of Maghreb origin as well as European origin. This interconnectivity poses several risks, such as cross-border smuggling, drug trafficking, human trafficking, illegal immigration and so on. In a region facing such conflict and crisis, activities like these flourish and can spread across to other countries from Maghreb.

The idea of countering violent extremism is a complex one. Experts often use this idea to talk about how violent extremism/terrorism is a swamp. The metaphor implies that in order to get rid of the malaria that comes from the swamp, instead of shooting the mosquitoes, one must dry the swamp. This can be done by finding out the root causes of terrorism and fixing them. Only by engaging with the quagmire can solutions for the same be found. There is a need to gain ideological consensus first, disseminate it and then work towards providing havens for counter-radicalising the youth.

There are several ways in which this can be done. Outreach can be built through dialogues and socio-political inclusion. There is a need to include the youth in all the socio-political processes. Increasing participation is the best way to ensure compliance and cooperation. It is the best way to prevent the growth of extremism. Further steps that need to be taken include establishing democracy, encouraging freedom of speech and engaging in dialogue with these groups. It is necessary to sit with them, engage with their ideological systems, examine their religious beliefs and attempt to begin a dialogue on religious moderation. Historical precedence can be found in the way Britain treated the Irish Republican Army (IRA). The IRA was a terrorist group that used to bomb London and other cities in England, but the British authorities engaged in dialogue with them in order to determine the cause for their violence, which helped them devise a solution together. There is a severe need for demobilisation, disarmament and reintegration, or DDR for short. A hypothetical case for this can be made in Libya. There is a problem with the spread of arms after the revolution and an increase in the militia spreading those weapons across the country. These menaces can either be combated and opposed through force or reintegrated into society by providing them with socio-economic alternatives to weapons smuggling. Reintegration and demobilisation would work to a great extent to help disarm the affected people, and the ensuing social stability would provide opportunities and resources for rebuilding the security sector.

Another key solution is security sector reforms, aimed at creating an environment stable enough to allow for interventions. Several experts have recommended conducting security interventions through military, intelligence, police and so on. The problem with such measures is that countries cannot intervene with security unless there are adequate security institutions that are accepted by the people and that the people abide by the law. If groups are already radicalised, they will not accept the mandates of overseeing institutions and will instead seek to disrupt them. Furthermore, those who have faced injustice at the hands of such institutions would be even less inclined to accept an arbitrary power body that is unjust, tortures people and kills them unlawfully instead of enforcing the law. Engaging in committed security sector reform is therefore a very important solution in countering and combating violent extremism. This is particularly true in Maghreb Al-Arabi because as previous experience demonstrates, there are certain key issues in the security sectors that need to be addressed. Problems involved are: the lack of professionality in the security section sector; an avoidance of the law; and the disregard for human rights. These are all lived issues that need to be tackled at structural levels before people have faith in the system again.

Conclusion

After examining the social, historical and economic drivers that move people towards terrorism, the various ways it can be countered and the complexities of engaging with such an ideologically complex structure, I would like to end by providing a current regional scan and examining the ways in which politics in the region has manifested in the recent past. Morocco has been more successful than other countries in combating extremism and countering terrorism. When the Arab Spring started in 2011, the first thing the king did was to discuss constitutional reforms with his people in order to give them a more empowered voice. Morocco also instituted a committee, called the Reconciliation Committee, where the authorities sat with political prisoners, provided them with compensation, gave them rights and tried to rehabilitate them back into society. They engaged in a dialogue and in a manner that was not a determination of guilt but an acceptance of failure on the part of the state.

An example that I would like to cite here is that of a very famous Jihad-al-Salafi cleric named Fazazi. The King of Morocco once attended a Friday prayer where Fazazi was the preacher but instead of condemning him, they entered into dialogue with him and his group. It was decided that reintegrating these people into society would be beneficial for Morocco, Islam and the people. It is only in the face of such committed acceptance that any of these problems can be solved.

In conclusion, I would like to state that "understanding" the root causes of radicalisation and violent extremism leading to terrorism, according to historical, cultural and socio-economic contexts of the Maghreb, is the first step in combating terrorism. Before fixing the problem, there is a need to understand and work on the background and the cause.

Short and long-term causes are different and can manifest in varying ways/ have different effects. It is essential to develop a holistic understanding of the same in order to develop sustainable solutions to the phenomena of terrorism. While one might not be able to combat terrorism, it might be possible to control the side effects, and eventually cut it off, by removing the socio-political reasons for its existence and proliferation.

Developing comprehensive and holistic institutional and cultural reforms that include the state, society, religion, religious thought and the individual can provide lasting solutions. Post the Arab Spring, Maghreb has the historical opportunity to overcome many of its challenges by creating a renaissance based on freedom, democracy and socio-economic development.

13

A Brief Survey of Total Strategic Failure
NATO in West Asia

Frank Ledwidge[1]

In 2006, Tony Blair said that "the future of world security [would] be decided in the Afghan desert." A decade later, such declarations ring hollow. At all levels, from the grand strategic to the tactical, the North Atlantic Treaty Organization's (NATO) approach to what was once called the "war on terror" in West Asia has resulted in a complete failure.

To begin, I would like to go back to 1912—not the deserts of southern Iraq where I served as a military intelligence officer or the "green zone of Helmand" where I worked as a part of the United Kingdom (UK) civilian mission—to the North Atlantic. The greatest ship, and in fact the largest man-made object at the time, *Titanic*, sank with the loss of 1,500 lives, poor and rich. Until recently, the cause was ascribed only to the fact that the ship struck an iceberg. It did, but there was every expectation that it would survive the strike. The reason that it did not was because a fire had been burning in the coal stores, which weakened the ship's structure so much that when the collision with the iceberg occurred, it could not bear the impact. We now know that the existence of that fire was covered up both before and after the sinking for commercial reasons.

In other words, it was a deep man-made flaw that compromised the ship and not an act of god or a terrible accident that was beyond human interference. When an ignorant and arrogant West was struck by insurgencies in the countries they invaded in Western Asia, it was seen in a similar way to the *Titanic*, that is, it was something that happened to us, not something that we had caused.

The West began a series of interventions in 2001 in Afghanistan. The United States (US) had been hit, and someone was going to get invaded. The attackers of 9/11 were mostly Saudi and all were Arab. They had planned the operation in

Germany and the US, and trained for it in the US itself. However, it was Afghanistan, where some training had been done and where, in fairness, the al-Qaeda was based, that was chosen for invasion and occupation. All went reasonably well until 2003. Then, on the specious pretext of weapons of mass destruction (WMDs), Iraq was made the next target. It did not take long before the inherent flaw in the logic of this "intervention"—you might call it aggression or invasion—became brutally apparent. It took less than a year before a serious insurgency erupted. The fact that the neighbouring countries were heavily involved in fermenting this insurgency, and supporting it in one way or another, is often used as an excuse. Yet one might reflect that one takes a problem as one finds it. If I set fire to a house and send in firefighters to put out the fire knowing that the house is filled with gasoline, I should hardly be surprised if the house explodes, taking the firefighters with it.

And then, of course, there is the perennial problem of all occupiers and invaders. As Robert Pape put it so pithily, "It's the occupation, stupid." Lawrence of Arabia made a similar point in his "27 Articles": "The foreigner and Christian is not a popular person in Arabia. However friendly and informal the treatment of yourself may be, remember your foundations are very sandy ones."

The case, however, was not hopeless and the question that must be asked is: could it have been salvaged? The answer is "Yes", if proper attention had been paid to the rather basic principle laid down by Clausewitz that war is a political act. The response was at almost all costs to double down with a military response. The "surge" of 2007–08 as it was called, which effectively comprised a reinforcement of the US force by several brigades, was said to have "opened up space" for a political solution. Sadly, the political solution arrived at by the Iraqi government was to conduct a sectarian clear-out, led by the leadership of the day, which resulted in further disenfranchising the Sunni minority. The results of those actions can still be seen today. The "surge" was accompanied by a ferocious "special forces" campaign of targeted killing and capture.

At the time, the British were embroiled in a disaster of their own making, well stoked by Iranian-backed militias in southern Iraq. Eventually, they cut and ran from Basra as they neither has the capability nor the will to hold that great city. The US had some of both, but not enough of either to hold Iraq together in the absence of a realistic regional strategy and they followed suit in 2011.

In the UK, the Iraq disaster was examined in some detail and with a good deal of honesty and integrity unusual for British inquiries, which are commonly set up to achieve certain predetermined results. Sir John Chilcot, who led—what by British standards was—an open and fair inquiry into the serious governmental failings around the Iraq War, was clear that criticism was not simply ex post facto rationalisation. He demonstrated that warnings had been evident, authoritative and plentiful prior to the war. They were ignored by a largely ignorant political and military elite who were set on their course of action regardless of the advice being given.

I now turn back to Afghanistan, which I left in 2003, and examine the landscape in a little more detail. At a strategic level, exactly the same features are to be seen. After the invasion, a puppet government was set up. It was almost what post-modernists might call a "simulacrum" of a government. It had all the accoutrements of a democratic state—elections, constitution and the rest—but none of the substance. It was, in fact, what several people have called, a vertically-integrated organised crime structure which functioned and continues to function exactly as it was intended to do: as a means of extracting money from outside donors and the people of Afghanistan itself. Was there an alternative? There certainly was. Further, that alternative—a system founded and built upon how Afghanistan actually worked rather than what the West *wanted it too look like*— was available. It was hijacked by criminal warlord interests, once again backed by a neighbouring power.

I do not propose to dwell on the details or what might have happened. The facts remain the same and history cannot be changed. As in Iraq, a political problem was seen to have an entirely military solution. The military campaign, which essentially began in 2007, was primarily undertaken due to acute confirmation bias. This serves as evidence that strategic failure was constantly available and apparent. It was totally ignored in favour of a constant stream of fictional "good news" which was proliferated at all levels.

By way of an example, friends of mine leading infantry companies found that their reports of serious problems were being watered down at every succeeding higher level, so that by the time they got to higher headquarters—brigade or divisional levels—"progress is being made, obstacles remain" became common parlance. In the British case, there was of course the idea that our colonial heritage in some way equipped us uniquely well for the supposed art of "counter-insurgency", an idea that soon proved misguided, unfounded and entirely misconceived. What some of the British saw as the "Great Game" was seen in a very different light by the southern Pashtun people, who watched, for a fourth time, as British soldiers marched uninvited into their provinces once again.

As in Iraq, there was a "surge", led by the same leaders, with even more deleterious results. Once the classical counter-insurgency rhetoric of the hearts and minds had floundered upon the rocks of Afghan reality, the British and the

US defaulted to so-called "kill–capture" missions by special forces; and this idea was inherited from the Iraqi experience. Once again, it had not sensibly been thought out, and the approach was therefore tremendously counter-productive. The NATO special forces acted unwittingly as "useful idiots" in local power struggles, of which many UK/US officers had not the slightest awareness. This was termed a "strategy", rather than the last-resort tactic that it actually was, and it had the entirely predictable result of further dislocating an already chaotic political environment, especially in the extremely volatile southern region of the country.

The approach taken in Afghanistan may be seen as an exemplar for the West's efforts in Western Asia as a whole. Bereft of historical or political awareness and beguiled by an internal narrative of proficiency in counter-insurgency, the US and particularly the UK entered an area where they had little to no understanding. They elected to fight a military campaign against a political problem. In so doing, they failed both to engage regional powers constructively and to set a sensible and achievable political strategy, which for success would have required the acceptance of certain realities.

All said and done, at the end of the day, war is a political act. The failure to appreciate this has led us to where we are now. The NATO is now in the sixteenth year of its war in Afghanistan, with no signs of any improvement. The only solution offered by the US, and to a far lesser extent by the Western advisors for whom the concept of self-deception seems entirely alien, is to deploy more troops. Presumably, the 30,000 requested for a few months will do better than the 150,000 Western troops present for a decade. Given that it is the presence of Western troops that is a primary cause of the war, there may be a perverse logic in that! The danger, of course, is that this new request is merely a precursor to another, larger, doomed deployment.

Let us return to the point with which this chapter began. Ploughing on with limited understanding of what lurks ahead is one thing, but doing so knowing that there is a fundamental problem with the whole, a fire so to speak in the heart of the vessel, is simply untenable. However, NATO and specifically the US are doing precisely that.

At the operational and tactical level, there is an awareness that reinforcing failure is a poor option. I hesitate to privilege experience in this or any context, since experience is often a false friend, with perspectives being necessarily narrow. However, it is certainly indicative that at and below the rank of Lieutenant Colonel—those who have some familiarity with matters "on the ground"—there is full awareness of this. One US Marine officer, writing recently in the *Marine*

Corps Gazette, echoes the views of what I believe is a majority of thinking Western military officers:[2]

> It is time that we, as professional military officers, accept the fact that we have lost the wars in Iraq and Afghanistan. Objective analysis of the US military's effectiveness in these wars can only conclude that we were unable to translate tactical success into operational or strategic success.

NOTES

1   Editor's Note: Frank Ledwige's presentation at the Asian Security Conference 2017 was formulated as more of an opinion from a former NATO officer's perspective having served in West Asia. Since the author speaks from experience and as an published expert on the subject academic references have not been provided in this chapter.

2   Thomas E. Ricks, "A powerful attack on the Marine Corps leadership—by a serving Marine captain," Foreign Policy, 7 February, 2017, available at https://foreignpolicy.com/2017/02/07/a-powerful-attack-on-the-marine-corps-leadership-by-a-serving-marine-captain/ accessed on 17 February, 2017.

14

What After Counter Insurgency?
Raiding in Zones of Turmoil*

Eitan Shamir

The Challenge Posed by Ungoverned Territories

Since the end of the Cold War, the international system has been increasingly divided between zones of peace and zones of turmoil.[1] This dichotomy has witnessed a tremendous growth of failed states[2] and ungoverned regions in which terror groups, guerrillas and criminal bands (at times a combination of all three) operate freely. The United Nations (UN) Fragile States Index (formerly the Failed States Index) now includes several countries, such as Afghanistan, Iraq, Libya, Nigeria, Pakistan, Somalia, Syria and Yemen, all of which serve as hubs for transnational terror and crime. Even if the security risks posed by these regions are not constant in terms of intensity, failed states nevertheless generate practices that destabilise social functioning, such as terrorism, weapons proliferation, crime, energy insecurity and regional instability, all of which cumulatively endanger international security.[3]

For a while the United States (US), with support from its allies, was engaged in occupying and state-building effort in two states, Afghanistan and Iraq. The aim of the exercise was to bring about stability, prosperity and even democracy. These efforts have failed to a large degree, and culminated in the US and its allies realising that foreign interventions under similar circumstances—despite the committed provision of manpower and resources—are often ineffective. As a result, the US and its allies have lost their appetite for long-term occupation,[4]

---

*Parts of this chapter were published in Efraim Inbar and Eitan Shamir, "What after Counterinsurgency? Raiding in Zones of Turmoil", *International Affairs*, Vol. 92, No. 6, 2016, pp. 1427–41.

leaving large tracts of land to determine their own fates. However, these areas, as indicated earlier, continue to pose threats to civilised society.

In the absence of a viable political solution to controlling and negotiating these ungoverned areas, this chapter argues that the military approach must be tailored in a way where it is used as a rebuilding mechanism and not just a monitoring mechanism. There is no quick solution to the problem and the civilised world must recognise that it is up against a long struggle. The strategy that needs to be followed would have to be one of patient attrition with repetitive raiding as a main component. It can be complemented by economic and diplomatic measures, but these measures by themselves can never hope to achieve anything other than limited effectiveness.

Surrounded by Ungoverned Areas

Israel, for that matter, is an excellent case in point. In the last two decades, following the changes in regional circumstances, Israel is surrounded by ungoverned areas. For example, since the 1990s, large areas of Lebanon have been under the de facto control of the Hezbollah—a radical and well-armed Shiite organisation supported by Iran. The Syrian civil war has led to the country's disintegration and consequently, Syria's border with Israel in the Golan Heights is being controlled by groups such as the al-Qaeda affiliate Jabhat Fateh al-Sham (formerly Al-Nusra Front) and Hezbollah. Israel's border in the east with Jordan is stable; however, Hamas continues to challenge the Palestinian authority by conducting terror attacks against Israel. Furthermore, south of Israel, despite Egypt's efforts, the Sinai Peninsula has become a safe haven for groups affiliated with the Islamic State of Iraq and Syria (ISIS), mostly aimed at Egyptian targets. Nevertheless, on occasion, these malicious elements spread and attempt to mount an attack across the border into Israel. In the south-west, since the Israeli disengagement from the Gaza Strip, the radical Islamist Hamas movement has taken over and continues to repeatedly provoke Israel. To sum up, excluding the border with Jordan, Israel's borders are either fully or partially controlled by non-state radical groups.

In July and August 2014, Israel fought Hamas in Gaza for the third time since its disengagement from the Gaza Strip.[5] Like the previous operations, its modest goal was to restore calm along its border and to end its limited military operation with a "weakened Hamas". Once again, the Israeli government "mowed the grass" in Gaza,[6] refraining from removing Hamas' grip on Gaza and refusing to give in to populist demands in Israel to reconquer the Strip, which it unilaterally left in 2005. It implemented a patient raiding strategy, primarily from the air, to coerce Hamas into accepting the Egyptian-sponsored ceasefire. It used ground troops only for a limited incursion, to destroy the attack tunnels dug by Hamas to send terrorists into Israel. While some point out that the need for repeated operations in Gaza represents a failure of Israel's policy, it is in fact congruent with Israel's notion of "cumulative deterrence".[7]

The relatively calm border that has been maintained with Gaza since the August 2014 ceasefire should be seen as an achievement in such a turbulent region. In the twenty-first century, Israel has no intention of ending the conflict by military means; it realises that radical Islamist elements cannot be vanquished by superiority on the battlefield. Unlike the Americans and their allies in Iraq and Afghanistan, Israel has refrained from attempting to win the hearts and minds of Arab insurgents. The political, cultural and religious gaps between Jews and Arabs are simply too wide to allow for a strategy aimed at ending the conflict by persuading the opponents that peaceful coexistence is preferable.

Despite the thirst for regional acceptance, Israel understands that it will be impossible to overcome the hostility and suspicions held by Arabs against Jews. This perspective has since been reinforced by the failure of the Oslo peace process with the Palestinians. The process was never followed through and this mistrust became apparent with the outbreak of the hostilities in 2000. Israel shied away from adopting a population-centric approach when it ruled over Arabs in the West Bank, Gaza and southern Lebanon. In essence, it viewed its military presence as a temporary expedient that needed to be continued until a political settlement became available.[8] Moreover, Israel, with very few exceptions, did not entertain the illusion that it could generate sympathy among the occupied Arab population. Even so, this did not prevent it from developing a carrot-and-stick system for minimising violent opposition and for fostering pragmatic cooperation with the local leadership.[9]

Following its bitter experiences in Lebanon, the West Bank and Gaza, Israel has become fully aware of the limited degree of control it can exercise over hostile populations. Therefore, since then, Israel has pursued a policy of disengagement from the territories inhabited by such populations. The Oslo peace process with the Palestinians was fuelled by the desire to depart from territories populated by Arabs. In May 2000, Israel withdrew unilaterally from southern Lebanon and two years later, it built a security barrier in the West Bank, signalling its disengagement from the main Palestinian population centres and marking a potential future border. In August 2005, it withdrew its civil and military presence from Gaza. However, it maintains a thin military presence in the areas that can be considered critical for its security—such as the West Bank. Given the security paradigms and the geopolitical nature of the region, Israel chooses to maintain a thin military presence, while avoiding the burden associated with a civilian administration. This approach maintains a separation between Israel's mainland and the hostile populations that lie beyond its border.

The Palestinians and Hezbollah in Lebanon are not the only sources of concern for Israel. Israel has also made preparations to cope with the chaotic situation existing along its northern borders as result of the civil war in Syria. Similarly, there may also be a change in the Hezbollah's strategic calculus despite the fact that they have thus far refrained from attacking Israel. In fact, as mentioned earlier, the only Israeli border that is under full control of the state is the one with Jordan. Israel fears the destabilisation of Jordan, with which it has its longest border and which is closest to its heartland (the Jerusalem–Tel Aviv–Haifa triangle). As noted, the Sinai Peninsula, beyond Israel's border with Egypt, has also become a safe haven for radical groups. Israel hopes that Egypt's President Al-Sisi's determination to change this situation will bear fruit.

Israel's Strategic and Military Response

Israel's use of force is designed to strike effectively in a short space of time, with no intention of capturing territory for strategic gain. The military activity designed and carried out as a large raid, with the aim of weakening the opponent, reduces the actual threat and buys important time with a relatively modest investment. A final political settlement is not expected.

Israel's approach for using force vis-à-vis this reality is often termed as "mowing the grass".[10] The new term reflects the assumption that Israel finds itself in a prolonged intractable conflict with extremely hostile non-state entities. The asymmetry in the relation makes it qualitatively different from an inter-state conflict. The use of force is therefore not intended to attain impossible political goals, but rather to debilitate the capabilities of the enemy attempting to harm Israel. Given the difficulties in affecting the behaviour and beliefs of radical ideological non-state actors, Israel's use of force can only achieve temporary deterrence. Therefore, Israel has adopted a patient military strategy of attrition designed primarily at destroying enemy capabilities. Only after absorbing a series of attacks and showing much restraint in its offensive actions does Israel act forcefully to destroy the capabilities of its foes, hoping that occasional large-scale operations will also have a temporary deterrent effect thereby creating periods of quiet along its borders. "Mowing the grass", in other words, is repetitive raiding.

In his study of the evolution of the art of war in Europe from the period of the Greeks to the twentieth century, historian Archer Jones designated all strategies as being either "persistent", if aimed at capturing and/or holding onto territory, or "raiding", if the occupation of land was transient.[11] A strategy of raiding, then, represents no intention to control land or population for any length of time. This approach stands in contrast to the counter-insurgency operations that call for seizing control of territories and then focus on gaining the support of the civilian population ("winning hearts and minds") in order to deprive the insurgents of their main source of support.[12]

In such a situation, where diplomatic and/or economic leverage hardly exists, raids are last-resort military measures aimed at degrading enemies' abilities to create havoc. Moreover, such raiding activities exhibit very limited political goals, owing to the understanding that ambitious political objectives are not attainable. Raiding also entails patience insofar as it represents an attempt to weaken adversaries over time.[13]

Israel has had a long history of using raids to deter its opponents. In the 1950s, Israel raided Egypt and Jordan in response to border infiltrations by irregular forces sponsored by those states.[14] These raids were relatively small, and were aimed at the military and government installations of the host states in order to put pressure on their respective governments. In the 1960s and 1970s, Israel conducted raids against the Palestine Liberation Organization (PLO) in Jordan and Lebanon.[15] Most of these raids were short and limited operations. In contrast, contemporary raids in Gaza and Lebanon are much larger both in terms of scope and duration. These raids are designed to degrade the enemy's capabilities sufficiently and deter them from renewing hostilities for as long as possible. These should not be seen as isolated events but rather as episodes in a protracted, long-term conflict. The 2006 campaign in Lebanon deterred Hezbollah from further provocations, while three big raiding operations (in 2008, 2012 and 2014) that took place in Gaza brought temporary quiet.

The Israel Defense Forces (IDF) is currently using raiding as more than just a small-scale operation involving a handful of special operations units. The operation could also cover larger conventional forces invading an area and possibly conducting operations for a period of weeks or even months. Should the IDF consider it, the raid could be defined as a strategic raid, through which a strategic impact could be produced or intended.

It should be mentioned here that limited political gains warrant only limited investment in military action. It is politically difficult to sustain large-scale operations that demand much blood and treasure when the benefits reaped are no more than modest. This dictates the limited military nature of the raids, which is tremendously attractive in terms of domestic politics. Raids carry limited risks, and reduce the potential for opposition at home. Moreover, they are relatively inexpensive as there is no need to commit large forces, resort to reserve formations or conduct large-scale recruitment. The limited character of such operations, in terms of extent, costs, risks and time, makes it easier to establish domestic legitimacy and avoid international criticism.

Raids are different from military interventions that are aimed at assisting a friendly government in distress. In the latter situation, the intervention is in support of a clear central authority. The French intervention in Mali (January 2012) is such an example.[16] In contrast, strategic but limited incursions or raids are employed when there is a lack of a legitimate state authority.

One important implication of this development is the refinement of the meaning of victory, which is not a military concept but a political one. Victory cannot always be measured in concrete terms. The military can measure the destruction inflicted and can tell when an opponent is defeated on the battlefield. However, other variables pertaining to the grand strategy and the politics of the state all cumulatively affect victory. Additionally, the outcome of a conflict can often be assessed only in retrospect. Such an example is the 2006 Lebanon War outcomes, which did not look promising from Israel's point of view initially, but its current evaluation is more positive.[17]

To call a war victorious usually implies acquisition of territory, control over natural resources, as well as political and economic subjugation of the defeated entity. Earlier, inter-state conflict was usually characterised by a "persistent" strategy and victory was often measured by the ability of the victorious power to bring about change in the status quo. This was true of the ancient empires of the Middle East in Greek and Roman times as well as for the Normans and Crusaders in the Middle Ages, and from the Napoleonic wars of the early nineteenth century to the two World Wars of the twentieth. Victory meant that one side could dictate the peace terms in its favour.

This definition is not valid in today's prolonged conflicts that are designed to either preserve status quo or minimise threats to the existing order. Furthermore, today's conflicts are not aimed at the total defeat of the opposing military force or control of its land, despite the offensive nature of the operations. In these types of conflict, there are no formal or ceremonial acts of surrender, no victory pictures and no imposition of peace terms. Victory within this framework is more elusive. In the absence of a clear victory, it is difficult to sustain legitimacy and support for military action. Therefore, military commanders and politicians have to find ways to "market" their victories at home.[18]

In conclusion, strategies like "mowing the grass"—short incursions and raiding such as the one that Israel's employs—are politically unambitious and limited in time and scope. Furthermore, they also serve as a containment policy through which borders can be secured. There is no attempt to attain a political agreement nor is there any attempt to terminate the conflict by annihilation or surrender. In overall cost–benefit terms, raids offer many advantages in return for a relatively modest investment. By employing a kinetic force over a short time, the state is able to destroy significant elements of the opposition's military capabilities. Also, determination in carrying out the attack instils fear and creates a deterrent effect, at least for a short time.

The military aspect of raiding, like its strategic dimension, is also limited. In contemporary conflicts, when there is a need for ground forces in addition to an aerial offensive, it involves limited deployment of forces for a limited period. These raids are also light on logistics due to the relatively short time span of the operation.[19] In the three consecutive operations in Gaza (2008, 2012, 2014), Israel has employed only a fraction of its total force. In the 2012 operation (Pillar of Defense), the ground forces were deployed on the border, but only the air force and standoff fire were eventually engaged.

Deterrence by denial is achieved by crippling the offensive capabilities of the challenger and disrupting status quo in ungoverned areas. Deterrence by punishment is usually achieved by exacting a high cost when destroying high-value targets. Non-state actors, by definition, offer a limited number of such targets; however, such an organisation's leadership is vulnerable to targeted killings. Targeted killing is not "a silver bullet" solution and its utility has been debated. Yet it is quite clear that under certain conditions, decapitation of the leadership could cripple a terror organisation, at least for a while.[20]

A precondition for a successful raid is high-quality intelligence. Without such intelligence, the chances of hitting the high-value targets of an elusive enemy are small. In the absence of reliable intelligence, the military operations might become what analysts call a "pounding dusk operation", that is, one in which technologically advanced and expensive weapons are launched and create an impressive effect in the media, but inflict little damage on the opponent.[21] Israeli intelligence has therefore developed expertise in penetrating radical organisations and acquiring accurate intelligence of the leaders' locations, plans of attack, location of weapons cache, etc. Without such intelligence, the operation could fail and become futile.

Another condition for successful raiding is the ability to escalate the use of force against non-state groups, particularly when resistance becomes stiff. The potential for inflicting greater pain is important as it puts a pause on the opponent's calculus. Escalation dominance is therefore a key requirement.[22] If the opponent considers retaliating, the state's ability to escalate might persuade him otherwise.

Historically, strategic land raids were based on mobile forces supported by fire capabilities. Since the advent of air power, however, a strategic strike can be executed from the air as well. However, employing ground forces could dramatically enhance the effectiveness of the expedition, as it signals determination and willingness to take greater risks. "Boots on the ground" facilitate the collection of real-time intelligence, exposing hideouts and leaders' whereabouts. The presence of ground forces, even for a limited time, could be more disruptive and destructive to the non-state actor than air strikes, despite the latter's state-of-the-art technology.

Implementing a raiding strategy requires military institutions to adapt their force structures. As the scope of military action varies, the military needs to be versatile and capable of conducting a variety of strategic raids, from large-scale ground operations, involving tanks, artillery and air support, to pinpointed counter-terrorism operations that rely mainly on the use of drones, precision air strikes and/or special operations forces.[23] While most advanced militaries have perfected their ability to carry out surgical strikes and commando raids, there is nevertheless a need for a similar reorganisation of the conventional forces. There is a need to establish new force structures that would enable them to carry out bigger and longer raids. Force design must conform to the needs of raiding operations, that is, of expeditionary and "in and out" missions.

The IDF in 2015 published a document, signed by the IDF Chief of Staff, offering an introspective glance.[24] One should bear in mind, when analysing this document, that it is the shorter, unclassified version of a comprehensive document that was designed as a conceptual framework for a new IDF five-year plan.[25]

The document elaborates several issues, but what is important for this chapter is that it explicitly states the fact that in the face of current and foreseeable threats, the IDF must maintain an effective force capability. The stated tasks of the IDF forces, specifically the ground forces, are:

1. Defending against small-scale or large-scale attacks into Israeli territory,[26] though mass offensives are deemed less likely for the time being given the internal Arab wars.[27]
2. Conducting small or large focused raids into enemy territory in order to destroy enemy military assets or pressure hostile leadership.[28]
3. Temporarily conquer large tracts of hostile territory in order to clear them of enemy artillery or other military threats.[29]

In order to accomplish these tasks, the IDF believes it needs military forces with better firepower, mobility and protection than its potential enemies.[30]

The Israeli military has developed advanced intelligence and surveillance techniques as well as the ability to close in on targets quickly, using precision fire. This requires close cooperation between military and intelligence units. Ground operations require combined arms and heavy brigades capable of conducting fire and manoeuvring with minimal losses in a battlefield saturated with mines, improvised explosive devices (IEDs), booby traps and advanced anti-tank guided missile systems. The need for heavily protected armoured personnel carriers (APCs) and tanks in order to increase survivability and reduce casualties emerged clearly during the 2014 campaign in Gaza.[31]

What can Others Learn? The US Case

Israel is not the only country that is facing terror emanating from ungoverned areas. After more than a decade of occupation in Iraq, the US is following a strategy similar to Israel's while fighting the ISIS in Syria and Iraq.

In September 2014, the US concluded that the ISIS was evolving into a significant threat to American interests and ordered its air force to raid ISIS installations and militants in Syria and Iraq.[32] One analysis estimated that a counter-insurgency campaign against the ISIS in accordance with US Army doctrine—that is, a long occupation—would need 160,000 troops, and even then success would not be assured.[33] This explains why Washington is reluctant to reinsert ground forces to occupy land, and probably hopes that it can reduce ISIS from a major insurgent force with serious military capabilities to a collection of terrorist cells with limited political or military impact. The hope is that a protracted air campaign could break the group's momentum while buying time and space for local forces to organise and conduct the ground operations that could contain it. Without the cooperation of capable local forces on the ground, the air campaign may prove insufficient.

Despite its declarations of intent to destroy the ISIS, the US in fact aims to reduce it to the scale of a manageable problem. The US Defense Minister, General Mattis, recently declared that the US is moving from a strategy of "attrition" to one of "annihilation", but at the same time he warned that the fight against the ISIS would be "a long fight" and "a fight about ideas", aware that this problem will not disappear in the short future.[34] Mattis' declaration probably came in response to the growing ISIS-inspired terror attacks in Britain, Belgium, France, Germany and the US, which have increased the perception of threat. Earlier, President Obama had called for patient attrition by air strikes and advocating a very "light foot print".[35] Yet, it seems that what we have seen so far is somewhat reluctant and hesitant operations carried out by the US military; the new administration has shown that it will step up the fight.

Thus, similar to Israel, the US is seeking to avoid a long occupation, and hence the optimal available strategic option is to develop a consistent and more vigorous raiding strategy. One US analyst advised the adoption of a strategy that might loosely be termed as "repetitive raiding".[36] Disappointed by the poor strategic results in Afghanistan and Iraq, one US General who commanded forces in both places sadly concluded that: "Perhaps the best we can or should do is to keep it [the enemy] busy, 'degrade' its forces, harry them or kill them, and seek the long game at the lowest possible cost."[37]

By using a raiding strategy, the US can leverage its relative areas of advantage: technology, firepower, mobility and intelligence. In contrast, when it fought counter-insurgencies using light forces in great numbers in conducting policing duties against irregular forces, it was waging war on its enemies' terms. Raiding allows the US to fight wars on its own terms.

The US might face security challenges on other fronts as well. Some areas are not really vital to the US' interests and their descent into chaos hardly affects America's fortunes. But distance may become less significant as developing military technologies become more accessible to substate organisations. We may see the emergence of ungoverned areas in the western hemisphere that could become very problematic for the US national security. The further deterioration of internal security in Mexico as a result of feuding among the drug barons is not a far-fetched scenario. Such a contingency could have devastating effects on the American side of the border. For example, missiles might be added to narcotics in the trafficking in which Hezbollah is involved.[38]

While it is still not clear what grand strategy is going to be chosen by the new US President Donald J. Trump, it is apparent, however, that raiding, as discussed here, remains an important tool for achieving US foreign policy goals under any grand strategy chosen.

Conclusion: How it is Relevant to Other State Actors

The leaders of the civilised world increasingly recognise that radical ideologies cannot be terminally defeated on the battlefield. Strongly rooted, rigid and radical religious ideologies, as well as tribal rivalries and economic disparities, prevent reaching a conflict resolution. Unwilling to pay the cost of occupation, and/or realising its futility, stable states are no longer prepared to attempt to hold, rule or occupy ungoverned areas.

Following the disappointing results of more than a decade of counter-insurgency and attempted state building, states are seeking alternative strategies to fight violent and extreme non-state actors. The continued disintegration of states in various regions of conflict provides more safe havens that serve as launching pads for attacking Western strategic interests. Raids offer a valid way to curb the threat and contain it at minimum risk and cost. In addition to continuous small raids from the air and by special operations forces, larger raids with heavy ground forces are needed periodically to "mow the grass", that is, to inflict heavy losses and impair the opponents' capabilities.

Historical experience from the Romans to the British Empire, and Israel's contemporary experience, shows that ungoverned areas require patience and persistence. In military terms, raids can serve, under the right circumstances, as an effective tool to manage the threat posed from ungoverned areas. Such military expeditions are designed not to conquer territory but to annihilate, so far as possible, the fighting force of the enemy, kill the leaders and create a modicum of deterrence. This course of action does not accomplish total victory, but does reduce problems to a manageable level.

In the present-day context, other states might have to face challenges similar to that of Israel. Italy, France and Spain are facing ungoverned areas to their south across the Mediterranean.[39] Libya, already a failed state, and the rest of North Africa, comprising a number of fragile states, could become a source not only of illegal immigrants but also of terrorism, missile launches and piracy. A raiding strategy is probably an option that European states might consider in self-defence.

Another example, this time in Asia, is India. India fears the implosion of Pakistan and a release of great radical and terrorist energies. Its other neighbour, Bangladesh, beleaguered with demographic and economic problems, is hardly an example of democratic stability. India has so far displayed a timid strategic culture and is unlikely to be tempted into the conquest of territories inhabited by Muslims. Therefore, raids also seem an attractive option for India in the event of the disintegration of its neighbouring states. A sign in this direction could be seen in India's recent raid into Pakistan. On 29 September 2016, India launched a commando raid into Pakistan's territory, searching and killing terrorists in retaliation for the killing of its own soldiers a few days earlier.[40]

As the evolution of conflicts in Afghanistan and Iraq shows, America's war against Islamic extremism is not winnable in the traditional sense of eradicating the enemy or forcing it to a complete surrender in which it eschews the stated political goals that provoked the conflict. The potential repercussions of state failure and the rise of extreme ideologies compels the West and other functioning states to develop a strategy for conducting a protracted and seemingly unwinnable conflict. Despite the natural tendency to look for political solutions, they must internalise the thought that conflict management, rather than conflict resolution, is the best approach for confronting many contemporary strategic problems. Within such an approach, repetitive raiding and "mowing the grass" is the appropriate strategic and military response.

NOTES

1   Max Singer and Aaron Wildavsky, *The Real World Order: Zones of Peace, Zones of Turmoil*, Chatham, NJ: Chatham House, 1993.

2   For the trend, list of countries and definition, see the Fund for Peace, *Fragile State Index 2015*, available at http://fsi.fundforpeace.org/rankings-2015. (Unless otherwise noted at point of citation, all URLs cited in this article were accessible on 4 October 2016.) The working definition of a failed state I use here, following Max Weber, is a political entity without monopoly over the use of force, unable to enforce its sovereignty over its territory and unable to deliver basic services, primarily security, to its population. For this phenomenon in contemporary international relations, see Robert I. Rothberg (ed.), *When States Fail: Causes and Consequences*, Princeton: Princeton University Press, 2004.

3   Patrick Stewart, "Weak States and Global Threats: Fact or Fiction?", *Washington Quarterly*, Vol. 29, No. 2, 2006, p. 49; James A. Piazza, "Incubators of Terror: Do Failed and Failing States Promote Transnational Terrorism?", *International Studies Quarterly*, Vol. 52, No. 3, 2008, p. 483.

4   See, for example, President Obama's address to West Point cadets: "Remarks by the President at the United States Military Academy Commencement Ceremony", US Military Academy West Point, West Point, NY, 28 May 2014, available at http://www.whitehouse.gov/the-press-office/2014/05/28/remarks-president-united-states-military-academy-commencement-ceremony.

5   Hamas' seizure of Gaza in 2007 was followed by continued rocket fire towards Israel; Israel responded by conducting three operations designed to impair and deter Hamas: Cast Lead (2008), Pillar of Defense (2012) and Protective Edge (2014).

6   Efraim Inbar and Eitan Shamir, "Mowing the Grass: Israel's Strategy for Protracted Intractable Conflict", *Journal of Strategic Studies*, Vol. 37, No. 1, 2014, pp. 65–90 and "Mowing the Grass in Gaza", Perspectives Paper No. 255, Begin–Sadat Center for Strategic Studies, Bar-Ilan University, Ramat Gan, 20 July 2014, available at http://besacenter.org/perspectives-papers/mowing-grass-gaza/; Moni Chorev, "'Deterrence Campaigns': Lessons from IDF Operations in Gaza", Mideast Security Policies No. 115, Begin–Sadat Center for Strategic Studies, Bar-Ilan University, Ramat Gan, Israel, March 2016.

7   Doron Almog, "Cumulative Deterrence and the War on Terrorism", *Parameters*, Vol. 34, No. 4, 2004, pp. 4–19.

8   Israel has refrained from annexing the West Bank and the political power of the "Greater Israel" ideology has greatly diminished. Every poll shows that over two-thirds of the Israelis are ready for partition. Moreover, the establishment of the Palestinian Authority in 1994 is a de facto partition, albeit a messy one.

9   For example, following the 1967 war, Moshe Dayan promoted the "Open Bridges" policy with Jordan and a degree of economic integration with Israel. See Eitan Shamir, "From

Retaliation to Open Bridges: Moshe Dayan's Evolving Approach toward the Population in Counter Insurgency", *Civil Wars*, Vol. 14, No. 1, 2012, pp. 63–79.

10   The Israel Defense Forces (IDF) officers often use the phrase "mowing the grass", usually in a tactical sense. An example is a briefing for academics by senior officers in the Central Command, on 20 February 2013. See also http://www.ynet.co.il/articles/0,7340,L-4340652,00.html and the IDF website: "Did We Bite Palestinian Terror?", available at http://www.idf.il/1613-15468-he/Dover.aspx. The use of this term, non-existent in any IDF doctrinal document, is typical of the organisational culture in the IDF, which allows the use of informal operational and doctrinal concepts. On the IDF's informal culture, see Dima Adamsky, *The Culture of Military Innovation: The Impact of Cultural Factors on the Revolution in Military Affairs in Russia, the US, and Israel*, Stanford: Stanford University Press, 2010, p. 111; Eitan Shamir, *Transforming Command: The Pursuit of Mission Command in the US, British, and Israeli Armies*, Stanford: Stanford University Press, 2011, p. 83.

11   Archer Jones, *The Art of War in the Western World*, Urbana-Champaign: University of Illinois Press, 2001, pp. 662–716.

12   Department of the Army, *Counterinsurgency*, FM 3-24/MCWP 3-33.5, Washington, DC, 2006, p. 51.

13   "Wearing down the enemy in a conflict means using the duration of the war to bring about a gradual exhaustion of his physical and moral resistance. If we intend to hold out longer than our opponent does we must be content with the smallest possible objects, for obviously a major object requires more effort than a minor one." See Carl von Clausewitz, *On war*, 1st edition, edited by Michael Howard and Peter Paret, Princeton: Princeton University Press, 1976, p. 93.

14   Ze'ev Drory, *Israel's Reprisal Policy, 1953–1956: The Dynamics of Military Retaliation*, London: Routledge, 2012.

15   Jonathan Shimshoni, *Israel and Conventional Deterrence: Border Warfare from 1953 to 1970*, Ithaca, NY: Cornell University Press, 1988.

16   On the characteristics of French interventions, see Michel Martin, "From Algiers to N'Djamena: France's Adaptation to Low-intensity Wars, 1830–1987", in David Charters and Maurice Tugwell (eds), *Armies in Low-intensity Conflict: A Comparative Analysis*, Washington, DC: Brassey's Defence Publishers, 1989, pp. 77–138.

17   Initially, the war was considered a total failure, but reassessment after a few years almost reversed this perspective. See Martin van Creveld, "The Second Lebanon War: A Re-assessment", *Infinity Journal*, Vol. 1, No. 3, 2011, pp. 4–7; Gur Laish, "The Second Lebanon War: A Strategic Reappraisal", *Infinity Journal*, Vol. 1, No. 4, 2011, pp. 22–25; Itai Brun, "The Second Lebanon War, 2006", in John Andreas (ed.), *A History of Air Warfare*, Washington, DC: Potomac, 2010, pp. 207–324.

18   Bruce Collins, "Defining Victory in Victorian Warfare, 1860–1882", *Journal of Military History*, Vol. 77, No. 3, 2013, pp. 895–929.

19   See Smith, *The Utility of Force*, p. 401.

20   For doubts about the utility of decapitation, see Paul Staniland, "Defeating Transnational Insurgencies: The Best Offense is a Good Fence", *Washington Quarterly*, Vol. 29, No. 1, 2005–06, pp. 21–40; Jenna Jordan, "When Heads Roll: Assessing the Effectiveness of Leadership Decapitation", *Security Studies*, Vol. 18, No. 4, 2009, pp. 719–55. For research that finds targeted killing useful, see Daniel Byman, "Do Targeted Killings Work?", *Foreign Affairs*, Vol. 85, No. 2, 2006, pp. 95–111; Patrick B. Johnston, "Does Decapitation Work? Assessing the Effectiveness of Leadership Targeting in Counter-insurgency Campaigns", *International Security*, Vol. 36, No. 4, 2012, pp. 47–79; Javier Jordan, "The Effectiveness of the Drone Campaign

against Al-Qaida Central: A Case Study", *Journal of Strategic Studies*, Vol. 37, No. 1, 2014, pp. 4–29.

21 For example, on the 1998 American assault against terrorist camps in Afghanistan (Operation Infinite Reach), see *The 9/11 Commission Report: Final Report of the National Commission on Terrorist Attacks upon the United States*, Official government edition, Washington, DC: US Government Printing Office, 2004, pp. 115–21, available at http://fas.org/irp/offdocs/911commission.pdf. On Israeli operations during the 1990s against Hezbollah in Lebanon, Operation Accountability (1993) and Operation Grapes of Wrath (1996), see Itay Brun, "Where has the Maneuver Disappeared?" (Hebrew), *Maarachot*, Nos 420–21, September 2008, pp. 420–21, p. 9.

22 For the notion of escalation dominance, see Herman Kahn, *On Escalation: Metaphors and Scenarios*, New York: Praeger, 1965, pp. 66–72.

23 Jordan, "The Effectiveness of the Drone Campaign", n. 20; Jon R. Lindsay, "Reinventing the Revolution: Technological Visions, Counterinsurgent Criticism, and the Rise of Special Operations", *Journal of Strategic Studies*, Vol. 36, No. 3, 2013, pp. 422–53.

24 IDF Chief of the General Staff, *IDF Strategy* (Hebrew), August 2015, available at http://www.idf.il/SIP_STORAGE/FILES/9/16919.pdf.

25 Michael Herzog, "The IDF Strategy Goes Public", Policy Watch No. 2479, The Washington Institute, 28 August 2015, available at http://www.washingtoninstitute.org/policy-analysis/view/new-idf-strategy-goes-public.

26 IDF, *IDF Strategy*, n. 24, p. 1.

27 Ibid., p. 28.

28 Ibid., p. 29.

29 Ibid., p. 28. Essentially, this is still a raid, albeit a more extended one, since the political intention is to return the territory to the enemy either by withdrawing during the war, when the clearing operation is deemed complete (as in summer 2014 in Gaza), or after the ceasefire (as in summer 2006 in Lebanon).

30 Ibid., p. 29.

31 Yossi Yehoshua, "Yaalon Approves Addition of 200 Advanced APCs for the IDF", *YNET News*, 22 September 2014, available at http://www.ynetnews.com/articles/0,7340,L-4573814,00.html.

32 See Eytan Gilboa, "The War against the Islamic State", *The Jerusalem Report*, 20 October 2014, pp. 8–9.

33 Stephen Biddle and Jacob Shapiro, "Here's Why We can Only Contain ISIS", *The Washington Post*, 3 December 2015.

34 Martin Pengelly, "Defense Secretary Mattis Says US Policy against ISIS is Now 'Annihilation'", *The Guardian*, 28 May 2017, available at https://www.theguardian.com/us-news/2017/may/28/james-mattis-defense-secretary-us-isis-annihilation, accessed on 28 May 2017

35 David Ignatius, "In Fighting the Islamic State, Obama is a Tortoise and the GOP is Harebrained", *The Washington Post*, 16 December 2015, available at http://www.washingtonpost.com/opinions/in-fighting-the-islamic-state-obama-is-a-tortoise-and-the-gop-is-harebrained/2015/12/16/0acc3ad8-a430-11e5-ad3f-991ce3374e23_story.html.

36 Bernard I. Finel, "An Alternative to COIN", *Armed Forces Journal*, February 2010, available at http://armedforcesjournal.com/an-alternative-to-coin/.

37 Daniel P. Bolger, "The Truth about the Wars", *The New York Times*, 10 November 2014, available at http://www.nytimes.com/2014/11/11/opinion/the-truth-about-the-wars-in-iraq-and-afghanistan.html?_r=0.

38 "Mexican Cartels Help Hezbollah Infiltrate US", *Judicial Watch*, 18 October 2013, available at http://www.judicialwatch.org/blog/2013/10/mexican-cartels-help-hezbollah-infiltrate-u-s/

39 For the new security problems in the East Mediterranean, see Efraim Inbar, "Israel's New Challenges in the Eastern Mediterranean", *Middle East Quarterly*, Vol. 21, No. 4, 2014, pp. 1–12, available at http://www.meforum.org/meq/pdfs/4804.pdf.

40 See *The Economist*, "Reversing Roles", 8–14 October 2016, p. 54, available at http://www.economist.com/news/asia/21708302-there-still-more-smoke-fire-heated-exchanges-how-long-reversing-roles, accessed on 28 May 2017.

SECTION FIVE

Regional Perspectives—South and
Southeast Asia: The Growing
Spectre of Terror

15

Countering Terrorism
Perspectives from Bangladesh

Lt. Gen. Chowdhury Hasan Sarwardy (Retd.)

Introduction

Terrorism in Bangladesh has been a recent phenomenon, compared to some other South Asian states. Globally, Asia is one of the biggest political, economic and culturally diverse regions to suffer from terrorist activities. Since the end of the Second World War, the southern half of Asia has seen numerous communist uprisings, Cold War era proxy wars, thriving transnational criminal groups and the emergence of non-state actors. However, in Asia, the rise of militancy and terrorism is a relatively recent phenomenon and, according to many, is a spillover effect of the Middle East crisis, the Afghan war, the Iraq war and other extra-regional factors. The Asian region has become increasingly prone to conflict, and developing countries have become the main stage for terrorist activities. The personal and political trauma that the citizens of Asian countries have undergone in the recent past breeds resentment and hatred, which pushes them towards becoming lone wolf actors or joining organised groups. Terrorism in Asia is an evolving phenomenon and continues to adapt to meet the challenges emerging from government responses, developments in technology and society. Terrorist groups have demonstrated an increasing ability to adapt to flexible counter-terrorism measures and techniques. They have also taken advantage of political failures within the region to spread their reach.

Bangladesh Experience

Since its independence, Bangladesh has experienced three kinds of terrorism. The first was political violence by left-wing terrorism, which was politically motivated with the intention of establishing communism in this country. The second was an insurgency spearheaded by Parbatya Chattagram Jana Samhati Samiti (PCJSS) in the early 1980s, with the demand for autonomy in the Chittagong Hill Districts. Lately, militancy in the name of religion has also emerged in Bangladesh under the banner of Jamaat-ul-Mujahideen Bangladesh (JMB), Harkat-ul-Jihad al-Islami Bangladesh (HUJI-B), etc. Recent activities undertaken by these extremist groups include the killing of several groups of people, including a few bloggers who criticised the Islamic ideology, non-Muslim religious preachers, foreigners involved in development projects, law enforcement agency members, etc. One of the key socio-economic drivers of terrorism is poverty. Poverty and ignorance provide the most valid scope of recruiting activists from rural areas for religious extremism. Their aspiration of social emancipation and establishing independent state pushes them towards terrorist activities. Furthermore, perceived injustices in the society, such as corruption, chaos and irregularities, are used as motivators to stimulate the emotions of youth from affluent families. The desire for order and change, conjoined with the misinterpretation of scripture, is utilised collectively to indoctrinate young ignorant minds in extremism. A survey[1] conducted by the Bangladesh Enterprise Institute (BEI) has identified poverty, misinterpretation of scriptures, social values degradation, the political use of Islam, illiteracy, unemployment, corruption, political violence, fragile democracy and the absence of social justice as major contributors to the cause of terrorism in Bangladesh.

Since 2014, there have been some sporadic incidents of terrorist acts perpetrated by home-grown activists. While they have insignificant financial and technological abilities and their capabilities are rudimentary, small-scale shooting attacks and a combination of shooting and knife attacks by small groups have been used to great effect. The usual targets of these terrorists are people they identify as atheists or blasphemers or writers and foreigners. The July 2016 terrorist attack in a Dhaka restaurant,[2] that caused the death of 23 innocent foreigners and Bangladeshis, was the first massive strike committed against the traditionally harmonious society of Bangladesh. It was an eye-opener for the people when the family members of terrorists came forward and helped members of law enforcement agencies in figuring out and locating a number of suspects. Furthermore, the local terrorist cell that was previously operating on a smaller scale became completely exposed by switching over to a big target. As a result, almost all of them were either apprehended or killed in action during the operations undertaken by law enforcement agencies.

This region has also observed the influx of a large number of Rohingya refugees, displaced from their homes in the wake of an ongoing crackdown in Myanmar, which is a matter of serious security concern. While Bangladesh has been host to an incredible number of Rohingya refugees, it remains vulnerable to traffickers and its local population remains vulnerable to recruitment by extremist Islamic groups taking advantage of prevailing disarray on the Myanmar border. The Rohingya youths, recruited by foreign terrorist groups, are treated as cannon fodder in the name of jihad. Meanwhile, regional online extremists have begun pledging their support through various provocative Internet sites and apps. The close nexus between Rohingya and terrorist outfits supplants the humanitarian call of refugees, which has ultimately served to develop new security dynamics in this region. The failure of regional and global focus on this issue may turn Bangladesh–Myanmar border into a new theatre of global jihad. This will not only affect Bangladesh's national security but also have an adverse impact on peace in the region.

Counter-terrorism: The Bangladesh Perspective

Bangladesh has made remarkable progress in countering terrorism thus far. The country has responded to the threat through robust law enforcement, undercover operations, intelligence-led operations, the prevention of terror financing, electronic surveillance and analytical support, as well as social measures aimed at addressing and fighting the root causes of terrorism. The next priority is harnessing citizen's support and security awareness in combating the scourge of terror. Further efforts, such as the introduction of information rendering apps for smartphones and campaigns against terrorism, are being undertaken through new media. Efforts are also being taken for building counter-narratives and deradicalisation—through segregation and counselling, community meetings by Islamic scholars and declaration of monetary reward for terrorist surrenders.

The government has banned a few militant organisations as well. Above all, the "zero tolerance" policy of the government is aimed at arresting the situation and ensuring lasting peace. The Bangladesh government's political will and firm commitment towards combating domestic and transnational terrorist groups is very evident. It has formulated a "National Counter-Terrorism Strategy". Furthermore, an Anti-terrorism Act, 2009 has also been enacted and it has been amended twice to bring the anti-terrorism legislation in line with the United Nations (UN) action plan on counter-terrorism strategy and other such resolutions. The National Committee for Intelligence Coordination, chaired by Honourable Prime Minister of Bangladesh, and the National Committee on Militancy Resistance and Prevention have also been formed to coordinate between law enforcement and intelligence services in order to counter terrorism and violent extremism in the most intense form.

As a part of the social measures against terrorism, the government has integrated educational institutions, civil society, cultural organisations, non-governmental organisations (NGOs) and the media for strengthening its campaign against terrorism. In 2010, the government formulated an anti-terrorism education policy, which highlighted the need to reform the madrasa curriculum. The government also introduced anti-extremism chapters in academic textbooks. Traditionally, the people of Bangladesh are ethnically harmonious and cultured people. They are intrinsically resistant to any religious extremism-based violence. While people are resilient to any political violence and welcome all ideological discourses, they also remain united to ensure the maintenance of religious and societal harmony. Even today, most of the successful drives undertaken by law enforcement agencies against terrorist outfits have been directly supported by information tips gained from the locals. Thus far, terrorists have not been successful in making inroads into the region due to people's hatred for all types of terrorist activities in the society. Above all, the government has been able to successfully raise the resistance perception of the people and fight terrorism with root-level public support. Finally, there is also a need to recognise the importance of global and regional cooperation in countering terrorism. Bangladesh is effectively participating in different regional and global forums. Some of the major cooperation initiatives are:[3]

1. the UN Global Counter-Terrorism Strategy;
2. South Asian Association for Regional Cooperation (SAARC);
3. the Bangladesh–India extradition treaty aimed at disrupting regional connections and networks among terrorist outfits in South Asia (signed on 28 January 2013); and
4. the Bangladesh–United States (US) agreement aimed at enhancing counter-terrorism cooperation which includes capacity building, information sharing and ensuring increased exchange between the respective law enforcement agencies (signed on 22 October 2013).

The Way Forward

Bangladesh is committed to subduing the terror groups and not allowing those groups to establish links with global terrorist networks through its counter-terrorism efforts. The country recognises the necessity of adopting a holistic approach involving all national and regional stakeholders towards eradicating terrorism from this region in general, and Bangladesh in particular. The devised strategy should encompass conceptual, physical and moral components.

The institutional set-up of law enforcement in Bangladesh is focused towards capacity building, particularly towards the widespread use of technology in countering terrorism. Bangladesh is a peaceful nation with a culture of fine arts, literature and music, which gives us an overarching advantage to align the moral compass. Good governance, development initiatives, political cohesion, best practices on inculcation of social values and the fostering of family values, all need to be encouraged to prevent the buds of terrorism sprouting within the region. Furthermore, emphasis should also be laid on proper religious education, awareness programmes, the use of media, monitoring systems in educational institutions, strict monitoring of the usage of information and communications technology and a proper implementation of the law as a means for countering militant activities. In the intellectual domain, prominent think tanks and organisations, like the Bangladesh Institute of International and Strategic Studies, as well as premier education institutes, like the National Defence College, and other universities should enhance the exchange of regional discourses and experiences through seminars and workshops.

Regional cooperation would be necessary to secure Bangladesh–Myanmar border, and address the Rohingya's citizenship status and grievances. It is necessary for the global community to come together and work with the Rohingyas as strategic partners in order to alert the authorities of terrorist or insurgent activities. Furthermore, it is also necessary to devise a long-term solution aimed at addressing the plight of the Rohingya refugees by funding support to Bangladesh in its rehabilitation efforts. Regional countries must cooperate with each other against the possible recruitment or radicalisation of the refugees. Regional governments and the international community need to call for an immediate seizure of the political atrocities being committed against the Rohingyas, with the focus on settling the issue in their own country rather than pushing them towards Bangladesh. The present position of Bangladesh is well maintained with a "zero tolerance" policy against terrorism in all its forms and manifestations. Bangladeshi culture is imbued with ethnic and religious tolerance, which will pave the way in combating terrorism. We emphasise on the united effort and mutual cooperation of all Asian countries against terrorism in order to cumulatively protect the global population against the scourge of this dreadful malice by all means.

Conclusion

Over the years, Bangladesh has made great progress in countering and containing terrorism within the country. Bangladesh pursues a value-driven foreign policy that promotes peace, democracy, communal harmony, human rights, good governance, social justice, a culture of peace and non-violence, intercultural dialogues, as well as ethnic and religious tolerance to combat extremism and fundamentalism. The country will continue to work with the various parties involved in maintaining peace and harmony within the region. It will also do everything within its power to prevent the proliferation of extremist ideologies and stop terrorism once and for all.

NOTES

1   Bangladesh Enterprise Institute, Mitra and Associates, and Saferworld, February 2013, "Safety and security in the South-East border area of Bangladesh A public perceptions survey", available at https://www.saferworld.org.uk/Safety--security-in-the-SE-border-area-of-Bangladesh accessed on 22 February 2017.

2   For more see a series of reports on the attack, available at https://www.thedailystar.net/tags/holey-artisan-attack, accessed on 22 February 2017.

3   United States Department of State, Country Reports on Terrorism 2017 - Bangladesh, 19 September 2018, available at https://www.refworld.org/docid/5bcf1fb6140.html, accessed on 11 February 2019.

16

The Sri Lankan Defeat of Terrorism

Lessons for Evolving a Regional Response for Combating Terrorism

Lt. 'Gen R.M. Daya Ratnayake (Retd.)[1]

Introduction

The post-Cold War period and the era of globalisation has witnessed the rise of internal armed conflicts of separatist, religious and ethnic nature, which has brought death, destruction and suffering to the affected nations. Democracies have struggled to come to terms with the resultant terrorism and insurgencies, including using military and peaceful means, which have not produced the desired end state of peace.

But in May 2009, Sri Lanka, an island nation plagued by terrorism for over three decades, defeated the Liberation Tigers of Tamil Eelam (LTTE)—considered one of the deadliest terrorist organisations in the world—to achieve peace. Almost 30,000 strong, the LTTE possessed a land force comprising a guerrilla army capable of conventional combat and the deadliest of suicide cadres; naval capability extending from shallow-water dominance to blue-water transnational logistics; and a limited but strategically disruptive air capability.

However, under assiduous political leadership that united the nation and a rejuvenated military, terrorism was decisively defeated, thereby establishing Sri Lanka as the only nation to have done so in the twenty-first century. But what is unique in this defeat is that it was achieved in a period of three-and-a-half years and was comprehensive in the fact that, after May 2009, the official completion of the conflict, no terrorist-related incident has being recorded. The retired head of India's Sri Lankan peacekeeping force characterised the defeat of the LTTE as having turned conventional counter-insurgency (COIN) theory on its head.[2] The

Sri Lankan government's defeat of terrorism has established beyond doubt that terrorism can be defeated by adaptive and innovative militaries, augmented by the synchronised application of political, social, diplomatic and economic means.

Extending the response to a regional application, crossing national geographical and political boundaries, can be accepted as next to impossible. The already complex, divergent international and regional environment, with its share of inter-state conflicts, complicates the cooperation imperative to formulating an effective regional response to terrorism. However, all is not lost and hope for the future exists with a slow but steady realisation by nation-states that terrorism is best managed through a comprehensive, whole-of-a-region approach. Of course, challenges will be more complex, opportunities fleeting and ideas conflicting, but greater rewards will accrue.

This chapter focuses on exploring the Sri Lankan experience of defeating terrorism with a view to identify critical lessons that could contribute to the formulation of an effective Southeast Asian response to terrorism. The discussion is framed in different sections. This section briefly sheds light on the Sri Lankan conflict, which was national in nature, whilst identifying the importance of a holistic regional approach to countering terrorism in the wake of its emerging transnational nature. The next two sections establish the context of the Sri Lankan conflict by setting out the activities of the LTTE and the Government of Sri Lanka (GoSL), respectively, which enables comprehension of the conflict and strategies and concepts adopted by the parties concerned. Further, the LTTE, which was supported by a global network and reach, is a classic example of a non-state actor with the soul of terrorism. The following section discusses the vital lessons derived from the conflict and its potential connection to a regional counter-terrorism mechanism. The penultimate section reflects on the outcome of the Sri Lankan conflict had a regional response mechanism to terrorism existed. In conclusion, the chapter summarises a few critical observations and related recommendations.

The LTTE: Hybrid Terrorist Non-state Actor

Composition of Violence

While many nations have witnessed and experienced the devastating effects of terrorism in different forms, no other nation has had to contend with a terrorist organisation that blended diverse and hybrid capabilities ranging from terrorism, guerrilla warfare, insurgency to sub-conventional combat. This blend of conventional and unconventional methods, along with a penchant for indiscriminate violence and terror, defined the uniqueness of the LTTE. Rising from a small band of petty criminals to a sub-conventional force comprising of a guerrilla army, a deadly Black Tiger suicide cadre, an effective Sea Tiger force and a fledgling air force, the LTTE was able to not only terrorise the entire nation but also compete for and retain geographical space and establish a "de facto" government. The ruthless efficiency of the LTTE compelled the Federal Bureau of Investigation (FBI) to describe the organisation as the "most dangerous and deadly extremist"[3] outfit in the world.

Suicide Terrorism: The Soul of the LTTE

The LTTE's fearsome reputation was born of its ruthless employment of the deadly suicide killers, as both a tactical and strategic weapon, which facilitated the retention of the initiative. The LTTE, unlike most terrorist organisations that grew out of terrorism as military and political power accumulated, continued the employment of indiscriminate violence against civilians for coercive purposes.

For the LTTE, terrorism, and at its epicentre, suicide, that delivered indiscriminate violence was more a logic than a tactic. Suicide terrorism was a culture with enormous popularity among its cadres, which inspired not only the suicide and military cadres but also the organisation as a whole, which in turn created and sustained a sense of ruthlessness. The culture of suicide and death was an identity that was worn around the neck of all members of the LTTE in the form of a cyanide capsule.

The LTTE was the first terrorist organisation to reinvent suicide terrorism by employing the suicide belt and women as a suicide bomb. The suicide element of the organisation was active in the land, naval and air dimensions of the conflict and cascaded with deadly effect in to the political, social, psychological and economic fabric of the nation. Terrorism in general, and the suicide bomber in particular, was utilised to destroy the political leadership and undermine the will of the nation to resist. The success of this concept is evident in the fact that the LTTE was able to assassinate a president, ministers and political figures, service chiefs and high-level military officials. The employment of the suicide bomber was not confined to national geography but was extended to India, with a suicide attack which killed the ex-prime minister of India, Rajiv Gandhi, thereby demonstrating to the world its reach. The assassination of the president of Sri Lanka by a suicide bomber, who was activated after living for two years as part of the presidential staff, is a classic example of the intelligence capabilities and motivation of its cadres. Tactically, terrorism and the suicide element were employed to augment guerrilla and sub-conventional operations by selective commitment at critical points in combat. The attacks on strategic assets, such as the international airport in Colombo and the air force base in Anuradhapura, which sustained damage, and the war efforts are classic examples of the effective blend of suicide terrorism and guerrilla warfare. The reconnaissance and infiltration methods of the LTTE were phenomenal and added force multiplication to all levels of warfare, in all dimensions.

Military Capabilities

Another addition to the military capabilities of the LTTE was its deadly women cadre and child soldiers, who were second to none in dedication to the cause. Raised from the culture of violence, these cadres not only augmented the hardcore cadres but also provided the much-needed recruits for suicide terrorism. The employment of traditional firepower, such as artillery, in unconventional ways to achieve objectives of military and political gain was traditional to the LTTE.

The brown waters of the Indian Ocean bordering the controlled areas of the LTTE were dominated by the Sea Tigers whilst contesting the naval presence even in the mid-seas. Specially designed boats with extra power and 30 mm cannons, supported by innovative tactics such as "wolf pack" attacks, enabled the Sea Tiger wing of the LTTE to be an effective force. However, the weapon of decision which provided an edge in the contest for the waters was the suicide boats of many designs which inflicted a heavy toll on the navy. The use of suicide boats to attack naval crafts, both combat and logistics, was pioneered by the LTTE. The successful suicide attack on the US naval craft, *USS Cole*, by al-Qaeda, off the coast of Algeria, is a classic example of emulation of this LTTE innovation. The war machine of the LTTE was supported by a fleet of almost 26 merchant ships owned by the organisation and based on a concept of floating dumps. This fleet of ships was employed extensively for human as well as arms smuggling.

It was this intricate system of external sustenance that enabled the LTTE to develop into a hybrid non-state actor with global reach. The LTTE also deployed a Sea Tiger force of land or coastal combatants, who augmented other land combat groups. It also included a combat diver unit that scored spectacular successes against the armed forces in general, and the navy in particular. Some of their successes included the destruction of naval crafts anchored in the harbour.

The air capability of the LTTE, although very limited in terms of superiority of equipment and range, possessed the ability to threaten vital installations in Colombo, including the power grid, international airport and the Parliament. Here too, it was the suicide dimension that posed the greatest threat and impacted on the nation politically, economically and most devastatingly, psychologically.

The ground attack capabilities of the air force were also threatened by the LTTE's use of anti-aircraft missiles and cannons. The threat also extended to the pilots who flew these aircraft.

All in all, it can be safely stated that the LTTE, which possessed both conventional and asymmetric capabilities, had developed into a hybrid non-state actor employing terrorism as logic through a culture of suicide terrorism. Gaining legitimacy from a separatist and freedom fighter image, the LTTE's centre of gravity was sourced by the external support from Tamil diaspora and sympathetic nations and its military strength.

Sri Lanka's Response to Terrorism

Blending National Power into Counter-terrorism Strategy and Operational Plans

The defeat of the LTTE due to the concentrated application of the instruments of national power by the GoSL sets an example for nations dealing with terrorism and makes the unwinnable, as propagated by the scholars, winnable. The theory of COIN and counter-terrorism, practised by the Western nations in recent conflicts in Iraq and Afghanistan, seems lacking and is yet to produce the desired end state of peace. Sri Lanka's strategy to defeat terrorism rose as result of a strong and decisive political leadership and the will of a nation, which had suffered for almost 30 years due to the conflict. The strategy was designed on several complimenting lines which aimed at achieving the end state of peace. International isolation of the LTTE through diplomacy and naval action denied the much-needed external support. The extension of naval operations for interdiction of the floating warehouses and armories impacted on the sustenance of the organisation. Political action mustered the nation's will to support the government in the campaign. The military campaign waged by the land forces, supported by the air force and the navy, focused on the defeat of the LTTE's military capability.

Identifying correctly the centre of gravity of the LTTE, which revolved around external support and military power, the Sri Lanka Army (SLA) focused its efforts on the destruction and dismantling of the organisation. After having experienced the protracted nature of the conflict due to population-centric strategies, the SLA shifted to a more attritional approach to dealing with the LTTE. The operational level focused on a policy of deliberate confrontation in which the simultaneous engagement of the LTTE, from the leadership to guerrilla, was emphasised.

Tactical Innovation

The control of terrain was avoided and the destruction of the cadres at the tactical level, although at times slow, gradually converted tactical victories into operational gains. The application of mass against an elusive guerrilla army had caused the military many casualties with no gain. Hence, this time, the SLA transformed into small groups to contest the LTTE in the jungles. It involved the training of the infantry to operate in small groups, relying on integral weapon systems rather than heavy weapons. The intent was to overload the LTTE by deploying a mass of small groups both forward and to the rear of its controlled areas. Employing tactics of guerrilla warfare, supported by the innovative application of support weapons, these groups were able to defeat the guerrillas at its own game. Tactically, the edge gained by the suicide cadres was neutralised by gaining and retaining the initiative through the use of small groups. The traditional advantage of surprise shifted to the army.

Force Multiplying with the Populace

The control of terrorism and suicide bombings in the depth of the nation was a result of a total security concept, which meshed the populace from all professions with the security forces thereby multiplying security effect. Civilian security committees, with the civilians adding to the "eyes and ears" of the security forces, played a valuable role in the total security concept. These were some of the many innovative means adopted and adapted to sustain security in rear areas and sustain the conflict. Other than a few suicide attacks, many were pre-empted and defeated. Attempts at Mumbai style of attacks too were defeated swiftly with the rapid and instantaneous use of special forces.

Force Multiplying with Special Operations Forces

Another force multiplier was the use of special operations forces (SOF) in the LTTE-controlled areas to destroy leadership and high-value targets. Operating behind the lines for periods exceeding 20 days, these elite forces were able to inflict enormous damage on the LTTE's ability to wage war. Taking the fight into the safe havens of the LTTE added to the psychological pressure and compelled the deployment of more cadres for rear area security, causing heavy manpower problems. Directing firepower assets, including air and heavy artillery, these small teams were able to inflict destruction far beyond their composition. The skills, drills and innovative tactics adopted by these groups, such as the innovative employment of the claymore mine, were unmatchable and contributed immensely to the concept of "fight a guerrilla like a guerrilla". Utilising specially prepared indigenous food and medicine for sustenance and inspired by the indomitable will to accomplish the mission, these SOF teams took the fight to the minds of the terrorist. Mastering the art of reconnaissance, these teams provided the much-needed intelligence and information, which shifted the initiative from the terrorists to the army.

Force Multiplying with Intelligence

An invigorated and restructured national intelligence, integrating all intelligence organisations including the tri-services, police and related organisations, was able to stay ahead of the LTTE. Organised by the Ministry of Defence (MoD) under the watchful guidance of the secretary of defence, the intelligence grew in reach and quality. The destruction of the LTTE's floating warehouses through integrated naval and air strikes is a case in point. The decapitating attack on an influential top-rung leader, Thamil Chelvam, speaks volumes of the effect of an improved intelligence apparatus. Counter-intelligence played an important role in tracking and identifying the LTTE intelligence network in Colombo, resulting in the detection and neutralisation of the suicide bombing strategy.

The intelligence focus at the tactical level improved tremendously with the transformation of the infantry operations into a small group setting. The traditional patrolling was redefined with new methods and longer range and sustainability, which enabled the extraction of battlefield intelligence, which in turn contributed to the enhanced effectiveness of firepower and overall application of combat power.

The Naval Power Application

The effectiveness of naval operations contributed significantly to the denial of external support and isolation of the LTTE. These naval operations extending into the high seas were based on quality intelligence and bold execution, resulting in the destruction of the critical lifeline of the LTTE. The development and employment of small boat equipment and concepts enabled the navy to gradually but certainly match, and subsequently defeat, the LTTE in the brown waters. Improvisation spiced with learning and adapting drove the navy's operational design. Resorting to building its own crafts added with affordable technologies, the navy confronted the deadly suicide boats of the Sea Tigers and gained the much-needed dominance of the sea.

The Air Power Application

The air force, equipped with capabilities which included improved target acquisition means, delivered accurate surgical strikes exacting a heavy toll on the LTTE. Reinforcements, gun positions and reserves of the LTTE were located and destroyed. The unmanned aerial vehicles (UAVs) were used extensively to support target acquisition for both air and land operations, thereby contributing to effective target engagement. Utilising laser-directed munitions, combined with accurate intelligence and innovative flying skills, the air force was able strike at high-value targets, such as the leadership and LTTE shipping, under the guidance of the navy. Close air support played an ever-so-important role in the attacks on LTTE strong points and larger engagements.

Lessons Learnt and Potential Connections to a Regional Response Mechanism

Deciding Strategy

The root of an effective counter-terrorism or COIN strategy lies in the populace and naturally should be politically led. The GoSL strategy was decided by taking into consideration the socio-political realities existing at that point in time. The Sinhala populace was divided as to what course of action was needed, with almost 50 per cent seeking defeat of the LTTE militarily and the rest dangerously seeking peace, even to the extent of permitting secession from the country. Hence, a population-centric strategy may have taken years to implement and reap dividends which, in the long run, would have eroded the will of the nation as a result of the protracted nature of the conflict. The LTTE, over the years, had managed to undermine the GoSL in the eyes of the people. Thus, the GoSL, considering the above and the centre of gravity of the LTTE which included its military capability sustained by an international network, decided on a threat-centric attritional approach as its strategy.

In considering a regional response, the challenge would be to formulate and integrate into a common multinational strategy (regional) or as a minimum, common understanding. Unlike integration which facilitated the effective response of the GoSL, a regional response would have to be based on the principle of cooperation and collective security. How far and to what extent is a key challenge that requires early attention. A mini version of the Indian proposal to the United Nations (UN), namely, Comprehensive Convention on International Terrorism (CCIT), tailored to the region is an option that could be considered. Whatever be the collective effort, for purposes of international legitimacy and reach, it is advisable that linkages be established with the UN Global Counter-Terrorism Strategy for South Asia (adopted at the UN General Assembly in 2006).[4]

Denying External Support

A critical prerequisite for defeating terrorism/insurgency is the denial of external support. The GoSL took almost 25 years to achieve this by exploiting events that took place both regionally and internationally. A key factor that contributed to the isolation of the LTTE externally was the post-9/11 environment which was unfavourable to terrorist organisations. Exploiting these conditions through astute diplomacy, the GoSL was able to suppress the LTTE support organisations and diaspora, specifically with regards to financial support. Arms, equipment and logistics essential to sustaining the fight against the GoSL were effectively reduced (LTTE was banned and proscribed in 30 countries). This was complemented by naval action against floating warehouses and major logistical ships of the LTTE.

It was principally diplomacy at the bilateral level that established the conditions which facilitated the international rejection of the LTTE. Thus, it was through diplomacy that the GoSL was able to access arms and support from Pakistan and China without antagonising India.

As a principle of a counter-terrorism strategy, the denial of external support signals the end of any terrorist organisation[5], and so it was in the case of the LTTE too. This is a classic example as to why regional cooperation and collective security approaches are of paramount importance to defeat terrorism, be it national or transnational.

No Safe Havens and Sanctuaries, No Terrorism

It is an established fact[6] that India provided space for, and initially trained, the separatist terrorist organisation that subsequently developed into a hybrid non-state actor capable of holding ground and building a de facto government supported by an international network. Just 32 km from mainland India, the people of northern Sri Lanka, ethnic Tamils, were motivated to fight for a separate state.

Sanctuaries in both governed and ungoverned spaces are prerequisites for any terrorist activity until, as in the case of the LTTE, a defensible controlled territory, including a sympathetic populace, is constructed. Hence, the defeat of terrorism is hinged on denying the terrorist a safe haven, which generally is outside the country of terrorist's focus.

The Will of the Nation

The political leadership was able to muster the will of the populace against the LTTE, which had deliberately violated and withdrawn from the Norwegian peace initiative. This enabled the empowerment of the people as a part of the counter-terrorist strategy, thus facilitating a collective and total security approach. The public opinion was strong enough to last the duration of the conflict.

A regionally supported national counter-terrorist strategy will add to the legitimacy of the national cause and multiply the public support for the country concerned. The regional support could include capacity building (counter-terrorism military aid) and economic assistance to enable the victimised country to sustain its strategy.

A Realistic Foreign Policy: Understanding the Concerns of Regional Big Power Neighbours

The guiding principle behind Sri Lanka's foreign relations and accompanying diplomacy is friendship towards all and enmity towards none, which inspires non-alignment, a core attribute advocated and practised by the nation since independence. This policy which accrued respect in international relations is manifested in the support the nation has received in troubled times from big powers, both regional and outside, despite their different ideologies. Examples in this regard can be found in the Indian support provided in 1956 during internal unrest; and Indian, Chinese and Russian military aid received to successfully suppress an insurrection in 1971. However, at times, Sri Lanka's foreign policy ignored Indian security concerns and its regional standing, which resulted in periods of strained relations impacting negatively on cooperation in areas of security that could have enabled the early defeat or better, the prevention of terrorism in the country. Sri Lanka's shift towards the West in 1977, at a time when India was aligned towards the East, is a case in point that inspired the rise of armed Tamil ethno-nationalism. A more balanced policy adopted by the GoSL, catering to India's security aspirations, would have changed the course of our nation's recent history.

Reflections of How a Regional Response to Terrorism could have Affected the Sri Lankan Conflict

To provide credence to the topic, an analysis of the key effects a regional response mechanism could have generated in support of the GoSL during the conflict will be undertaken in this section. It is, in essence, a reflection of a past conflict, aided by a futuristic response mechanism. The discourse also continues into the bilateralism which enabled Sri Lanka to win the war on terrorism.

Denial of External Support

A regional response would have denied the LTTE a sanctuary and the necessary logistic support to wage terrorism. Access to international forums in search of legitimacy through disinformation could have being better managed by collective diplomacy instituted by regional arrangements. The LTTE's arms smuggling, which escalated the conflict, could have being drastically reduced with naval assistance from India.

Neutralising the Cause and Reaching for Peace

The separatist agenda, the roots of which were local in construction and inspired due to deficiencies in post-independence nation building, also has linkages with the southern Indian Tamil population. Geographically separated by a short stretch of the Indian Ocean, the Tamils of northern Sri Lanka have traditionally and historically shared a common and binding culture with Indian Tamils. Hence, the Tamil cause of the Sri Lankan Tamils was supported vigorously by the south Indians. It is important to highlight that the Indian influence in the Sri Lankan conflict was adequate to bring about a peaceful termination to the same. Most importantly, the LTTE's cause for a separate state could have being neutralised and watered down to an internal power-sharing arrangement.

Missed Opportunity for Early Defeat of the Tigers

The military operation by the GoSL in the Northern Province to clear the LTTE's last bastion (Operation Vadamarachchi) was prevented due to intervention by the Indian government. Had a counter-terrorism commitment at regional level existed, the opportunity to terminate what later became the world's deadliest terrorist organisation would not have being missed. However, the 1971 insurrection by a southern communist/Marxist organisation comprising of Sinhalese youth was amply supported by India, resulting in the comprehensive defeat of the Janatha Vimukthi Peramuna (JVP).

Bilateralism and the Defeat of the LTTE

Sri Lanka's successful termination of the conflict evidences the fact that governments of poor nations with the support of a few allies, if committed, can defeat terrorism. The application of the critical instruments of national power, namely, diplomacy, military and economy, is more effective when applied with a boost by regional allies. It can be safely stated that although a formal South Asian regional counter-terrorism mechanism was not active, fair interaction and cooperation between South Asian Association for Regional Cooperation (SAARC) and other countries provided Sri Lanka tremendous support at a bilateral and informal level. Despite lacking a coherent, coordinated and collective response as a region, the common dislike of terrorism existed.

Diplomatic support negotiated by Sri Lanka on a bilateral basis with regional allies and the Western nations, whose perception of terrorism and Sri Lanka changed in the wake of 9/11, provided adequate breathing space in the form of non-interference to facilitate the counter-terrorism campaign back home.

Further, diplomacy with traditional friendly nations, China and Pakistan, facilitated the acquisition of the much-needed military hardware which was not accessible due to Western embargoes. Diplomacy and economic support go hand in hand. This was evident in the relationship with China which enabled the GoSL to procure military equipment on concessionary and easy credit lines, thus easing the burden on the country. It is to the credit of the GoSL that the nation, though committed to a major counter-terrorism campaign involving the whole nation, was still able to maintain an average economic growth rate of 6.08 per cent. The Chinese diplomacy protected the nation's interest at the UN and other international forums, which provided the time and space to execute the counter-terrorism campaign to a favourable termination. Russia, too, played a significant role in international forums by supporting the country's interest.

Military capacity building is one strand of cooperation that continued despite differences in other politically sensitive areas. The cooperation included two principle aspects, intelligence sharing and training. The Sri Lankan military was able to train in all countries of the region and a few outside the region, including the United States (US). It is to the credit of India that despite enormous pressure from its southern constituency to stop training the Sri Lankan armed forces, the central government never ceded to these demands, risking internal political stability, and continued with the training. Pakistan wholeheartedly supported Sri Lanka on all fronts and remains a key ally to this day. The intelligence shared enabled the neutralising of LTTE financing, arms smuggling and disinformation. The navy's success in destroying the LTTE's international shipping in high seas was based on intelligence provided by a friendly country, who for obvious reasons cannot be identified.

Conclusion

The conclusion identifies critical observations and related recommendations which should be the focus of any concept of regional response mechanisms. One of the core observations of this chapter is that Sri Lanka's defeat of terrorism in the final three-and-a-half years of the conflict can be credited to a strong political leadership, pragmatic strategy, national will, empowering the populace as partners, economic stability, military innovation and external support. External support included mustering own external support whilst denying the LTTE external support. The true finesse in diplomacy was keeping India out of the conflict, a feat achieved through the personal efforts of the president and a specially designated team. Another observation is that poor or developing nations cannot defeat, or as a minimum manage, internal or transnational terrorism without organised external support in the form of common regional or international responses.

The Sri Lankan experience is that nations in instances of counter-terrorism cooperation prefer to cooperate bilaterally rather than multilaterally. A core or common understanding based on broadly agreed objectives may shape policy, but cooperation would generally water down to bilateral interaction. However, a common stand on issues of contention is required. The common stand should extend to international forums to expand own influence and gain legitimacy for the cause at hand.

The support generated from regionally coherent responses should focus on boosting the instruments of national power of the nation supported, which would enhance capacity to deal with related complexities. A classic example in the Sri Lankan context was the sustainment of a stable economy through China and other friendly countries. This also contributed to continuing development whilst in contact with the threat, which facilitated rapid post-conflict recovery.

A frequent area of discussion is whether the Sri Lankan conflict could have been terminated much earlier, specifically during 1987 when the LTTE was cornered and at the brink of destruction. In analysing the circumstances, both political and military and the internal dynamics, I personally feel that the LTTE could have been contained effectively had the Indian government not intervened. However, during the final days of survival, the LTTE expected and requested for Indian intervention, which went unanswered possibly because of the better and common understanding on terrorism with Sri Lanka. Further, it is recommended that regional cooperation should be not confined to just combating terrorism but also include supporting nations with conditions that breed terrorism. A preventive approach based on capacity building of such vulnerable nations is also a vital requirement. Finally, the Sri Lankan experience should stand as an example as to how a nation suffered due to the big power hegemony, an unbalanced and unrealistic foreign policy and the lack of a common regional understanding on dealing with terrorism.

NOTES

1   Editor's Note: Lt. Gen R.M. Daya Ratnayake (Retd.), WWV, RWP, RSP, USP, NDU, PSC was the 20th Commander of the Sri Lanka Army. All facts about the LTTE represented in this chapter are drawn from the author's personal understanding of the LTTE and experience in the army fighting it.

2   Niel A Smith, "Understanding Sri Lanka's Defeat of the Tamil Tigers," *Joint Forces Quarterly*, No. 59 (Quarter 2010): 40–44.

3   Taming the Tamil Tigers (2008), "Federal Bureau of Investigation archives," available at https://archives.fbi.gov/archives/news/stories/2008/january/tamil_tigers011008, accessed on 26 February 2017.

4   Available at https://www.un.org/sc/ctc/news/region/asia/south-asia/, accessed on 26 February 2017.

5   Connable, Ben and Martin C. Libicki, "How Insurgencies End. Santa Monica," CA: RAND Corporation, 2010, available at https://www.rand.org/pubs/monographs/MG965.html.

6   See Note 1.

17

A 9/11 for South Asia?

Ayesha Siddiqa

South Asia has changed from a place where multiple ideas and numerous communities and faiths could live peacefully side by side to a region with greater intolerance and radicalism. While faith-based ideological differences resulting in some form of violence is not a new phenomenon, the tone and texture of this vitriol that infiltrated the region after the 1980s has only grown both quantitatively and qualitatively. In the years since, faith-based violence has generally increased throughout the region, and states have attempted to reduce the actuality of these changes by dumbing them down and labelling them as communal or sectarian violence. The reality of the situation, however, is that the systematic use of religious ideology compounded with violence has been aimed at achieving particular political goals. Despite the fact that most regional states tend to ignore their respective spate of radicalism, this is a problem that cannot be ignored or denied. It is important to note that this trend is prevalent throughout the region, and yet governments would like to hide behind the argument that violence is reducing on the whole. The reduction in violence notwithstanding, it needs to be contextualised by taking into account the increased capacity of security and law enforcement organisations. The fact of the matter is that this could be a trend that could change at any point, whenever certain shifts in the goals of global terrorist organisations occur, which could lead to the further perpetuation of radicalism in the region. I argue in this chapter that the continuation of such a threat can be attributed to the fact that states continue to see non-state actors and violence as a policy tool and have no vision for the region to come together to fight the menace. Despite the rhetoric, there is no reckoning regarding the ways in which terrorism and radicalism pose a huge threat to stability of the society.

Violence in South Asia

Since its peak in 2009, violence in South Asia has experienced a downward trend. Figure 17.1 demonstrates the aforementioned pattern, and the decline can be attributed to an overall reduction in violence in most countries. A significant aspect of the figure is the almost total end in countries like Sri Lanka and Nepal that earlier suffered from political violence, terrorism and civil war.

Figure 17.1: Terrorism Trends in South Asia

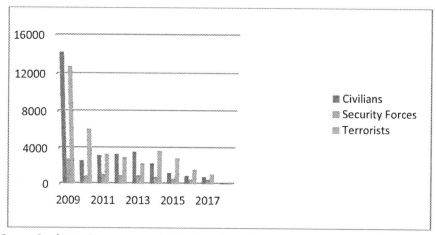

Source: South Asia Terrorism Portal, "Fatalities 2005–2018".[1]

However, such a figure is not holistically representative as the reduction is not evenly divided. Afghanistan suffered from the highest number of attacks and fatalities in 2017 where the Taliban carried out most of these attacks. Despite the fact that several other terror networks like the Islamic State of Iraq and Syria (ISIS) or Daesh have also made inroads into the country, it is the Taliban that continues to pose a major threat in the region. Reportedly, in early 2017, 57 per cent districts were under the Taliban control.[2]

As mentioned earlier, the reduction reflected in the figure ought not to be viewed as an end of violent extremism, but instead should be seen as linked with continued presence of violent extremist groups and radicalism. In fact, there are visible footprints of global terrorist organisations such as Daesh in most major states of the region. In Afghanistan, for instance, out of the 105 terrorist attacks in 2017, about 24 were by Daesh.[3] Similarly in Pakistan, out of the 48 terrorist attacks that occurred in the same period, Daesh and its affiliates carried out 13.[4] In Bangladesh, on the other hand, three out of the five attacks that occurred were by Daesh. While Daesh has not managed to penetrate India, there remains a threat from certain forces presenting themselves as Daesh and al-Qaeda subsets, claiming their intent to intervene in Kashmir.[5] Even states adjacent to South Asia, like China and Russia, have expressed concerns about the presence of Daesh in the region.[6]

This is a worrying development as it indicates the growth of an organisation born and nourished in the Middle East, expanding in South Asia and benefiting from the commonality of faith. When forced out of the Middle East, Daesh leader Abu Bakr al-Baghdadi called upon his followers to go and "strike at home".[7] This was a significant message for Daesh members from South and Southeast Asia. Furthermore, the Middle East and South Asia are already involved in a pendulum-like movement in which extremist elements or trained fighters have shifted from one region to the other depending on where the pressure points have been. For instance, a considerable number of militants initially linked with freedom struggle in the Middle East moved to Afghanistan during the 1980s after they were unable to operate in their own countries. The Afghan war of the 1980s saw Palestinians, Egyptians, Iraqis, Syrians, Yemenis and Saudis come to South Asia. However, much after 9/11 when Afghanistan came under attack, and it was not feasible for transnational terrorist organisations like al-Qaeda to operate freely, many of the militants shifted back to the Middle East, taking along militants from Afghanistan, Pakistan and other parts of South Asia as well.

Al-Baghdadi's above-mentioned message was for non-Arab fighters that were trained by Daesh in Iraq, Syria and other parts of the Middle East. This says a lot about the capacity of transnational violent extremist outfits and the ways in which they connect with local issues as the method to expand their influence. The al-Qaeda, for instance, propagates the need for the creation of an independent Islamic state of Baluchistan and uses it as an attempt to poach on the separatist instincts amongst certain segments of the population in both Iran and Pakistan.[8] The global militant infrastructure has become more localised and this has occurred through introductory franchising of local organisations, groups and individuals. Thus, the element of violent extremism being external to the region is gone.

Reasons for the Continued Existence of Terrorism in South Asia

The fact is that there are three critical elements due to which violent extremist infrastructures continue to exist in South Asia. First, there is sustained use of non-state actors by regional states as tools to be used in proxy wars. The intelligence agencies of a number of regional countries tend to deploy politically or religiously motivated non-state actors against rival states. The sponsorship of violent extremists comes from both within the region and from outside. The continued hostility between India and Pakistan, for example, has resulted in Pakistan using non-state actors against India. But there are other state actors too, like Iran, China and Russia, that are in conversation with the Taliban for their respective motives. The fact that the United States (US) has tilted towards talking to the Taliban to figure out Afghanistan's future will have its consequences. Furthermore, the competition between the great powers in Afghanistan continues to make the Taliban relevant. Besides, the Saudi–Iran conflict could also spill into the region at some stage. According to Antonio Giustozzi, Visiting Professor at King's College London and Fellow at RUSI, the Saudis now have contact with Taliban and other warlords in Afghanistans.[9] As long as the Afghanistan conflict continues and state actors have the propensity and will to use extremist elements, containing violent extremism will be difficult.

Second, the expansion of communal politics in larger states like India has encouraged the growth of right-wing extremist organisations. This has led to an alleged acceptance of the usage of violence as a tool to subjugate minorities, which is what fuels the narrative and appeal of local and transnational terrorist organisations. The rise of Hindutva, and its terrorism, as a phenomenon has only served to escalate the terrorism problem.[10] Other examples are the Rohingya crisis in Myanmar and its impact on Bangladesh, or the rising tension between Buddhists and Muslims in Sri Lanka in which the dominant religious ideology targets the minority.[11] While states continue to use violence as a precursor to any negotiation in a political conflict, it strengthens the influence of extremist ideologies. In this regard, the responsibility is not entirely that of non-state actors or the aggrieved population, but also of governments that are trying to introduce political solutions to political and socio-economic problems.

Third, it is difficult to dissipate violent extremism in the absence of measures to checkmate radicalism. The fact of the matter is that in today's South Asia, radicalism of all colours and hues has been exacerbated. In countries like Afghanistan and Pakistan, extremist ideology dates back to the mid-1970s and in certain other cases, even earlier. The conceptualisation of this ideology has expanded significantly since then. The anti-American sentiment has played a significant role in anchoring extremist ideology. Over the years and with the subsequent use of militants on other war fronts, the extremist narrative has got streamlined. As a result, there has been larger expansion of Deobandi and Ahl-e-Hadith ideologies. Furthermore, the popularity of various militant groups connected with aforementioned ideologies has encouraged various other schools of thought like the Barelvis—that constitutes the largest number of Muslims—towards extremism. In this case, the emphasis is on implementing the blasphemy law in the country and preventing violence by masses against blasphemy accused.

In fact, the popularity of implementing the blasphemy law has turned into a key influence in countries like Bangladesh. The killing of bloggers and the rise of blasphemy-related cases indicate the impact of radicalism in Bangladesh,[12] which was considered a secular state despite its Muslim identity. Blasphemy-related violence in Pakistan and Afghanistan is also an indicator of extremism in these states. However, other countries have not remained safe either. As mentioned earlier, there has been a rise of Hindutva in India and Buddhist extremism in Sri Lanka and adjoining Myanmar.

The Need for Introspection

The question that counter-terrorism scholarship needs to ask itself right now is: whether reduction in violence is in itself a guarantee of lasting peace? Unless the internal sources of discontentment are addressed and radicalism contained without any exception, societies in South Asia, or even rest of the world, will continue to be threatened. There is a need for genuine political, social and cultural pluralism and an increased capacity of groups to ensure that they coexist for peace to stabilise. The South Asian region has been in a constant state of war since 1979 and that has fundamentally changed the mood of most societies. It is not just the states but the societies that have transformed as well. The internal societal competition for power in most states has fanned extremist ideologies and encouraged right-wing ideologies and politics to grow. For peace and counter-terrorism objectives, it is essential to have a new vision for deradicalisation.

Therefore, it seems that despite the violence in the region on the whole, the region has not arrived at its 9/11 moment of catastrophe. It is safe to assume that this might not happen until various stakeholders see greater benefit in abandoning proxy wars as tool of war fighting, or prefer to develop a joint vision for fighting terrorism and radicalism. Thus, unless consensus is developed amongst most regional states, it would not matter for individual states to claim that they have been victimised by terrorism. A larger agreement is essential.

NOTES

1   Datasheets Fatalities, South Asia Terrorism Portal, available at http://old.satp.org/satporgtp/southasia/datasheets/Fatalities.html accessed on 18 August 2018.
2   Vanda Felbab-Brown, "President Trump's Afghanistan Policy: Hopes and Pitfalls", Brookings, September 2017, p. 4.
3   Available at https://storymaps.esri.com/stories/terrorist-attacks/?year=2017, accessed on 17 December 2017.
4   Ibid.
5   Daesh influenced forces trying to create chaos in Kashmir: Geelani, *Al-Masdar News*, 22 July

2017, Available at https://mobile.almasdarnews.com/article/daesh-influenced-forces-trying-create-chaos-kashmir-geelani/ accessed on 22 February 2018.

6   Russia voices worries over US, NATO denial of Daesh in Afghanistan, *Press TV*, 21 February 2018, available at http://www.presstv.com/Detail/2018/02/21/553065/russia-afghanistan-daesh-us-nato, accessed on 22 February 2018.

7   Nadine Awadalla and Eric Knecht, "Islamic State's Baghdadi, in Undated Audio, Urges Militants to Keep Fighting", *Reuters*, 28 September 2017.

8   Qari Abdul Hadi, "Yeh Kis Ki Fauj Hey? (Whose Army is This?)", *Hittin* (Al-Qaeeda journal), Vol. 8, Shaban 1433 (Islamic calendar), pp. 24–56.

9   Discussion with Antonio Giustozzi in London, September 2017.

10   Sudha Ramachandran, "Hindutva Terrorism in India", *The Diplomat*, 7 July 2017, available at https://thediplomat.com/2017/07/hindutva-terrorism-in-india/, accessed on 18 August 2018.

11   "Sri Lanka: Police Inaction as Muslim Shops Torched by Buddhists", *Al-Jazeera*, 6 March 2018, available at https://www.aljazeera.com/news/2018/03/sri-lanka-muslim-shops-mosques-targeted-buddhist-hardliners-180305165900594.html accessed on 18 August 2018.

12   Emma Graham-Harrison and Saad Hammadi, "Inside Bangladesh's Killing Fields: Bloggers and Outsiders Targeted by Fanatics", *The Guardian*, 12 June 2016.

18

The Evolving ISIS Threat to Southeast Asia

*Kumar Ramakrishna**

The ISIS Threat I: The Physical Dimension

In August 2016, media reports emerged of a plan by a cell of Indonesian militants associated with the so-called Islamic State of Iraq and Syria (ISIS) to fire a rocket from Batam island—south of Singapore—at the iconic Marina Bay Sands (MBS) complex on Singapore island itself. The five-man cell was colourfully called Katibah Gonggong Rebus (KGR), meaning "Boiled Snails Cell" in Bahasa Indonesia. While KGR was apparently influenced by the incarcerated Indonesian extremist cleric Aman Abdurrahman, it was operationally directed by a Syria-based Indonesian ISIS militant called Bahrun Naim, also an associate of Aman's. Moreover, KGR had intended to launch the projectile from a point on Batam island called Habibie Hill, about 17 km from Singapore's shoreline and 18 km from MBS. Investigations revealed that the Batam cell leader, Gigih Rahmat Dewa, had coordinated the planned strike with Bahrun Naim via social media. Planning for the attack reportedly began in October 2015, and Singapore aside, the cell had also intended to attack Indonesian targets, such as an international seaport in Batam, shopping malls and other places in the archipelago, using suicide bombers. Some reports suggested that the KGR cell members did possess some technical skills that may have enabled them to build a rocket capable of striking Singapore's MBS from Batam; in any case, the cell could also have potentially relied on expertise brought

*Elements of this chapter were adapted from Kumar Ramakrishna, "The Threat of Terrorism and Extremism: 'A Matter of "When", and Not "If"'", Daljit Singh and Malcolm Cook (eds), *Southeast Asian Affairs 2017*, Singapore: ISEAS Publishing, 2017, pp. 335–52 and "The Growth of ISIS Extremism in Southeast Asia: Its Ideological and Cognitive Features—and Possible Policy Responses", *New England Journal of Public Policy*, Vol. 29, No. 1, March 2017, pp. 1–22. Despite the military setbacks incurred to ISIS, post the presentation of this paper in March 2017, there is no doubt that the threat of ideological expansion, especially to Southeast Asia, has only multiplied.

in from outside Batam by Bahrun Naim. In this connection, it emerged that one of the latter's protégés, Dodi Suridi, had—based on information gleaned from YouTube—built and successfully test-fired a makeshift rocket launcher employing a plastic tube, potassium nitrate extracted from fertiliser and other substances. Most analysts, however, expressed scepticism that the KGR cell could have built or easily acquired the military-grade rocket system that would have been needed to hit MBS from Batam, such as Russian-built Katyusha and Grad, as well as Chinese-type WS-1E rockets. Still, some observers conceded that a home-made rocket could have been launched from a boat just off the Singapore coastline.[1]

The ISIS Threat II: The Ideological Dimension

It was not just in the physical sphere that the ISIS threat presented itself to the worried Singaporean security officials. Far more insidiously, it evinced a potent ideological dimension as well. This was driven home on several occasions throughout 2016. First, on 20 January, news broke of the arrests under the Internal Security Act (ISA) of 27 Bangladeshi foreign workers employed in the local construction sector, who had been arrested between 6 November and 1 December 2015 for being involved in a "closed religious study group" that "subscribed to extremist beliefs and teachings of radical ideologues like" the late al-Qaeda ideologue Anwar al-Awlaki, as well as the extremist ideological output of the ISIS—exemplified by its members' support of the Sunni terror group's drive to kill members of the Shia minority sect of Islam. The group had viewed video footage of children being trained in "terrorist military camps" and had, in its possession, literature graphically demonstrating various methods of "silent killings". While some of the radicalised Bangladeshis had plans to join ISIS in the Middle East, a number of them also contemplated returning to Bangladesh itself to wage war against the government and sent donations to domestic extremist groups in that country. While 26 of the group's members were repatriated, one was jailed for attempting to flee Singapore illegally on learning of the arrests of other group members.[2]

Four months later, in early May, it was reported that another six Bangladeshi workers, purportedly belonging to a group called Islamic State of Bangladesh (ISB), had been detained under the ISA in April. The ISB cell had initially sought to join up with ISIS in the Middle East, but due to the difficulty of travelling there, its members had switched plans, now seeking to return to Bangladesh "to topple their government through violence, set up an Islamic State there, and bring it under the self-declared caliphate" of ISIS. The ISB cell leader, Rahman Mizanur, apparently possessed "a significant amount of ISIS and Al-Qaeda radical material that he used to recruit ISB members in Singapore", and had identified specific targets in Bangladesh for liquidation, including "disbelievers", "media peoples", as well as Bangladeshi government and military figures. Significantly, Singapore government leaders noted that while the city-state itself had not figured in ISB targeting plans, Mizanur had expressly indicated that "he would carry out an attack anywhere if he was instructed by ISIS to do so"—and the ISIS had certainly identified Singapore as a target in several social media posts in 2015.[3]

The ISIS: A "Mutation" of Al-Qaeda

Before proceeding further, a concise recapitulation of the ISIS phenomenon is warranted. To be sure, the ISIS did not pop out of thin air. It is simply the latest "mutation" of the wider al-Qaeda ideological movement in the face of intense global security force pressure since the 11 September 2001 attacks in the United States (US).[4] Following terrorism scholar Bruce Hoffman, it could be said that the current configuration of the global al-Qaeda movement comprises "four distinct, but not mutually exclusive, dimensions" in "descending order of sophistication".[5] The first of these dimensions is "Al-Qaeda Central", comprising the "remnants of the pre 9/11 al-Qaeda organization". Second, "Al-Qaeda Affiliates and Associates",[6] including its regional franchise networks, such as Al-Qaeda in the Arabian Peninsula (AQAP), Al-Qaeda in the Islamic Maghreb (AQIM), Al-Shabab in Somalia, Jamaat-e-Islami (JI) in Southeast Asia, Al-Nusra in Syria and, of course, ISIS, which straddles both Iraq and Syria, and since mid-2014 has rapidly grown into a global rival to al-Qaeda itself, chiefly because of its highly symbolic and strategic inauguration of the caliphate. Anthropologist and terrorism scholar Scott Atran has argued that the caliphate idea "represents a very real and powerful attractor for the disaffected across the Muslim world" and is "the only systemic, countercultural global movement" that "represents in the minds of tens of millions a history and destiny denied".[7]

A third dimension of the al-Qaeda global movement could be regarded as "Al-Qaeda Network", comprising "amorphous groups of al-Qaeda adherents who are likely to have had some prior terrorism experience" and connection with "Al-Qaeda Central",[8] such as the so-called 7/7 bombers who struck the London rail and bus network in July 2005. The leader of the four-man militant cell that carried out the London attacks that killed 52 civilians, Mohammad Siddique Khan, and one other cell member had received paramilitary training by "Al-Qaeda Central" in Pakistan prior to the attacks.[9] What Hoffman calls "Al-Qaeda Galaxy", comprising "home-grown Islamic radicals who have no direct connection with al-Qaeda" but are "prepared to carry out attacks in solidarity with or support of

al-Qaeda's radical jihadi agenda"—"lone wolves" or "wolf packs" in short[10]—
represents the fourth dimension of the global al-Qaeda movement.[11] As Hoffman
cogently avers, what holds this complex, diverse and multilayered al-Qaeda global
movement—which includes the ISIS—together is a broadly shared ideological
narrative of "a shared sense of enmity and grievance towards the United States
and the West in general, and their host-nations in particular".[12]

The ISIS Threat in Wider Geopolitical Perspective

The developments on the Singaporean home front, described previously, very
much reflect the general trends globally. The ISIS has, throughout 2016, been on
the strategic defensive in both Iraq and Syria, and its so-called caliphate, epicentred
in Mosul in Iraq and Raqqa in Syria, has been subjected to tremendous military
pressure by an international coalition of military forces led by the US and Russia
and including Iraqi and Syrian government troops and pro-government militias.
By October 2016, by some estimates, the ISIS had lost almost 28 per cent of
"strategically significant" territory it had held in both Iraq and Syria since January
2015, six months after it inaugurated the caliphate at the end of June 2014.[13]
This has prompted its leadership to seek other relatively poorly governed and
restive zones to establish some sort of *wilayat* or province in, to act as alternate
fallback positions should the current territorial infrastructure within Iraq and
Syria collapse. While some analysts have pointed to areas particularly within Libya
but also, inter alia, Yemen, Egypt, West Africa, Pakistan and Afghanistan as
potential wilayat,[14] others have suggested that Southeast Asia, which straddles
important sea lines of communications and importantly, a quarter of the world's
Muslim populations, could also be another area the ISIS planners would logically
consider—all the more so as Southeast Asian fighters currently fighting with ISIS
may return to the region if the ISIS loses critical territorial mass in the Middle
East.[15]

The Southeast Asian Context

In particular, reports have suggested that, in April 2016, an ISIS wilayat was
declared in Mindanao in the southern Philippines, which has been the arena for
a decades-long insurgency by Muslim separatists agitating for independence from
a central Christian government in Manila. Furthermore, some of these separatist
entities, such as the Abu Sayyaf Group (ASG), have had links with transnational
terrorist networks such as the al-Qaeda and JI in the not-too-distant past. One
reason the southern Philippines appears to have become "the fulcrum of IS activity"
in the region is because the leader of the East Indonesia Mujahidin (*Mujahidin*

Indonesia Timur [MIT]) network operating in Poso, Central Sulawesi, Santoso—who had pledged allegiance to the ISIS—was killed in July 2016. Hence, the titular leader of the ISIS groups in the southern Philippines and by implication, potentially the region, may well be Isnilon Hapilon, a senior ASG leader who himself has pledged allegiance to the ISIS. There have been reports that Arabs, Uighurs from Xinjiang in China and even Caucasians have begun arriving in Mindanao,[16] while Indonesian militants who have been thwarted in their plans to travel to Syria to fight have also turned eastwards towards Mindanao instead, marrying up with their Philippine counterparts and triggering concerns about "cross-border violence".[17]

Little wonder that IHS Jane's Terrorism and Insurgency Centre went so far as to declare that "it is only a matter of time before ISIS controls swathes of southern Philippines with its base on Mindanao, the country's second-largest island with a population of 20 million."[18] The residual vulnerability of the southern Philippines—taken together with ISIS-orchestrated strikes on the Jakarta business district in January 2016, in which eight people including four militants were killed,[19] as well as on a nightclub in Puchong, near Kuala Lumpur in late June, injuring eight people, and a raft of other smaller-scale incidents in both countries over the course of the year—has not been lost on the Singapore authorities.[20] In March, the Singaporean Home Affairs and Law Minister, K. Shanmugam, responding to the ISIS-orchestrated attacks on the Brussels international airport and nearby subway that killed more than 31 people, argued that this incident showed just how difficult it was to protect cities from terrorist attacks, as Brussels had been on the highest state of alert and it was still attacked. Hence, he assessed that realistically speaking, an attack on Singapore "was a matter of 'when' and not 'if'".[21] Part of Mr Shanmugam's concern no doubt stemmed from the fact that the ISIS has gone so far as to create a Malay/Indonesian military unit called the ISIS Malay Archipelago Unit or Katibah Nusantara (KN), staffed with volunteers drawn from the more than 700 Indonesian and 200 Malaysian fighters—as of November 2015 according to some estimates—that have decided to head to Syria. It has been suggested that KN has provided assistance to Indonesian terrorist groups, including allegedly funding several thwarted bomb plots in the country.[22]

The KN—Majmuah Al Arkhabiliy in Arabic—was apparently raised in Shaddadi, Hasakah, in Syria, in September 2014. It started out as a 100-strong unit of Indonesian and Malaysian fighters and by October 2015, it had grown sufficiently to form three geographical subunits led by Indonesian nationals: KN Central led by Bahrumsyah; Katibah Masyariq led by the Homs-based Salim Mubarok At-Tamimi, alias Abu Jandal; and Katibah Aleppo, led by Abu Abdillah.

Bahrumsyah, till his death in Syria in March 2017, was the amir of KN and had developed a reputation for dealing harshly with Indonesian ISIS fighters that attempted to defect and undermine KN unity. Reports indicate that as of late 2015, about 450 Indonesian and Malaysian fighters and their families were in the Iraq/Syrian region under ISIS/KN control.[23]

More ominously, KN has apparently set up the Abdullah Azzam Academy for the education and military training of children of Malaysian and Indonesian fighters. The medium of instruction is the Malay language, and it is clear that KN is quite deliberately and self-consciously training a new generation of Malay-speaking militants indoctrinated from young to be committed to the core belief that the setting up of the Southeast Asian wilayat of ISIS is a long-term God-given mission. In March 2015, the ISIS posted a two-minute video showing Malay children training with weapons in ISIS-held territory. The video declared that these children will "finish all oppressors, disbelievers, apostates", and ended with a child firing a revolver. The underlying theme was as ominous: "These children will be the next generation of fighters. You can capture us, kill us, we will regenerate, no matter how hard you try."[24] Greatly aiding the ISIS/KN cause is its extensive and clever use of social media. Analysts have noted a "surge in Indonesian- and Malay-language material posted by ISIS online",[25] as its media division, Al-Hayat, has ramped up targeted content in the form of media statements, videos and periodicals like the online magazine *Dabiq*—which has an Indonesian-language version—with a view to intensifying its outreach to vulnerable Southeast Asian Malay-Muslim communities. To this end, Al-Hayat "relies on its online 'fan base' in closed chat groups of forums" to soak up such content and ensure that it is "pushed across social media spheres like Twitter, Facebook and Google+".[26]

At one level, such a barrage of virulent ISIS ideological and mobilisational social media content may well inspire lone wolf activity (see next section); the August 2015 issue of *Dabiq*, for example, called upon supporters to attack the embassies of countries engaged in the global anti-ISIS coalition, a group which notably includes Singapore, Malaysia and Indonesia.[27] At another, more fundamental level, such ISIS propaganda—which often features an extreme anti-Shia bias—may ultimately compel a worrying deterioration of wider Sunni–Shia relations in Southeast Asia. As it is, the virulent ISIS message already finds fallow ground in Indonesia, where rising sectarian intolerance prompted the Setara Institute for Democracy and Peace in Indonesia to report a worrying threefold increase in anti-Shia violence between 2012–13.[28] Signs that the ISIS narrative is taking root in Malay-Muslim communities in the region are rife. Malaysia carried out more than 100 arrests of people suspected of having links to Daesh and foiled seven terrorist plots in 2015, while Indonesia made at least 74 terror-related arrests and prevented nine plots in 2015. By the end of 2016 moreover, 150 militants, imprisoned in Indonesian jails for terror-related offences, had been released—without any assurance that they had responded well to rehabilitation efforts. In addition, at least 100 Indonesians have returned from Syria, while 200 others were deported by Turkey whilst trying to enter Syria via the porous border. Thickening the plot further, it is not lost on regional analysts that 220,000 Muslim Rohingya refugees, formerly residing in the Arakan region in Myanmar, languish in camps in Malaysia and Thailand.[29] The Rohingya have sought to flee persecution at the hands of a Buddhist-dominated Myanmar military egged on by influential Buddhist extremist figures.[30] These displaced people are highly vulnerable to radicalisation—and ISIS is well known to exploit sectarian conflicts to replenish its ranks.

Social Media, the Rise of the "Lone Wolves" and the Insider Threat

In line with the given analysis, it is noteworthy that Mr Shanmugam himself identified three groups that could pose a threat to Singapore and for that matter, Southeast Asia: "battle-hardened" returning fighters from Iraq and Syria: "those freed from detention but who still harbor radical inclinations"; and finally, those radicalised online by "ISIS propaganda".[31] In recent times, a great deal of attention has been focused on the latter issue of self-radicalised lone wolf terrorists. Lone operators or lone wolves are becoming significant players, despite the lack of a physical support network, because the Internet gives indiscriminate access to information about targets and ways to construct various types of weapons. For instance, the article, "How to Make a Bomb in the Kitchen of Your Mom", in the English-language online magazine *Inspire*—put out by Awlaki's AQAP group in Yemen—apparently aided the April 2013 Boston marathon bombers to construct the pressure cooker bomb they used. The article has reportedly—and worryingly—also been translated into Bahasa Indonesia by the militant groups in that country as well.[32] On the one hand, the lone wolf militant may employ improvised explosive devices (IEDs), like the Tsarnaev brothers in the Boston attacks, and some analyst warn that downstream, lone wolves armed with chemical, biological, radiological and nuclear (CBRN) weapons and materials could strike population centres and generate enormous numbers of civilian casualties. On the other hand, the lone wolf strike may be very simple in practice, making use of everyday items like kitchen knives—the Woolwich, London, murder of the British soldier Lee Rigby in May 2013—or cars and trucks, as in the cases of Nice in July 2016, Berlin six months later and most recently, London in March 2017 and Stockholm a month later. It is for good reason, therefore, that the Soufan Group has referred to the ISIS-inspired "weaponization of everyday life" as a key feature of the growing ISIS threat to civilised, multicultural societies everywhere.[33]

The emergence of the lone wolf or lone actor has been facilitated by several converging trends. First, increasingly efficient Internet broadband access and cheaper 4G smartphone technology has been a boon to transnational terrorist networks like al-Qaeda and ISIS, enabling them to efficiently broadcast their ideologically extremist appeals in cyberspace, at minimum cost to themselves. The results have been significant. In Singapore, for instance, in mid-2010, a full-time National Serviceman, a freelance religious teacher and one of the teacher's students were detained. They had all been radicalised by the al-Qaeda ideologue, Anwar al-Awlaki—the so-called "bin Laden of the Internet".[34] The ISIS has, in fairness, been an upgrade on al-Qaeda in the social media domain. This is primarily because the ISIS has a professional media department devoted to pumping out messages that, in contrast to the long and frankly boring al-Qaeda spokespersons, are simple, easy to understand and "sticky".[35]

Second, the ISIS adroitly exploits the gaming culture of young people with skill. The ISIS propaganda comes across as slick messages via 50,000 Twitter accounts and 100,000 tweets a day.[36] Their propagandists on social media make the effort to promote the image of "jihadi cool"[37] and the appeal of "jihad tourism"[38] so as to attract young, bored, stimulus-seeking young men and women seeking meaning in life. This is why astute observers like Fawaz Gerges consider ISIS to be a "youth movement".[39] Young males aside, ISIS is also targeting a broader social base for recruitment: young women, doctors, judges, professionals and military personnel. This is simply because the ISIS is serious about building the Islamic State into a viable political, economic and administrative entity.[40] The Western-led anti-ISIS coalition still has some ground to cover in the social media battle versus the ISIS.[41] Nevertheless, by October 2016, thanks to the combination of intensified action taken by social media companies to remove extremist material from their platforms, as well as increasing military pressure on ISIS territorial strongholds in Iraq, studies showed that the organisation's propaganda output was gradually declining. However, circumspection is called for: some analysts cautioned that "that the psychological effects of the group's control over what people read, watched, and heard will likely outlast its physical control of the territory".[42]

The Lone Wolf "Insider Threat"

One particularly serious manifestation of the ISIS lone wolf problem could be in the form of the so-called "insider threat". Lone wolves may take the form of "insiders", that is, people who can harm a society not from outside, like returning foreign fighters, but from "within the system". Insiders have arguably demonstrated their terrible cost-effective potential to the ISIS and wider violent Islamist cause. In October 2015, a Russian Metrojet commercial aircraft flying from Sharm el-Sheikh to St Petersburg crashed in Sinai, killing all 224 passengers. An Egyptian ISIS affiliate claimed responsibility and Western investigators surmised that a bomb had been smuggled onboard either via airport baggage handlers or even staff at the hotels where the passengers had been staying in. Then, in February 2016, a Daallo Airlines flight from Mogadishu to Djibouti was struck by an apparent suicide bombing onboard. Fortunately, as the plane had not reached cruising altitude, the flight avoided the catastrophic decompression that had befallen the ill-fated Metrojet aircraft a few months before. Hence, only the suspected suicide bomber was killed when the blast created a small hole that caused him to be sucked out of the aircraft. Investigations revealed that the suspected bomber had been handed a package by someone beyond the security checkpoint just prior to boarding. Another example is of Abdirahmaan Muhumed, an American ISIS fighter killed in Syria in 2014, who once worked as a cleaner at the Minneapolis–Saint Paul Airport in Minnesota. The insider threat has manifested over the past year in Southeast Asia as well. These have included radicalised armed auxiliary airport police and immigration officials, Malaysian military personnel and even Indonesian commercial airline pilots. The respected Soufan Group observed that aviation aside, the insider threat is equally real for "power grids, water supplies, and other critical infrastructure".[43]

The insider threat has also surfaced in Singapore. In late 2015 and the first months of 2016, there were two separate arrests of radicalised Bangladeshi foreign workers in the construction and marine industries. Al-Qaeda and the ISIS materials on weapons and bomb making, as well as funds earmarked for purchasing weapons for use in Bangladesh, were also seized. Both cells had apparently no plans to attack Singapore, but had targeted the Bangladeshi government, military, media and "disbelievers" instead. Nevertheless, one of the Bangladeshi cell leaders conceded his willingness to "carry out an attack anywhere if he was instructed to do so by ISIS to do so". Thus, although the Singapore government reiterated that there were "no specific indications that Singapore had been selected as a target", analysts pointed out that ISIS has identified the city-state as a possible target on social media postings as well as its online magazine *Dabiq*.[44]

Three Strategic Implications

Effective risk assessment and operational counter-measures are needed to guard against the physical modalities of the expanded ISIS threat to Southeast Asia described here. In Singapore, for instance, "tell-tale indicator training" has been in place for several years now, in the form of the Threat-Oriented Passenger Screening Integrated System (TOPSIS). The TOPSIS "mobilises cleaners, cashiers, retail staff and counter staff at Changi Airport and other checkpoints to look out for suspicious individuals". There are indications that TOPSIS may be extended further to "other sectors such as shopping centres, office buildings and education institutions".[45] Such measures, while necessary, are nevertheless insufficient. It has been persuasively argued that the centre of gravity of the ISIS and the wider violent Islamist threat is not its organised and self-radicalised cells and lone wolves scattered throughout the world, including Southeast Asia. Rather, seasoned analysts like Jonathan Evans, former Director General of the British Secret Service, and Michael Chertoff, at one point Secretary of the US Department of Homeland Security, have argued that the "root" of the challenge is "ideological".[46] Hence, there is a need to fight fire with fire, by countering this violent ideology effectively through effective use of social media platforms to put out effective counter-ISIS messaging. Such a strategy would be multifaceted and involve considerable coordination at the national, regional and even global level. In essence, the foregoing analysis suggests three strategic implications.

First, it is utterly necessary to "cognitively immunise" multicultural societies in Southeast Asia—or for that matter beyond—against the attempts of ISIS to split them into warring sectarian divisions.[47] The basic operational strategy of the ISIS has been to sow communal discord in multicultural societies with significant Muslim populations, in an attempt to create mass social polarisation, for it is in such inclement conditions that its propagandists can most effectively recruit to its virulent cause. As seen in this chapter, its propagandists have been effective and adroit in the use of social media to radicalise vulnerable communities in Southeast Asia, and for that matter elsewhere, turning them against other communities in the wider body politic. As one Iraqi observer commenting on the destructive impact of al-Qaeda in Iraq, the forerunner of ISIS, noted: "We didn't know the difference between Sunnis and Shiites until [Al Qaeda in Iraq leader Abu Musab] Zarqawi came, and now, every day, there is a killing".[48] In order to forestall such an outcome, enhanced strategic communications programmes to promote social cohesion and resilience in the most-affected multicultural societies of Southeast Asia, particularly Indonesia, Malaysia, the southern Philippines, southern Thailand and of course Singapore, are much needed. In Singapore, for example, initiatives such as Total Defence and more recently, SG Secure are attempts to create mental firewalls against extremist ISIS appeals.[49]

In Indonesia, moreover, the largest traditionalist Muslim mass organisation, Nahdlatul Ulama, has promoted the concept of "Islam Nusantara", or "Islam of the Malay archipelago", in an effort to shore up the well-known "Islam with a Smiling Face" of Indonesia and the Malay archipelago against the ISIS and other violent Islamist attempts to transmogrify it into a more hardline, intolerant version.[50] A caveat is in order though. Sir Robert Thompson, the famous British counter-insurgent of the 1950s who cut his teeth in the Cold War contest for Malayan hearts and minds with the Communist Party of Malaya, used to argue that "You cannot make bricks without straw." In other words, effective strategic communications and counter-narrative efforts cannot succeed in a political and socio-economic vacuum. Hence, such "hearts and minds" campaigns presuppose a context of good or at least discernibly improving governance so that all communities feel a stake in society and would not dismiss government communications efforts as "propaganda".[51] In like vein, in April 2017, Malaysian Prime Minister Najib Razak affirmed the criticality of good governance, stressing that "Southeast Asian countries needed to ensure their economic growth is inclusive, or risk marginalized populations turning to violent extremism or even overturning political systems."[52]

A second strategic implication is this: given that the ISIS is by and large a "youth organisation", it is equally essential to help our young people build mental and theological firewalls against the ISIS narratives. In this respect, critical thinking skills are important to ingrain in young people. They need to learn not to blindly accept everything they hear, see or read online, or even in the real world, at face value. Instead, they must have the habit of critical enquiry ingrained in them from an early age as they enter the national schooling system. In fact, they need to learn to evaluate and analyse online content as second nature—a process of developing what the British think tank Demos calls "digital fluency".[53] In addition, another way young people, and for that matter their elders, can build mental firewalls against ISIS extremism is via exposure to their counterparts of other faiths and backgrounds from an early age. As Fawas Gerges argues, toleration should "be enshrined as the foundation of the religious and educational curriculum".[54] The idea is to deliberately foster broad acceptance of the importance of "common space" for all faiths and cultures to interact and mingle on a daily basis. Social distancing and the emergence of what Cass Sunstein calls "insulated enclaves" in the multicultural societies of Southeast Asia and beyond are to be avoided.[55]

Finally, rather than relying on overworked counter-terrorism practitioners alone, young people should also be tapped to provide ideas for counter-ideological struggle against the ISIS. This approach has been tried in Singapore. In October 2015, at an event organised by the Indian Muslim community, 20 outstanding Indian Muslim young people were appointed "Ambassadors of Peace", trained to reach out to other Muslim youth to answer their concerns about religion, extremism and terrorism. Another idea with considerable potential is the "Countering Violent Extremism (CVE) Hackathon". During such hackathons, small groups of young people from within the country, or even around the world, would compete with one another to come up with innovative counter-narrative products, such as social media apps or online games. The composition of each group would comprise a strategic mix: one member would be a carefully selected former extremist; one a graphic designer, an information technology practitioner or gaming specialist; and the rest tertiary students keen to contribute to the counter-ideological battle. Government agencies, civil society and social media agencies like Google, Twitter and Facebook could work together with youth on such hackathons, devising authentic themes and products that are more likely to give ISIS propagandists a real battle for the hearts and minds of that most strategic resource: young people.[56]

A third strategic implication involves the role of religious community leaders. Precisely because the ISIS exploits the relative lack of religious knowledge of young people, especially to manipulate them, religious community leaders must play a leading role in providing the theological baseline against which extremist ideological assertions can be benchmarked and exposed. Religious scholars—rather than counter-terrorism practitioners—are best placed to advise on how best to contextualise the faith within a globalised, plural society and by implication, detect signs of extremist interpretations. For instance, in August 2016, some Singaporean Muslim scholars observed that the owner of a Batam-based Indonesian station called Radio Hang had apparently become "influenced by the ideas of a puritanical Indonesian scholar Abdul Hakim Abdat in the mid-90s and decided to start airing" his lectures. The station had since then become known for "promoting religious scholars from a puritanical sect of Islam."[57] It was observed that while Radio Hang's "teachings may not directly encourage violence, they ask believers to stay apart from non-Muslims and Muslims who don't share their views"—prompting even Batam-based Indonesian listeners to criticise the station "for divisive leanings" that, inter alia, "say Muslims should isolate themselves to maintain their purity".[58] Hence the concern amongst Singaporean Muslim and governmental authorities was that in the context of a multireligious society like Singapore, the "exclusivist preachings' put out by Radio Hang, "even if they don't preach violence overtly", could nevertheless influence people to be "less tolerant and more receptive of violent preachings".[59]

In order to enhance their effectiveness however, it behooves religious scholars to master social media and produce messages that key audiences such as youth can relate to. This represents another way in which Muslim civil society, governments and social media companies in Southeast Asia can cooperate as part of the counter-ISIS messaging effort. Finally, judicious exploitation of selected former ISIS militants from Southeast Asia that have been disillusioned by their experiences in Iraq and Syria should also be explored.[60]

In sum, the struggle against the violent ISIS threat in Southeast Asia will not be easy. However, here as elsewhere, the key would be whole-of-society coordination in devising effective counter-narratives and concomitant social media strategies to neutralise the deadly work of ISIS propagandists. Sun Tzu, the ancient Chinese strategist, put it well: to prevail against such a committed foe, we would have to fight with wisdom—and not merely force alone.

NOTES

1   Francis Chan and Wahyudi Soeriaatmadja, "Plotter's Plan: Strike Singapore from Batam Hill", *The Straits Times* (Singapore), 28 September 2016, available at http://www.straitstimes.com/asia/se-asia/plotters-plan-strike-spore-from-batam-hill; Francis Chan, "Suspect in Foiled Marina Bay Rocket Attack Planned to Get Job on Sentosa", *The Straits Times*, 6 September 2016, available at http://www.straitstimes.com/asia/se-asia/suspect-planned-to-get-job-on-sentosa; Arlina Arshad and Lee Seok Hwai, "Indonesian Police Foil Rocket Attack Plot on Marina Bay; Singapore Steps Up Security", *The Straits Times*, 10 August 2016, available at http://www.straitstimes.com/asia/se-asia/indonesian-police-arrest-six-batam-militants; Arlina Arshad, "IT Guy Who Plotted Terror from Batam", *The Straits Times*, 14 August 2016, available at http://www.straitstimes.com/singapore/terror-in-batam-it-guy-who-plotted-terror-from-batam; Jeremy Koh, "'Military-grade Rocket Needed' to Hit S'pore from Batam", *The Straits Times*, 6 August 2016, available at http://www.straitstimes.com/singapore/military-grade-rocket-needed-to-hit-spore-from-batam; V. Arianti, "Gigih Rahmat Dewa: The IT Jihadist in Batam", *Counter-Terrorist Trends and Analysis*, Vol. 8, No. 11, November 2016, pp. 11–14.
2   Lee Min Kok, "27 Radicalised Bangladeshis Arrested in Singapore under Internal Security Act: MHA", *The Straits Times*, 20 January 2016, available at http://www.straitstimes.com/singapore/courts-crime/27-radicalised-bangladeshis-arrested-in-singapore-under-internal-security-act.
3   Zakir Hussain, "Bangladeshis Plotting Terror Attacks Held under ISA", *The Straits Times*, 4 May 2016, available at http://www.straitstimes.com/singapore/bangladeshis-plotting-terror-attacks-held-under-isa.
4   Kumar Ramakrishna, *Islamist Terrorism and Militancy in Indonesia: The Power of the Manichean Mindset*, Singapore: Springer, 2015, pp. 108–9.
5   Bruce Hoffman, cited in ibid., p. 109.
6   Ibid.
7   Lim Yan Liang, "Why are Some People Attracted to ISIS?", *The Sunday Times* (Singapore), 1 November 2015, p. B2.

8   Bruce Hoffman, cited in Ramakrishna, *Islamist Terrorism and Militancy in Indonesia*, n. 4, p. 109.

9   "July 7 Bombings were Last Successful Al-Qaeda Attack Osama bin Laden Played a Role in, US Claims", *The Telegraph* (UK), 13 July 2011, available at http://www.telegraph.co.uk/news/uknews/terrorism-in-the-uk/8633919/July-7-bombings-were-last-successful-al-Qaeda-attack-Osama-bin-Laden-played-a-role-in-US-claims.html, accessed on 2 November 2015.

10 See Raffaello Pantucci, "A Typology of Lone Wolves: Preliminary Analysis of Lone Islamist Terrorists", in *Developments in Radicalisation and Political Violence*, London: International Centre for the Study of Radicalisation, 2011.

11 Bruce Hoffman, cited in Ramakrishna, *Islamist Terrorism and Militancy in Indonesia*, n. 4, p. 109.

12 Ibid. For a deeper analysis of the aggressive, apocalyptic Islamic religiosity driving the ISIS, see Graeme Wood, *The Way of the Strangers: Encounters with the Islamic State*, New York: Random House, 2017.

13 Jenny Awford, "New Setback for ISIS as it is Revealed They have Lost a QUARTER of the Territory They Seized since 2015", *Daily Mail* (UK), 9 October 2016, available at http://www.dailymail.co.uk/news/article-3829345/ISIS-lost-quarter-territory.html.

14 Brian L. Steed, *ISIS: An Introduction and Guide to the Islamic State*, Santa Barbara: ABC-CLIO, 2016, pp. 145–6.

15 Bilveer Singh and Kumar Ramakrishna, "Islamic State's Wilayah Philippines: Implications for Southeast Asia", *RSIS Commentary*, 21 July 2016, available at https://www.rsis.edu.sg/rsis-publication/rsis/co16187-islamic-states-wilayah-philippines-implications-for-southeast-asia/#.WEJkbUtVpPo.

16 Ibid.; Francis Chan, "Indonesia Terror Cell was Planning Dec Holiday Strike", *The Straits Times*, 1 December 2016, p. A8.

17 Kanupriya Kapoor and Agustinus Beo Da Costa, "Some Indonesians 'Joining pro-Islamic State Groups in Philippines'", *Reuters*, 25 October 2016, available at http://news.abs-cbn.com/news/10/25/16/some-indonesians-joining-pro-islamic-state-groups-in-philippines.

18 David Harris, "ISIS Sets Eyes on Creating 'New State'", *Clarion Project*, 1 December 2016, available at http://www.clarionproject.org/analysis/isis-sets-eyes-creating-'new-'state'.

19 Saifulbahri Ismail, "Indonesia Jails Bomb Maker Linked to Jakarta Attacks", *Channel NewsAsia* (Singapore), 20 October 2016, available at http://www.channelnewsasia.com/news/asiapacific/indonesia-jails-bomb-maker-linked-to-jakarta-attacks/3221424.html.

20 Akil Yunus, "Local IS Fighter Claims Movida Bombing is 'First Attack on Malaysian Soil'", *The Star* (Malaysia), 4 July 2016, available at http://www.thestar.com.my/news/nation/2016/07/04/local-is-fighter-claims-movida-bombing-is-first-attack-on-malaysian-soil/.

21 "Attack on Singapore a Matter of When, Not If, Says Shanmugam", *Today* (Singapore), 24 March 2016, available at http://www.todayonline.com/singapore/unless-we-turn-city-prison-not-possible-counter-every-terror-attack-shanmugam.

22 Lim Yan Liang, "How Much of a Threat is ISIS to the Region?", *The Straits Times*, 1 November 2015, available at http://www.straitstimes.com/singapore/how-much-of-a-threat-is-isis-to-the-region.

23 V. Arianti and Jasminder Singh, "ISIS' Southeast Asia Unit: Raising the Security Threat", *RSIS Commentary*, 19 October 2015, available at https://www.rsis.edu.sg/rsis-publication/icpvtr/co15220-isis-southeast-asia-unit-raising-the-security-threat/#.Vlkcv2DFH-Y, accessed on 28 November 2015; Francis Chan, "Indonesian Commander Killed in Syria", *The Straits Times*, 15 March 2017, available at http://www.straitstimes.com/asia/se-asia/indonesian-commander-killed-in-syria.

24 Zakir Hussain, "ISIS Posts Footage of Boy-trainees from South-east Asia", *The Straits Times*,

17 March 2015, available at http://www.straitstimes.com/asia/se-asia/isis-posts-footage-of-boy-trainees-from-south-east-asia, accessed on 5 November 2015.

25 Ibid.

26 Liang, "Why are Some People Attracted to ISIS?", n. 7.

27 Liang, "How Much of a Threat is ISIS to the Region?", n. 22.

28 Zachary Abuza and Bridget Welsh, "Draconian Laws' False Sense of Security", *Rappler.com*, 15 April 2015, available at http://www.rappler.com/thought-leaders/89698-draconian-laws-false-sense-security, accessed on 5 November 2015.

29 Zakir Hussain, "Singapore a 'Prime Target' for Terrorist Attack", *The Star*, 19 March 2016, available at http://www.thestar.com.my/news/regional/2016/03/19/singapore-a-prime-target-for-terrorist-attack/.

30 Kumar Ramakrishna, "Religious Extremism: The Case of the Monk Wirathu", *The Nation* (Thailand), 7 August 2013, available at http://www.nationmultimedia.com/news/opinion/aec/30212037.

31 Chong Zi Liang, "ISIS Terror Threat Greater Now, Says Shanmugam", *The Straits Times*, 3 December 2016, p. A6.

32 Kumar Ramakrishna, "From Global to Micro Jihad: Three Trends of Grassroots Terrorism", *RSIS Commentary*, 7 May 2013, available at https://www.rsis.edu.sg/rsis-publication/cens/1978-from-global-to-micro-jihad-th/#.WQYPAVfYr-Y, and "Countering the Self-Radicalized Lone Wolf: A New Paradigm?", *RSIS Commentary*, 28 January 2014, available at https://www.rsis.edu.sg/rsis-publication/cens/2144-countering-the-self-radicalise/#.WQYR71fYr-Y.

33 Kumar Ramakrishna, "When Everyday Items Become Terror Weapons", *Today*, 30 March 2017, available at http://www.todayonline.com/commentary/when-everyday-items-become-terror-weapons.

34 "Online Preachers of Hate: Anwar al-Awlaki, 'bin Laden of the Internet'", *The Telegraph* (UK), 7 July 2011, available at http://www.telegraph.co.uk/news/uknews/terrorism-in-the-uk/8560438/Online-preachers-of-hate-Anwar-al-Awlaki-bin-Laden-of-the-internet.html.

35 Ramakrishna, *Islamist Terrorism and Militancy in Indonesia*, n. 4, p. 228.

36 Vikram Dodd, "Europol Web Unit to Hunt Extremists behind ISIS Social Media Propaganda", *The Guardian* (UK), 21 June 2015, available at https://www.theguardian.com/world/2015/jun/21/europol-internet-unit-track-down-extremists-isis-social-media-propaganda.

37 Douglas Ernst, "'Jihadi-cool' Subculture Drives Youth to Islamic State, Says Muslim Council of Britain Adviser", *The Washington Times*, 22 August 2014, available at http://www.washingtontimes.com/news/2014/aug/22/jihadi-cool-subculture-drives-youth-to-islamic-sta/.

38 Jonathan Owen and Brian Brady, "Theresa May Urges Action on 'Jihad Tourism'", *The Independent* (UK), 6 July 2013, available at http://www.independent.co.uk/news/world/politics/theresa-may-urges-action-on-jihad-tourism-8692590.html.

39 Fawaz A. Gerges, *ISIS: A History*, Princeton and Oxford: Princeton University Press, 2016, p. 282.

40 Ibid., pp. 264–66.

41 For instance, see Mark Mazzetti and Michael R. Gordon, "ISIS is Winning the Social Media War, U.S. Concludes", *The New York Times*, 12 June 2015, available at https://www.nytimes.com/2015/06/13/world/middleeast/isis-is-winning-message-war-us-concludes.html?_r=0.

42 Daniel Milton, *Communication Breakdown: Unraveling the Islamic State's Media Efforts*, New York: Combating Terrorism Center at West Point, US Military Academy, October 2016, available at https://www.ctc.usma.edu/v2/wp-content/uploads/2016/10/ISMedia_Online.pdf; see also Jack Crosbie, "ISIS is Losing the War on Social Media", *Inverse.com*, 24 October 2016, available at https://www.inverse.com/article/22646-isis-losing-twitter-war.

43   This section draws upon Kumar Ramakrishna, "The ISB Arrests: The Transnational Terrorist 'Insider Threat'", *RSIS Commentary*, 5 May 2016, available at https://www.rsis.edu.sg/rsis-publication/rsis/co16103-the-isb-arrests-the-transnational-terrorist-insider-threat/#.WQYS5lfYr-Y.

44   Ibid.

45   Damien D. Cheong and Kumar Ramakrishna, "Why Reporting Every Security Incident Matters", *Malay Mail Online* (Malaysia), 27 April 2017, available at http://www.themalaymailonline.com/what-you-think/article/why-reporting-every-security-incident-matters-damien-d-cheong-and-kumar-ram.

46   Michael Chertoff, "The Ideology of Terrorism: Radicalism Revisited", *Brown Journal of International Affairs*, Vol. XV, No. 1, Fall/Winter 2008, pp. 11–20.

47   Kumar Ramakrishna, "The Four Mutations of Violent Muslim Extremism in Southeast Asia: Some Implications for a Cognitive Immunization Policy", *Asia Policy*, No. 12, July 2011, pp. 13–19.

48   Joby Warrick, *Black Flags: The Rise of ISIS*, London: Corgi, 2016, p. 290.

49   Kumar Ramakrishna "The Threat of Terrorism and Extremism: 'A Matter of "When", and Not "If"'" in Daljit Singh and Malcolm Cook (eds), Southeast Asian Affairs 2017, Singapore: ISEAS Publishing, 2017, pp. 335–52

50   Alexander Raymond Arifianto, "Islam Nusantara: NU's Bid to Promote 'Moderate Indonesian Islam'", *RSIS Commentary*, 17 May 2016, available at https://www.rsis.edu.sg/rsis-publication/rsis/co16114-islam-nusantara-nus-bid-to-promote-moderate-indonesian-islam/#.WQYZslfYr-Y.

51   Sir Robert Thompson, *Defeating Communist Insurgency: The Lessons of Malaya and Vietnam*, New York: F.A. Praeger, 1966.

52   Christina Mendez, "Philippines, Indonesia to Step Up Fight vs Terror, Kidnapping", *Philstar Global*, 29 April 2017, available at http://m.philstar.com/314191/show/07add8b3dcd2d79f2ef7e250b5574dc6/.

53   C. Miller and J. Bartlett, "'Digital Fluency': Towards Young People's Critical Use of the Internet", *Journal of Information Literacy*, Vol. 6, No. 2, 2012, pp. 35–55.

54   Gerges, *ISIS*, n. 39, p. 292.

55   Cass R. Sunstein, *Going to Extremes: How Like Minds Unite and Divide*, New York: Oxford University Press, 2009, pp. 153–54.

56   See Kumar Ramakrishna and Stephanie Neubronner, "Engaging Youth as a Bulwark against ISIS Extremism", *The Straits Times*, 22 April 2017, available at http://www.straitstimes.com/opinion/engaging-youth-as-a-bulwark-against-isis-extremism.

57   Amanda Lee, "Extremist Ideology a Staple Item on Batam's Radio Hang", *Today*, 20 August 2016, available at http://www.todayonline.com/singapore/radio-0.

58   Lim Yan Liang, "Exclusivist Teachings could Prime Listeners to ISIS Propaganda", *The Straits Times*, 20 August 2016, available at http://www.straitstimes.com/singapore/exclusivist-teachings-could-prime-listeners-to-isis-propaganda.

59   Ibid.

60   Kumar Ramakrishna, "Engaging Former JI Detainees in Countering Extremism: Can it Work?", *RSIS Commentary*, 4 January 2012, available at https://www.rsis.edu.sg/rsis-publication/cens/1665-engaging-former-ji-detainees- accessed on 2 March 2017.

SECTION SIX

Constructing Effective Counter Narratives: The Need for a Global Response

Special Insight IV
Crafting a Narrative for Kashmir

Lt. Gen. S.A. Hasnain (Retd.)[*]

The subject of this chapter is Kashmir, particularly crafting a narrative for it. Normally, a person with my background would be expected to focus more on the military aspects and how the situation is faring, given the fairly turbulent military scenario. However, I am not going to do anything of the sort. In fact, I will be taking a different approach.

The fact remains that the kind of conflict that we are looking at in Kashmir is a hybrid one and not the usual conventional conflict. Hence, there are varied domains within the spectrum of conflict which can be exploited in different ways. While one could choose to craft a narrative out of any of these domains, my emphasis is on the strategic culture part of it, which, to my mind, is the most important thing under the current circumstances. The public at large, mainly guided by the media's persistence on the robust aspect of operations, continues to consider the key takeaway in terms of kill ratios, which has currently come down to 1:1, or one soldier lost for every terrorist killed, the worst such ratio in 27 years. However, as much as any army may try, killing the last terrorist is almost impossible. Even though there may be 300 terrorists left where there were 5,000–8,000 of them in the past, the reduction does not logically lead to eradication. We may have reduced their number down to 300, but to kill the last 300 is going to take a very long time and a large amount of resources. Therefore, while all of this is happening, one cannot wait for counter-narratives in other domains of hybrid conflict to emerge. These domains are of as great importance, but they are not in public focus and intellectuals rarely talk about them.

What should thus concern us are the other constituents of the conflict

---

[*]The views expressed here are the author's own, based on his distinguished service as a veteran of the Indian Armed Forces.

spectrum (not just the military), as just brought out. The political and the people's dimension is what dominates this conflict today, and that is where narratives are necessary to be created. When Zia-ul-Haq conceived his plan for jihad in Jammu and Kashmir (J&K), one of the major elements of the plan was the exploitation of ideology in the hope that pan-Islamism would override all other considerations. Pakistan's leadership could just as easily have used Islam as a binder, but it chose to employ the most radical strain of Islam for various reasons. That strategy was a hangover from the Islamic jihad employed successfully in Afghanistan, which was fought in the 1980s. However, Kashmir's Islam is different. Kashmir's Islam—the mystic Sufist Islam, which is much more syncretic and tolerant—is an evolved form of Islam that has been transformed. It has taken approximately 20–22 years of deliberate effort on the part of Pakistan and other agencies, combined with a tremendous amount of financial backing and the transplantation of a full clergy, to change Kashmir's faith from Sufi to almost Sunni–Wahhabi. It happened right under our nose, and the reason for that is because we had no idea about the employment of religion and ideology as a strategic weapon in modern times. Our reluctance to study the cultural terrain is the reason responsible for our discomfort today. You can even extend this argument to encompass the fact that we always considered the exodus of the Kashmiri Pandits in 1990 to be something political, without realising how ideological it was and without understanding the major ideological links tied to that event.

Understanding the Crafting of Pakistani Narrative on Kashmir

There are, therefore, a few things that characterise Pakistan's narrative that has been weaved around this larger issue of pan-Islamism. These are:

1. The creation of a pan-Islamic identity.
2. The extermination of a local minority, thus the Kashmiri Pandits, as their presence would have meant the non-attainment of the Islamic brotherhood.
3. Evolving the mosque as the centre of the clarion call to create alienation towards other faiths and towards mainstream India.
4. Making the mosque the centre of vigilantism of its own kind.
5. Introducing the "Intifada" model, the supposed non-violent way of fighting a superior adversary. The stone was adopted by separatists as a symbol of non-violent resistance, much to the discomfiture of our security forces.

All these factors have led to a few trends which have been adopted in the Kashmir narrative at the behest of the deep state of Pakistan, the entity within

Pakistan which controls the proxy war. To support classical operations, they had to immerse themselves in the *fidayeen* type of operations, which could further provide impetus to other operations such as ambushes. These suicide-oriented operations were conducted primarily by foreign fighters. Street turbulence has since been brought in as a norm, and this street turbulence is implemented in a manner aimed at drawing the ire of the security forces so that a level of desperation is reached that leads to state violence. This level of desperation has been responsible for a number of civilian casualties over the last few years. However, the fear of death among young Kashmiris seems to have virtually disappeared. But, at the same time, what is interesting is that there have been very few cases of suicide bombing in Kashmir involving youth, especially the type of model witnessed in Iraq, Afghanistan and Pakistan. To be specific, only three cases are known: two at the gates of Badami Bagh and one in 2004 on the road to Pattan. Apart from these incidents, there has never been a suicide bombing in Kashmir by the Kashmiri youths despite the fact that young Kashmiris today are not afraid of dying. These are very contradictory things that we have to look at and keep in mind if an effective counter-narrative is to be framed.

The Islamic flag—the green flag with crescent and star—is one which many people in India confuse with the Pakistani flag (the Pakistani one has a white band on the left). The Pakistani flag and the Islamic flag are symbols used to inspire and bond the Kashmiri public with the ummah. The Friday sermons are known to have become more radical, with calls for resistance to security forces. The separatists have followed the calendar system to bring the people to the streets and try to jump-start a kind of non-cooperation movement. The intent is to create triggers that could snowball into larger clashes to power the movement. These acts, however, do not remain peaceful, as has been evident over the last few years. Initially, this movement was led by people who were in their twenties. Lately, it has been observed that it has come down to youth as young as 10–14 years old. They also act as extremely vicious vigilantes to enforce their rules for Kashmiri society, including the bureaucracy. Many members of the local bureaucracy, it has been learnt, report to the mosques in the morning and pay allegiance to the cause of the vigilantes. Also, targeting the ranks of J&K Police is the ploy adopted to intimidate it, prevent its cooperation with the army and possibly instigate an insubordination. To the credit of the police, and that of the leadership in particular, this ploy has not succeeded.

The end of 2016 witnessed a return to the fidayeen type of operations, which had earlier placed considerable pressure on the security forces in J&K. The Jaish-e-Mohammad (JeM) of Masood Azhar was primarily responsible for this, the intent being a return to primacy in the J&K proxy war. These fidayeen type operations were combined with the new phenomenon of flash mobs, generated through clarion calls from mosques and use of social media. The flash mobs descended at encounter sites to intimidate the security forces and prevent them from optimising their operations. However, to the credit of the security forces, they have evolved standard operating procedures to deal with the mobs and have effectively minimised the effect, but not without inflicting some inadvertent civilian casualties. The latter have been used as symbols for further instigation. This is what the army chief was referring to when he spoke about the situation and outlined the necessity of treating the vigilantes and flash mob leaders as anti-national elements, in the same light as terrorists.

The fruition of the Pakistani strategy has been largely achieved by focus on making the population and the idea of *azaadi* the centres of gravity of this entire campaign; for Pakistan, *azaadi* is the first step towards eventual integration with Pakistan. Our centres of gravity of the counter-campaign have to be similar, that is, the population and the idea of *azaadi*—mainstreaming the former and diluting the latter. It is important to examine the purpose and structure of a counter-narrative in the first place. A counter-narrative, it must be remembered, is an argument—an argument that basically disputes a commonly held belief. So far, all that I have spoken of is commonly held beliefs or commonly held ideas of carrying forward this movement. If we are to build a counter-narrative to it, then we have to make sure that these beliefs are diluted. I think the first place where the Indian establishment, especially the security establishment, went wrong is that we never evolved for ourselves a clearly defined aim. An aim is necessary for almost everyone involved in the proxy war because, without an aim, there is little clarity on how to go about countering it. We do not have an aim in/for Kashmir, nor do we have a long-term strategy. Furthermore, a strategy itself needs to be divided into long term, medium term and short term. But this has eluded our approach in Kashmir as most of our strategy is situational, catering for a just emerged situation or something likely to emerge in the immediate future, thereby robbing us of a long-term perspective. Those who have served in Kashmir would remember, from the military point of view, that there has always been a summer strategy and a winter strategy. But there has never been a strategy 2025. What do we want the end state of Kashmir to be in 2025? There is a need to work towards this, which has never happened before.

Hybrid Threat Requires Whole of Government Approach for Counter Narrative to Succeed

As stated earlier, this proxy conflict is hybrid in nature. Conceptually, in such conflicts, unless the whole-of-government approach is accepted as the core strategy, no counter-narrative can succeed. Hybrid conflicts are all about the whole of government. If anyone thinks that hybrid conflict only involves terror groups, with an army required to neutralise them and nothing further, they would be sadly mistaken. The military domain is a subset of this entire politico-cultural spectrum. There are various domains in the spectrum which are being exploited. So, the first change that needs to be implemented is the change of mindset, and the understanding that counter-terrorist operations go well beyond just the military domain. The second step is the question of the control of the mosque. This control refers to the combination of the clergy, the messages they preach and the finances that they receive, internally or from external sources. This combination needs to be examined carefully and a depoliticisation of the mosque system in the Valley needs to be attempted. In the face of very vicious vigilantism, it is difficult to directly engage with the youth. Earlier, I was in direct engagement with the youth as a corps commander, but today, I think it is not possible for the army to be able to directly engage with them. It can only be done by leaders who are extremely confident of the ideological and cultural aspects of the proxy conflict.

There is also a need for diversions in the Valley, but these cannot be restricted to one-off events. Sports events are a great diversion, music festivals are another, but these things do not take place in the Valley. It is incredibly difficult to make them happen, but they are necessary to keep the cultural spirit of the Valley alive. Anything artificial or events not in sync with the mainstream events of the past must not be attempted as these will be resisted. Opening cinema halls is anathema, so there is no need to try that initially; however, screening acceptable films at some schools and colleges, or even at the Sher-i-Kashmir International Convention Centre (SKICC), could be experimented with to set the tone for long-term changes. It is my belief that it is sports, more than films, which will help to divert the obsessive negativity in the current environment.

There is also a crying need for mainstreaming the madrasas (seminaries). I am not proposing anything radical, that is, no interference with religious discourse at these institutions, but introduction of an environment of happiness is essential to prevent the emergence of brooding young men obsessed only with faith and ideology. I did experiment with encouraging some madrasas to participate in district sports tournaments and even get them to be a part of the march-past on national day celebrations on 15 August and 26 January. Another way to do this could be through the integration of madrasas into the curriculum through sports activities, inclusion in national day events and introducing some subjects such as information technology. Most security practitioners and the leadership are uncomfortable in dealing with these institutions and we need to be in consultation with local elders and intellectuals on this issue.

In an environment which has not witnessed grassroots political activity for many years, it is important to introduce some political empowerment at municipal and panchayat level. The last successful panchayat elections, as you are aware, took place in 2011, but actual empowerment has never taken place. Since then, the elections have also been deferred time and again. Panchayati Raj has been stymied with just the conduct of elections and nothing else beyond. Due to existence of security threats, political activity at the lowest levels is difficult as political meetings and events involving public interaction remain vulnerable. Thus, the lowest levels of society remain politically disempowered beyond just elections. In such a situation, I did find great enthusiasm for town hall type of meetings where the gentry could feel empowered enough to place their grievances at the doorstep of the political leadership or the civil administration. Enabling this is not easy. This is where the initiative can be taken by the army, with its organisational skills and its ability to provide security.

Craft Narratives Focusing on Key Constituents

The next issue that needs to be examined very strongly is gender equation. The role of women, of late, has been extremely negative. Even female counselling by fellow Muslim women is unlikely to be accepted today. There is a need, therefore, to look for role models; however, in Kashmir, role models are sometimes difficult to find.

The one element of who little is known is the clergy. It is common to hear many security practitioners talk of the "Jamaatis", but rarely do we do any analysis on them, their ideology or philosophy. The black-and-white policy we follow in terms of engagement prevents us from being in touch with the highest religious authorities, such as the amir of the Jamaat-e-Islami. It is not the responsibility of the security forces, but thought should be given from within the establishment to remain in touch and be in communication with the clergy all the time. The interpretation of religious texts to suit the environment of peace and tranquility is something that needs to be encouraged. The texts that are being used to incite terrorists need to be reinterpreted and put out across social media. Direct outreach with groups of youth could be possible, provided leaders have the courage to accept serious criticism. I have sat a couple of times and listened to the youth bombarding us with criticism. The same youth have then come outside and asked us how they can join the Kashmir police or the Indian Army. This sounds like a dichotomy, but there is a need to understand the psyche underlying it. These interstices are where the narratives have to be re-researched and built into. Experts from the field of psychology are needed to conduct studies on subjects in the field, which we in the security forces can identify for them.

A simple example for the above would be that Burhan Wani came from Tral. Tral is a township where security operations take place every other day. It is a township that has given us 300 or 400 terrorists. But what ends up being forgotten is that Tral has also given the country more than 500 JAK LI soldiers and you cannot find fault with a single JAK LI soldier. They are patriotic to their core and remain so till their last breath. So, there is a need to reinterpret this narrative too. What drives the patriotic soldiers from Tral and their families?

Conclusion

To sum up, it needs to be examined whether the enlightened ulema of the rest of India can be accepted in Kashmir. If so, dialogue between them and Kashmiri Muslims needs to be instated. There is a disconnect between the Indian Muslim and the rest of J&K. The Indian Muslim has very conveniently kept himself away from it and there has been no linkup between the two. Somehow, if we can bring this linkage a little closer, it would be easier to bring home the message to the Kashmiri population that being an Indian and being an Indian Muslim is probably today the best thing for a Muslim. This is particularly necessary when contrasted with the kind of problems you see around the world today. Therefore, the most important element for the implementation of a "hearts doctrine" kind of a programme is the restoration of self-esteem of the public. Having spoken about the various facets of the ideological conditioning of the Valley, the final step would be to redevelop the self-esteem of the public. Any public that has suffered for the better part of thirty years in an environment such as this will always suffer from low self-esteem, as will their children and their whole generation that has grown up in such an environment. We can keep blaming them sitting in Delhi and Kolkata and Mumbai, but without having lived in that environment, we will never understand how it impacts the psyche of a child. That is what we have to look at in terms of counter-narratives and our public perceptions.

I would like to end by recapitulating that unless security is seen holistically, we are not going to go beyond the stage of reduction of terrorist strength. There is a need to incorporate the whole-of-government approach, which will serve as a comprehensive mechanism to bring the Kashmiris closer to the mainstream. I would like to recount a small anecdote that demonstrates this need for holistic strategy and the various benefits it could offer. The army conducted the Kashmir Premier League, a cricket tournament, in 2011. Almost 390 matches were held and Rs 1.45 crore was spent on it. We had Bishan Singh Bedi, the famous cricketer, advising us on the protocol that ought to be followed. While organising the event, I asked him how much the Board of Control for Cricket in India (BCCI) would have spent if they had organised a 390-match tournament. He said the sum would have gone up to approximately Rs 1,000 crores. During this time, the army managed to keep a huge mass of people off the roads, as they were engaged in playing, talking, watching, clapping, etc. The reason I am bringing up this anecdote is to remind everyone that given the predominant air of negativity in that environment, anything that provides a positive change will contribute to a counter-narrative. However, despite the many merits and the relatively economic nature of the tournament, it had a short life and ran for only two years. In 2012, the audit authorities put an end to it. They said that the army was not being given money to play cricket. This reinforces the need to change mindsets and adopt a more comprehensive approach to problem solving.

19

Deconstruction of the Jihadist Narrative[1]

Adil Rasheed

In order to develop effective counter-narratives against global jihadism, we need to first focus on the salient facets of the existing global jihadist narrative itself. Ironically, any survey of some of the main strands of the contemporary jihadist literature reveals that it is in essence less about Islam and more of an antithesis to the prevailing mainstream international discourse on contemporaneous global events and the global order. Therefore, the present jihadist narrative, much like communism in its time, has been struggling to develop an effective counter-narrative to the civilised discourse of the modern world and gives us the opportunity to revisit, review and recommit to the fundamental principles of human rights and individual freedom which are being opposed by the forces of obscurantist bigotry and hate.

Not surprisingly, like any violent movement, the jihadists have the advantage of being aware of not only the grand ideological discourse on which modern liberal values are based, but also of mainstream socio-political narratives, which are often discussed and analysed threadbare by our own free press. Ironically, this allows the radical extremists to exploit any of the publicised weaknesses and flaws in our existing discourse about the state of polity and society in various parts of the world.

What is a Narrative?

In order to deconstruct the jihadist narrative and develop effective counter-messaging content and techniques of dissemination, it would be more appropriate

---

*Elements of this chapter were adapted from Adil Rasheed (2016): Countering the Threat of Radicalisation: Theories, Programmes and Challenges, Journal of Defence Studies, Vol. 10, No. 2 April-June 2016, pp. 39-76.

for us to first understand here the meaning of the term 'narrative'. In broad terms, a narrative is a spoken or written account of connected events or thoughts, say, as in a story, which in the case of an extremist political narrative justifies a violent social and/or religious campaign for achieving radical geopolitical goals and agenda. Thus, a political narrative presents an ideological case for justifying the rationale of a political movement for the purpose of radicalisation and recruitment to the political cause. Narratives are built up by gradually sequencing events and thoughts of universal appeal and putting them on an escalating ladder of complex ideas that build an ideological superstructure and climax into the movement's desired end state.

All ideas and concepts put forward in any political narrative, even if they might initially appear to be separate and at times disjointed from each other, are often carefully designed and calibrated as part of a whole and point to their hierarchical conclusion in a precise end state, such as a global caliphate in the case of global jihadism. Thus, at an incipient level, political narratives work on and develop several small but essential concepts that serve as the staircase for a grand ideological superstructure. Sometimes disparate streams of arguments, concepts and interpretations—coming from affiliate sources—serve as the toeholds for a great ideological ascent. For instance, modern liberalism is weaved around a gamut of concepts such as individual liberty, equality, secularism and democracy. Conversely, concepts of *tawheed*, sharia, *khilafah*, *al wala wal-bara* (loyalty and disavowal), jihad, etc., are fundamental concepts to the Islamist political ideology. These basic concepts serve as essential cogs in the grand narrative of a giant ideology, and so they are in themselves inviolable, for their desecration could bring down the carefully constructed ideological edifice.

Thus, the general method employed for deconstructing a narrative involves exposing the causal anomalies in the chain of ideas presented in a narrative. It should be noted that just as in literary fiction, a religious or political narrative is built around a chain of ideas that need to rationally connect to each other and justify their progression. Therefore, any counter-narrative needs to be adept at finding flaws in the narrative chain of thoughts, smart at identifying causal anomalies— weak links, outright lies and generalisations—as well as capable of exposing propaganda fallacies like red herrings, ad hominems, demagogy, non sequiturs, bandwagoning, card stacking, cognitive distortions and straw man techniques.

Crafting of the Extremist Narrative

Extremist movements often strengthen these ideological or religious concepts by seeking, somewhat rationally or emotively, to establish their relevance in the light of prevailing circumstances and socio-political conditions. These organisations seek to generate a highly emotional and violent reaction to their revolutionary message as they prey on the dark side of human sensibilities and seek to intensify feelings of fear, hate, anger, jealousy and other insecurities to purposely draw a violent response. Some of the more odious concepts, ideals and goals of certain political movements are often developed late, or kept hidden and revealed only after the target audience is presumed ready to receive them. It should be noted that the purveyors of faith are often found smarter than modern public relations executives, for they have been selling a commodity that is not apparent (that is, god) for thousands of years.

In fact, there are several commonalities in all forms of violent extremist discourse and jihadism. Almost all of them have a "persecution by the 'Other' and need to avenge" narrative, "the supremacism or exceptionalism" narrative, "the holy war and martyrdom narrative", the "anti-moderate takfiri and traitorous insiders" narrative, "the end-time reversion to post-modern utopia" narrative, etc. When it comes to jihadism, it is important to understand that for all its traditional trappings, it is essentially a modern construct which has derived many of its ideals and concepts from Islam, but mainly subsists on contemporary political perceptions and real/perceived socio-political grievances. Thus, the introduction of terrorism into the concept of jihad is in principle a modern innovation, ironically initiated by al-Qaeda that ostensibly opposes all innovation or *bidaa* in Islam as cardinal sin, except for those altered by it.

In fact, modern jihadism has made its own version of "khilafah" and espouses an "aggressive" and "terrorism"-based non-Islamic jihad as an essential article of faith, in variance with Islamic injunctions. Many jihadist organisations of the day circulate a set of books to their young recruits and neophytes. These include: Abu Bakr Naji's *Management of Savagery* that explores ways of employing terrorism to whittle down state armies in a protracted war of attrition; *The Economic System of Islam* by Taqiuddin Nabhani that details the "inherent structural" problems dogging the debt and speculation-based financial system of our times; Sayyid Qutb's infamous *Milestones (Ma'alim fi Al-Tariq)* that calls for overthrowing regimes in various Muslim states; and the *Laws of Islamic Governance (Al-Ahkam As-Sultaniyyah)* by Al-Mawardi.

The Need for Effective Counter-narratives

Efforts to develop anti-jihadist counter-narratives have picked up pace only recently. However, these efforts have mainly concentrated on developing Islamic counter-narratives, but the problem is that there has been little attempt at developing political counter-narratives, historical counter-narratives, psychological counter-narratives, tactical and insidious counter-narratives and humour and satire-laced counter-narratives in areas infested with global jihadist radicalisation. In fact, there is a need for evolving institutions, perhaps national or regional nodal agencies, that generate a counter-narrative database as part of a comprehensive and meticulously calibrated strategic communications initiative against all forms of radicalisation, particularly jihadist radicalisation, and whose function should be to launch public relations campaigns for disseminating counter-narratives through a variety of mass media, such as Internet, public platforms, educational forums and curricula and prison programmes, as well as to provide specialised solutions for specific contingencies erupting in any given time and space.

Thus, there is a need for both overt and covert counter-messaging programmes, for highly specific, localised exigencies, such as riot-affected areas, Internet and social media-related campaigns for national-level contingencies, as well as for regional and globalised events and phenomena. In devising these counter-narratives or what is known as "strategic rhetoric", three components are essential. The first is the "ethos", which means the credibility of the channels of communication. The second component is the "logos', which means the authenticity and effectiveness of the message itself. The third aspect is "pathos", which refers to the deep emotional and subliminal resonance and cultural connect in the language.

In the end, counter-narratives should never appear favouring one sect over the other, even if one sect or ideology appears to be pacifist and moderate. A board outside the Jama Masjid Sadar, in Jabalpur, instructs Wahhabis and Deobandis to keep out of the Sunni mosque. While devising counter-narratives, it should be noted that the narrative should never demonise any sect, nor prescribe any sectarian ideology as a counter-narrative to the other. Sometimes, Wahhabism, Salafism and Ahl-e-Hadith draw a lot of flak in the global media for espousing ideals which facilitate various terrorist groups to emerge. Conversely, Sufi Islam is often projected as a more tolerant, universalist, non-violent and more acceptable face of Islam. However, differentiation of law-abiding people based on their sectarian affiliations can be a recipe for disaster. Terrorism has no religion and is a disease that can infect members of any sect or community. Naming and shaming sects only polarises and alienates members of a society already struggling with radicalism.

20

Understanding Sufism to Influence Extremism in Kashmir

S.M. Sahai

Understanding Sufism and its influence in Kashmir requires a detailed understanding of the region as well as the context. There is a need to understand the overall concept of Islam in Kashmir, examine how Islam spread in Kashmir, the nature of Kashmiri society before this religious proliferation, the key triggers that led to the current state of radicalisation as well as solutions regarding how best they can be countered.

Origins of Sufism in Kashmir

The first issue that needs to be examined is the origin and spread of Sufism in Kashmir. As a part of religious ideology, Sufism should not be treated as a concept outside Islam. Reducing the entire debate to how Sufism differs from what the Muslims in Kashmir are doing is futile and borders on reductive generalisation. Sufism came to Kashmir under the reign of Suhadeva (1301–1320 CE), the last king of the Lohara dynasty. Sayyid Sharfudin, commonly known as Bulbul Shah, was the first amongst many preachers from Iran and Central Asia to bring in the concept of devotion to god to Kashmir. The concept seemed very similar to existing Hindu practices and found resonance amongst the local population. The religion itself was far simpler than the Hinduism then being practised in Kashmir. Along with religious salvation, these preachers also brought in crafts like carpet weaving, paper mache, woodwork, copper work, shawl weaving and embroidery. Thus,

---

*The views expressed here are the author's own. Mr. S.M. Sahai serves at the Additional Secretary, National Security Council Secretariat and shared his views based on his extensive experience in his prior appointment as the Inspector General of Police in Kashmir.

not only was Sufism a simpler religion to follow but it also had its own economic benefits as it provided Kashmir with economic linkages to Central Asia and Iran.

Sufism and Politics in Kashmir

It is in this background that a fairly moderate form of cultural practice evolved in Kashmir, which was acceptable to both Hindus and Muslims and provided a syncretic ethos which was in evidence till recently. Events in Kashmir preceding the partition of the subcontinent witnessed the development of a movement along religious lines, starting in 1931. This was quickly thwarted by Sheikh Abdullah when he converted the Muslim Conference into the National Conference in 1938 and gave the party a secular character.

Following the allegedly rigged elections of 1987, the Indian National Congress–National Conference coalition government came to power. Those who were denied political power initiated the current militancy with the help of Pakistan, a glaring example being that of Syed Yusuf Shah (aka Syed Salahuddin, Hizbul Mujahideen's [HM] supreme commander), who was defeated in Amira Kadal, and his agent Yasin Malik, who became the chief of the Jammu and Kashmir Liberation Front (JKLF). The secular nature of politics in Kashmir did not quite change until the onset of militancy in the late 1980s, when the JKLF targeted Kashmiri Pandits resulting in their mass migration from the Valley. Although the JKLF claimed to be a secular organisation, through this act of ostracisation, the seeds of radicalisation had been sown.

This was by far the biggest blow to the tolerant religious culture of the Valley. In one stroke, "Rishism", the Kashmiri form of Sufism, died. The traces of this entire thought structure were eradicated to such an extent that the word can no longer be found in the lexicon of the Kashmiri language. Rishi culture was unique in being able to absorb the devotional aspect of Hinduism, which metamorphosed into an inclusive culture acceptable to both Hindus and Muslims.

Recent Developments

This historical background was followed by a series of events, which were also influenced by global developments. Given the recent proliferation and rise of extremism, it is unsurprising that we are now in a situation, where Zakir Musa, an HM commander, openly advocates the cause of the caliphate as well as the cause of the al-Qaeda, and he is also being supported by the Jaish-e-Mohammad (JeM). Though the HM and Pakistan are opposed to the idea of a caliphate, HM commanders have shown a tilt towards the Islamic State, as evinced by the narrative brought out by Burhan Wani in his very first video.

Much of this radicalisation has been a result of the half-baked education Kashmiri youths receive through informal structures like the *darasgah*. Youngsters are exposed to a selective interpretation of history and religion that has been crafted to reinforce radical ideology and create a rift between Kashmiri Muslims and the rest of India. This was also done, very deliberately, as a part of Pakistani-sponsored militancy when, after the defeat of the Soviets in Afghanistan, mujahideen organisations like Harkat-ul-Ansar, Hizb-e-Islami, Tehreek-e-Mujahideen and Harkat-ul-Mujahideen were diverted towards the state of Kashmir.

Impact of Global Events on Sufism in Kashmir

In order to trace the impact of global events on Sufism in Kashmir, it is necessary to examine them in the context of the events of 1979. Four major events changed the political system and politics of the region that year and will be examined here briefly. The first seminal event was the Islamic Revolution in Iran (7 January 1978–11 February 1979) wherein Ayatollah Khomeini replaced the ruling secular Shah in Iran. The siege of Mecca (November–December 1979), wherein hajis were held hostage and evacuated with French help, was the second event. The crisis created a major upheaval in the Arab world and exposed the latent dissent in the existing political order in West Asia.

The third event of consequence was the Soviet invasion and occupation of Afghanistan (25 December 1979–15 February 1989). With the help of Pakistan, the United States (US) raised the Afghan Mujahideen to fight the Soviets, thereby giving political ownership to the concept of jihad. The fourth event that had an impact on the region was the hanging of the Pakistani Prime Minister Zulfikar Ali Bhutto (4 April 1979). General Zia-ul-Haq, who was the then Army Chief, subsequently became the President of Pakistan and began implementing his Islamist agenda, the impact of which is being felt even today.[1] Zia-ul-Haq sent Maulana Abdul Bari, the Jamaat-e-Islami (JI) chief in Azad Jammu and Kashmir (Pakistan-occupied Kashmir), to mobilise support for the JI in Kashmir. Bari, as per his own confession, had assured the JI in Kashmir of Pakistani support.

After the hanging of Zulfikar Ali Bhutto, the ire against the JI in Kashmir increased. The cadres as well as their houses were targeted and the orchards of JI cadres were cut down. Given the volatile scenario, in order to ensure its survival, the JI collaborated with the Pakistani establishment and brought the fundamentalist militant organization, HM, into the Valley. These developments, that took place in the mid-1980s and early 1990s, laid the foundation that ensured the spread of orthodox groups, which in turn led to the suppression of local moderate religious institutions and propagated the more orthodox versions of Islam.

Radicalisation in Kashmir also prospered due to the political vacuum created by the instability prevailing in the aftermath of the resignation of the coalition government in 1990. From a strategic perspective, radicalisation can generally be attributed to the unfulfilment of citizens' hopes and a lack of communication between those governing and those being governed. The withdrawal of governance only encourages this phenomenon and the building frustration leads to the consolidation of an identity primarily based on religion, which is what has happened in the case of Kashmir.

Sufism also came under attack due to the increased corruption of Sufi leaders (called "Pirs"). Their hierarchical privilege ensured that there was already an undercurrent of resentment against the exploitative nature of pir system, which further culminated in extremist opposition. This foundation of dissatisfaction ensured that the radical Islamist narrative easily found currency in Kashmir. The 2011 burning of Sufi shrines was a consequence of this opposition and the act was actively promoted by the Lashkar-e-Taiba (LeT).

Reviving Sufism in Kashmir: The Immediate Deliverables

The question that confronts us now is how to construct a counter-narrative? Or, if not to construct one, find one within the vast ideological corpus of Islam. In order to do so, there is a need to engage deeper in doctrinal study and examine the core concepts of the various strains of the religion. There is a need to understand and reiterate the fact that Sufism is not a concept that is outside Islam and that it has its legitimacy and genesis in the *Hadees-e-Jibreel*.

In the *Hadees-e-Jibreel*, the Prophet explains the three stages of faith wherein the first stage of faith is "Islam", that is, practice of religion by offering of namaz, paying zakat, going on haj, reading the *kalma* and fasting during Ramzan. The next is "*Iman*", that is, having faith, including belief in the Prophet, belief in all messengers of god, belief in religious books and maintaining constant faith in god. The last stage of faith is "*I'hsan*", wherein a person has to conduct himself in a manner as if he was being observed by god. This, according to the Prophet, was the highest form of faith in Islam and it is from here that the concept of Sufism evolved, wherein doing good was more important than the actual ritualistic practice of Islam.

While this is the doctrinal origin of Sufism, there is also a need to examine its physical roots. The advent of Sufism should be seen in the context of the proselytisation of Islam. Shortly after the death of the Prophet, the spread of Islam in West Asia took place by active promotion and the use of arms. The usage of lethality meant that victims were left with the dictum of either submitting or fleeing. Almost 500 years after the death of the Prophet, there was an ideological reorganisation in the Islamic world on the efficacy of such proselytisation. Debates emerged regarding a movement going back to the concept of persuasion (*Tasawwuff*) to spread Islam. Tasawwuff that evolved was promoted primarily by Imam Ghazali, also called Hujjat-e-Islam and considered to be the greatest authority on Islam after the Prophet himself. Sufi preachers established seminaries all over West Asia and several of these preachers and theologians came to Kashmir and established seminaries, which can still be seen in almost all the districts.

Unfortunately, over a period of time, after the founder preachers died, these seminaries became corrupted and their successors, instead of focusing on the essence of Sufism, gravitated towards mysticism, exorcism, charms and other materialistic manifestations. This was increasingly seen as a movement towards polytheism and considered akin to idolatry.

It was in reaction to this that a revival of madrasas in Kashmir began, with parents wanting to give their children access to a pure religious education. The concept of action in religion, from which the Muslims had moved away since the time of Imam Ghazali, began again. Currently, this active version is the form of religious preaching taking place in the Valley. Furthermore, the political uncertainty in Kashmir has only furthered the alienation of the people and deepened the identity crisis in the region. The disparity in education and comparative human development indices has created an aspirational gap, which has led to the consolidation of religious identity.

This consolidated identity and its perceived grievances are further accentuated by the ready availability and access to social media. Subscription to mobile phones in the Valley is the highest in the country. The only outlet for most Kashmiri youth today is the smartphone, which has isolated them from the real world. Their entrapment by the radical narrative in the virtual world (abundantly available) is thus a natural corollary to the prevailing uncertain times.

The question that remains is how to deal with the situation. The important thing to understand is that religion is not the fundamental issue and subscription to religion is only a means towards an end. It is the social, economic and political disenfranchisement that has caused this resonance. If we go to the beginning, it starts from an aspirational deficit. The Kashmiri youth, like youth across the country, have got global aspirations. Priority must be given to providing avenues for these aspirations, and this can be done by encouraging active political linkages for opportunity elsewhere in the country and having a political outlet.

Education needs to be given particular attention. It is important to end the insulation of the madrasas. Children going to government or private schools have an opportunity to interact and mingle with others from different walks of life. This gives them exposure to different thoughts and ideas and helps them develop an open and receptive personality.

The government too needs to reinvent itself in the post-modern times. Today's youth are politically active and seek an opportunity to make themselves heard. A platform must be provided to them for expressing their thoughts and grievances. Promotion of grassroots-level governance, involving the entire community, particularly all the youth, in local developmental issues would help in encouraging the sense of participation. These platforms could be in the form of a more associative, participative, horizontal government, which manifests itself in robust local organisational reconfiguring giving people a say in their governance, in making things better. Such an inclusive approach would also help reduce the socio-political alienation that people of Kashmir are experiencing. Cognisance must be taken of the dreams of the Kashmiri youth and a commitment to help him/her pursue these needs to be keyed in while governing the state.

The presence of social media has only helped to reinforce identities and the Kashmiri child, in comparison with the rest of the world, feels deprived. The routine construct of a school-going, play-dating, engaged in extracurricular activities spanning from theatre to tennis teenager is not applicable to the Kashmiri child, who is constantly living a life of uncertainty. The chance, the opportunity and the possibility of a career, or a constructive engagement, should not be denied to the Kashmiri youth. As a country, ensuring parity for children and access to a better future is exigent. And while attempting to assure this, we must simultaneously endeavour to bring back the elements of tolerance, cooperation and assimilation in society. There is a need to build emotional and economic linkages by providing visible and glamorous role models, especially as Kashmiri youth pride themselves in their appearance and find themselves right candidates for advertising and appearing on the big and small screen. If such aspirations remain unfulfilled, it leads to further expression of grievance, which over a period of time festers and eventually gets mapped onto random expressions of angst.

The concept of "I'hsan" needs to be given priority. The concept served to provide legitimacy to Sufism, which is currently being contested by several sources. It needs to be reiterated that Sufism is not outside the ambit of Islam and it is not a Sufism versus Islam debate. It is an attempt to understand the assimilative nature of Islam. A beginning can be made by putting the moderates in dialogue with the extremist interpretation of the Qu'ran to challenge the radical narrative. Support of the majority community usually helps in creating the narrative for minority communities. If the government and other social organisations were to encourage this aspect of religion, it would be universally acceptable and help in finding the counter-narrative to the radicalisation that is taking place in the Valley and elsewhere in the country.

Conclusion

In my opinion, Sufism is the summation of all religions. This is what "Kashmiriyat" has stood for thus far. A revival of this paradigm needs to be attempted to create a viable ecosystem for society to thrive in. The concept of I'hsan holds far more relevance in the land of Pir Vaer today, than perhaps at any other time in history. Sufi seminaries have always been a part of Kashmiri culture and ethos; they just need to be resuscitated.

> Declare your jihad on thirteen enemies you cannot see—Egoism, Arrogance, Conceit, Selfishness, Greed, Lust, Intolerance, Anger, Lying, Cheating, Gossiping and Slandering. If you can master and destroy them, you will be ready to fight the enemy you can see.
>
> —Imam Ghazali

NOTES

1   Editor's Note: For more on this see : Josy Joseph, "MEA totally misread General Zia-ul-Haq's intentions after coup, show declassified papers", 7 November 2011, *The Economic Times*, available at https://economictimes.indiatimes.com/news/politics-and-nation/mea-totally-misread-general-zia-ul-haqs-intentions-after-coup-show-declassified-papers/articleshow/10638292.cms, accessed on 22 July 2017.

List of Contributors

Shruti Pandalai is an Associate Fellow at IDSA, primarily working on India's strategic thought and practice. Great power politics, neighbourhood relations, developments in military affairs and new emerging threats to national security are her areas of research interest. She also specialises on the issue of strategic communication in defence and diplomacy. She has worked on task force projects with the National Security Council Secretariat, Ministry of External Affairs and Home Afffairs. Shruti frequently presents her research at conferences in international think tanks and military institutions and has published in academic journals, edited volumes and in the media. Shruti was honoured with the IDSA President's Award for excellence in research in 2015. She is part of many global emerging leaders' fora including The Asian Forum of Global Governance, The Munich Young Leaders Programme and is 2017 Raisina Fellow. Previously, Shruti was a broadcast journalist, a News Anchor and Senior Correspondent with a leading national English news network specialising in international affairs. She is an alumna of St Xavier's College Calcutta, The Asian College of Journalism and The Centre for International Studies and Diplomacy, SOAS, University of London.

H.E. Mhd. Hanif Atmar

National Security Advisor to President Ashraf Ghani, Afghanistan (2014-2018)

Mr. Mhd. Hanif Atmar served as one of Afghanistan's leading Ministers during his terms in office as the Minister of Interior (2008-2010), Minister of Education (2006-2008) and as Minister of Rural Rehabilitation and Development (2002-2006). He was one of the youngest members of the cabinet and became a thorough leader in shaping numerous development, education and security policies and programs for Afghanistan. Having served as a high level advisor to various international organisations. In his role as National Security Advisor of Afghanistan he emerged as one of Afghanistan's most articulate voices for progressive change, conflict resolution and accelerated development. Mr. Atmar holds advanced degrees in Public Policy and Information Technology from the University of York and has written and spoken extensively on security, peacebuilding, politics, humanitarian aid and the role of non-governmental organizations.

Maj. Gen. Mahmud Ali Durrani (Retd.)
Former National Security Advisor, Pakistan

General Durrani was commissioned in the Pakistan Army in 1961 and retired as a major general in 1998. In June 2006 he was appointed as Pakistan's Ambassador to the United States of America for a period of two years. Following his assignment in Washington D.C. he was appointed as the National Security Advisor to the Prime Minister of Pakistan, with the rank of a Federal Minister; a post he held till January 2009. He specializes in military strategy, defence production and international security issues. General Durrani is the author of a book titled "India and Pakistan - The Cost of Conflict and the Benefits of Peace", published by John Hopkins University, USA in 2000.

Abdel Bari Atwan
Editor-in-chief, Rai al-Youm, an Arab world digital news and opinion website

Abdel Bari Atwan is the editor-in-chief of Rai al-Youm, Arabic Independent newspaper. The established author, broadcaster and former editor of al-Quds al-Arabi was born in a refugee camp in the Gaza Strip two years after the Nakhbah. Having left to Jordan in 1967, Atwan has lived most of his life in exile. He is the author of The Country of World, The Secret History of al-Qaeda, After bin Laden and Islamic State: The Digital Caliphate.

Praveen Swami
Group Consulting Editor, Network18

Praveen Swami is Group Consulting Editor at Network18. He was previously National Editor for Strategic and International Affairs at The Indian Express, one of India's most respected investigative newspapers. He writes on regional security and intelligence issues. He has earlier worked as Resident Editor of The Hindu in New Delhi, as and as Diplomatic Editor of The Daily Telegraph in London. He is the author of *India, Pakistan and the Secret Jihad: the Covert War in Jammu and Kashmir, 1947-2002*, published by Routledge in January, 2007. The book was written while he was a Jennings Randolph senior fellow at the United States Institute of Peace in Washington, D.C., in 2004-2005. His other work includes a 1999 book, *The Kargil War*, chapters in several edited volumes, and papers in journals including *The India Review, Contemporary South Asia*, the *CTC Sentinel* of the Combating Terrorism Centre at West Point, *Faultlines* and the *South Asia Intelligence Review*.

Ehsan Monawar

Counter Terrorism Expert, Afghanistan

Ehsan Monawar is an Afghan-American security sector specialist with over 18 years of background in security and counter terrorism, with 4 years dedicated operational experience in Afghanistan working with the Joint Terrorism Task Force (JTTF) under the Federal Bureau of Investigation (FBI) from 2002 - 2006. Mr. Monawar provided on the ground expertise to SAIC (Science Application International Corporation) during the development of the National Security Council. Based on his successes, Mr. Monawar was tasked by JTTF to resolve complex security challenges in the most remote and challenging tribal areas of Afghanistan. Following his tenure and achievements in Afghanistan, Mr. Monawar was provided with an honorary position at New York City (NYC) detective unit for JTTF. During his time with the unit, he was involved in counter terrorism, threat financing, and high value targeting. In 2006, Mr. Monawar resigned from his efforts with JTTF due to the organizations focus outside of Afghanistan. Over the next decade, Mr. Monawar has worked with communities throughout the country to develop a path toward peace and stability

Waiel S.H Awwad

Writer and South Asia Political Analyst

Dr. Waiel is a writer, political analyst and South Asia based Journalist since 1979 and has travelled extensively in most of South and South East Asian countries. As a war reporter he covered Sri Lanka, Kashmir, Afghanistan, West Asia and Gulf Region. Dr. Waiel was detained in Afghanistan before the fall of Taliban government and was also captured in an ambush during the American invasion of Iraq in 2003 while he was embedded with American Troops. He served as President of the Foreign Correspondents' Club of South Asia (FCC) for two terms 2003-2005 and 2013-2015 and as a President Emeritus for FCC South Asia. In 2104 he was awarded the 5th Rajiv Gandhi Excellence Award for his work as the best journalist from overseas.

Baker Atyani

Al Arabiya News , Bureau Chief South and East Asia

Mr. Baker Atyani is a veteran journalist, covering conflict zones in Asia for the past 18 years. He is an expert on militant groups in Asia. He has produced numerous documentaries, articles, and investigative stories and was the last journalist to interview Osama Bin Laden before 9/11. He was kidnapped by one the sub factions of "Abu Sayyaf Group" in Sulu Islands in south of the Philippines while working on a documentary on the Conflict in Mindanao Islands in the Philippines. Baker spent 18 months in the jungles of Sulu from 12 June 2012, till he got his freedom back on 04 December 2013. He is currently Al-Arabiya News Channel Senior International correspondent, and the channel's expert on South and South East Asia Affairs. He has been honoured by Al Arabiya News Channel and MCF with "Exceptional Courage in Journalism" awards. The UN honored him in December 2013 for his contributions as a journalist.

Atul Goel, IPS

National Investigative Agency, GoI

Mr. Goel served as Superintendent of Police in the National Investigation Agency, an agency of the Government of India set up after the Mumbai terror attack of November, 2008 to investigate and prosecute important and complex terrorism related cases. In the present role, he has been involved in the investigation of several terrorism related cases of the North East and Jammu and Kashmir

C. Christine Fair

Associate Professor, Peace and Security Studies Program Georgetown University, USA

Dr. C. Christine Fair is a Provost's Distinguished Associate Professor in the Security Studies Program within Georgetown University's Edmund A. Walsh School of Foreign Service. She previously served as a senior political scientist with the RAND Corporation, a political officer with the United Nations Assistance Mission to Afghanistan in Kabul, and a senior research associate at USIP's Center for Conflict Analysis and Prevention. Fluent in English, Hindi, Urdu and Punjabi, Dr. Fair is a frequent commentator in print as well on television and radio programs. Her research focuses on political and military affairs in South Asia.

Lamya Haji Bashar

Public advocate of the Yazidi community, Iraq

Lamya Haji Bashar is a survivor of sexual enslavement by the Da'esh and has become a spokesperson for women afflicted by the groups campaign of sexual violence. She is a public advocate for the Yazidi community in Iraq, a religious minority that has been the subject of a genocidal campaign by Da'esh militants.

Anne Speckhard

Director of the International Center for the Study of Violent Extremism (ICSVE), USA

Dr. Anne Speckhard, is Adjunct Associate Professor of Psychiatry in the School of Medicine, Georgetown University, and Director of the International Center for the Study of Violent Extremism (ICSVE). Dr. Speckhard has been working in the field of counter-terrorism and psychology since the 1980's and has extensive experience working in Europe, the Middle East and the former Soviet Union. Dr. Speckhard has interviewed over 500 terrorists, their family members and supporters in various parts of the world including Iraq, Jordan, Turkey, Gaza, West Bank, Chechnya, and many countries in Western Europe. In 2007, she was responsible for designing the psychological and Islamic challenge aspects of the Detainee Rehabilitation Program in Iraq to be applied to 20,000 + detainees and 800 juveniles. She has consulted to NATO, OSCE, foreign governments and to the U.S. Senate & House, Departments of State, Defense, Justice, Homeland Security, Health & Human Services, CIA and FBI. She also appears frequently on CNN, BBC, NPR, Fox News, MSNBC, and publications like in Time, The New York Times, The Washington Post, and The London Times. She is the author of seven books including: Talking to Terrorists: Understanding the Psycho-Social Motivations of Militant Jihadi Terrorists, Mass Hostage Takers, Suicide Bombers and "Martyrs", Fetal Abduction: The True Story of Multiple Personalities and Murder, Brides of ISIS.

Saikat Datta

Director, Centre for Internet & Society, India & Editor, South Asia, Asia Times Online

Saikat Datta has been a journalist and a researcher on issues related to terrorism, Intelligence, Special Forces and cybersecurity. His book on India's Special Forces was released in May 2013. He is currently an editor with a news website and a Director with Centre For Internet & Society, a research organisation.

Sanjeev Singh

Addl DG (anti-Naxal Operations), Madhya Pradesh Police

As Inspector General (Investigation) at the National Investigation Agency (NIA) since 2010, Mr. Sanjeev Singh has led investigations into the most significant cases of terrorism in India. These cases span the entire spectrum of terrorist threats in India - Jihadi terrorism, left wing extremism, north-eastern insurgency and terrorist financing. Notable amongst these are the Patna/Bodh Gaya blasts (2013) and the David Coleman Headley case. He directly led investigation of Pathankot attack case and Bahadur Ali case Mr. Singh also chaired the India-Bangladesh Joint Task Force on Fake Indian currency notes which has streamlined and strengthened the law enforcement cooperation between the two countries.

Manjula Sridhar

Founder ArgByte - a cybercrime analytics software

Ms. Manjula Sridhar is the Founder of ArgByte a cyber crime analytics software. She is a techie with two decades of work experience in tech industry with specific focus on networks and security. She has been founder and CTO of Aujas Networks and has worked with many MNCs such as Lucent, Bosch, Huawei and Arcot. An Engineer by education, She did her M.S. from IIT Chicago. She is a mentor at Indian Institute of Bangalore's Incubation centre and MS Accelerator. She is a Fellow at iSpirt a think tank for Indian Entrepreneurship and runs iKenStartup a bootcamp for early Entrepreneurs.

Mr. Mustafa El Sagezli

General Manager, The Libyan Program for Reintegration & Development

Mr. Sagezli is the General Manager of the Libyan Programme for Reintegration and Development (LPRD), a project for the reintegration, demobilisation and disarmament of Libyans. As General Manager of The Libyan Programme for Reintegration and Development (LPRD), Mustafa has overseen the establishment, management and execution of Libya's ex-combatant reintegration programmes, which has served over 162,000 beneficiaries to date. Mustafa has twenty years' experience of entrepreneurship in the IT sector and four years of experience in politics, public management, social services management and SME's development

Frank Ledwidge

Former Military Intelligence Officer who served in Iraq, Afghanistan and Libya

Senior Lecturer in Strategic Studies and Law of Armed Conflict for the University of Portsmouth at the Royal Air Force College, Cranwell; Dr. Ledwidge is a fully qualified and experienced barrister with a strong record in provision of excellent advice on justice and rule of law reform in conflict and post-conflict zones, most recently Libya and the Somali Region of Ethiopia. He is the author of two bestselling, well-reviewed and controversial books on Britain's recent wars, in all of which he has served in one front line capacity or another. In 2016 he delivered one of the annual Darwin Lectures at Cambridge University. As a senior reserve military officer, Dr. Ledwidge served several combat tours in the Balkans and Iraq and retired as head of the most deployed unit in the Royal Navy.

Eitan Shamir

Senior Research Fellow, Begin Sadat Center for Strategic Studies, Israel

Dr. Eitan Shamir is an Associate professor at the Political Studies Department,

Bar Ilan University and a Senior Research Fellow with the Begin Sadat Center for Strategic Studies (BESA Center). Prior to his academic position, he was in charge of the National Security Doctrine Department at the Ministry of Strategic Affairs, Prime Minister Office. He is the author of Transforming Command: The Pursuit of Mission Command in the US, UK and Israeli Armies, Stanford UP, 2011. His most recent book (ed.) is Insurgencies and Counterinsurgencies: National Styles and Strategic Cultures, Cambridge UP, 2017, (with Prof. Beatrice Heuser). Shamir has published many articles in leading journals and various book chapters on the topics of military strategy and national security. Shamir has been interviewed in some of Israel's leading media outlets and in the international media. He holds a PhD from the Department of War Studies, King's College London.

Lt. Gen. Chowdhury Hasan Sarwardy (Retd.)

Commandant, National Defence College, Mirpur, Bangladesh (2015–2018)

Lieutenant General Chowdhury Hasan Sarwardy, BB, SBP, BSP, NDC, PSC, took over as the Commandant of National Defence College (NDC), Bangladesh in February 2015. Lieutenant General Chowdhury Hasan Sarwardy received gallantry award 'Bir Bikrom' for displaying indomitable courage during a counter insurgency operation in the Chittagong Hill Tracts where he was injured with enemy bullet but captured their camp without fearing his life.

Lt. Gen. R.M. Daya Ratnayake (Retd.)

Former Commander of Army, Sri Lanka

Gen. Daya Ratnayake is the only military officer in the Armed Forces of Sri Lanka who has been awarded with gallantry medals number of times. He has also held the appointment as Chief of Staff of the Sri Lanka Army and had the privilege of becoming the first Commissioner General of Rehabilitation in Sri Lanka, responsible for rehabilitation of hundreds of LTTE combatants. He previously held the appointment as Military Spokesman for the Ministry of Defence, Senior Intelligence Officer at the Operations Headquarters at Ministry of Defence, Commanding Officer of the Sri Lanka Military Academy, Chief Instructor in the Military Intelligence School and Chief Instructor of the Army Training School. He was also the Senior Intelligence Officer in charge of the Northern Peninsula during 1991-1992. Gen. Daya Ratnayake has graduated from the National Defence University, Beijing, People's Republic of China and Defence Service Command and Staff College, Dhaka, Bangladesh and is currently reading for a PhD at Kotelawala Defence University.

Ayesha Siddiqa

Political commentator, Pakistan

Dr. Ayesha Siddiqa is currently a research associate with the SOAS, University of London's South Asia Institute. She is a Ph.D. in War Studies from King's College, London and is an author of two books on Pakistan's military: (a) Pakistan's Arms Procurement and Military Buildup, 1979-99 and (b) Military Inc, Inside Pakistan's Military Economy. She was the inaugural Pakistan fellow at the Woodrow Wilson International Centre for Scholars, a Ford Fellow, a research fellow at the CMC, Sandia National Laboratories, and a Charles Wallace fellow at St. Antony's College, Oxford. Her current work pertains to radicalism and militancy in Punjab and Sindh.

Kumar Ramakrishna

Head of Policy Studies & Coordinator of National Security Studies Programme RSIS, Singapore

Dr. Kumar Ramakrishna is a tenured Associate Professor, Head of Policy Studies and Coordinator of National Security Studies Programme in the Office of the Executive Deputy Chairman, at the S. Rajaratnam School of International Studies (RSIS), Singapore. His current research interests include British propaganda in the Malayan Emergency; propaganda theory and practice; history of strategic thought; and counter-terrorism with a focus on radicalization.

In July 2015 he served as a member of the External Reference Group for the United Nations Secretary General's draft Plan of Action for Preventing Violent Extremism. In "recognition of the international contribution" he has made to research into violent extremism, in January 2016 he was also appointed as an honorary Visiting Senior Research Fellow at the Centre for the Resolution of Intractable Conflict, based at Harris Manchester College, Oxford University, UK. His book, Radical Pathways: Understanding Muslim Radicalization in Indonesia (2009) was identified by Perspectives on Terrorism in May 2012 as one of the top 150 books on terrorism and counter-terrorism as well as "an important and insightful case study on the pathways to extremism and violent jihad in Indonesia". His recent books include Islamist Terrorism and Militancy in Indonesia: The Power of the Manichean Mindset (2015), Original Sin? Revising the Revisionist Critique of the 1963 Operation Coldstore in Singapore (2015) and Singapore Chronicles: Emergency (2016).

Lt. Gen. S.A. Hasnain (Retd.)

Former GOC 15 Corps, Srinagar, Fellow, Vivekananda International Foundation and Member, Governing Council, Institute of Peace and Conflict Studies, India

Gen. Hasnain, is a retired Three Star General of the Indian Army. His last assignment in service was as the Military Secretary of the Indian Army. Prior to that, he commanded an Army Corps in the Indian state of Jammu and Kashmir, amongst other appointments. Gen. Hasnain introduced the Scholar Warrior concept to the Indian Army and after superannuation has extensively promoted the necessity of incorporating military intellectualism and strategic culture in India. In this regard he is a popular speaker at corporate events. Among the companies that he has addressed include Deloitte, Ashok Leyland, Larsen & Toubro (Design), Amdocs Pune, Atoc and Sanofi Pasteur

Adil Rasheed

Research Fellow, IDSA India

Dr. Adil Rasheed is a research fellow at the IDSA and an expert in West Asia strategic affairs and counter terrorism. Before joining the IDSA, Dr Adil Rasheed was Senior Research Fellow at the United Service Institution of India. He served at the Abu Dhabi-based Emirates Center for Strategic Studies and Research for eight years (2006-2014) and was Editor (Newsdesk) and political commentator at the Dubaibased daily Khaleej Times from 2000 to 2005. He has authored the book ISIS: Race to Armageddon (2015).

S.M. Sahai, IPS is serving as Additional secretary, National Security Council Secretariat (NSCS), Government of India.

Index